Vote of Faith

CATHOLIC PRACTICE IN THE AMERICAS

John C. Seitz and Jessica Delgado, series editors

SERIES ADVISORY BOARD:
Emma Anderson, Ottawa University
Kathleen Sprows Cummings, University of Notre Dame
Jack Lee Downey, University of Rochester
Thomas Ferraro, Duke University
Jennifer Scheper Hughes, University of California, Riverside
Brianna Leavitt-Alcantara, University of Cincinnati
Mark Massa, Boston College
Kenneth Mills, University of Michigan
Paul Ramirez, Northwestern University
Thomas A. Tweed, University of Notre Dame
Pamela Voekel, Dartmouth University

Vote of Faith

DEMOCRACY, DESIRE, AND THE TURBULENT LIVES OF PRIEST POLITICIANS

Maya Mayblin

FORDHAM UNIVERSITY PRESS
New York 2025

Copyright © 2025 Fordham University Press

All rights reserved. No part of this publication may be reproduced, stored in a retrieval system, or transmitted in any form or by any means—electronic, mechanical, photocopy, recording, or any other—except for brief quotations in printed reviews, without the prior permission of the publisher.

Fordham University Press has no responsibility for the persistence or accuracy of URLs for external or third-party Internet websites referred to in this publication and does not guarantee that any content on such websites is, or will remain, accurate or appropriate.

Fordham University Press also publishes its books in a variety of electronic formats. Some content that appears in print may not be available in electronic books.

Visit us online at www.fordhampress.com.

Library of Congress Cataloging-in-Publication Data available online at https://catalog.loc.gov.

Printed in the United States of America

27 26 25   5 4 3 2 1

First edition

Contents

	Introduction	1
1	Politics: Endless and Addictive	31
2	Celibacy as Theopolitics	53
3	Faith, Desire, and Machismo	75
4	Virile Celibacy	99
5	Votes of Faith: Force, Power, and Political Form	125
6	The Miraculous and the Mundane	150
	Conclusion	177
	Epilogue	187
	Acknowledgments	191
	Notes	193
	Bibliography	217
	Index	235

Vote of Faith

Introduction

The first time I met Padre Jorge, the air was sticky and the sky overcast. I introduced myself to him after Mass and, explaining my purpose as a researcher, asked if he might spare me a window of time for a brief conversation about his current situation. A friend who knew Padre Jorge well had reassured me beforehand that such a request would not be an intrusion—"He'll talk—he'll tell you about his dilemma!" he said, grinning widely. "No, he won't mind! His situation is common knowledge." It was two years before the next election was to take place, and everyone knew that Padre Jorge had been invited to run for mayor. Not in Jupi, the small town in Northeast Brazil where he was currently parish priest, but in Iati, an impoverished rural municipality further north, which had been the seat of his first-ever post as a priest.

The people of Iati were desperate. For the past two decades, their municipality had been governed by a wealthy landowning family. Over the course of that administration, roads had become deeply potholed, schools and health posts had struggled, and water was in short supply. From certain angles, Iati's situation appeared intractable. Once a powerful family gained control of the municipality's machinery, it was a Herculean task to wrest it away from them. People claimed that much of the wealth flowing into Iati's public coffers was being illegally siphoned off, used by the governing elite to bolster their control over the region's inhabitants.

Although priests are officially forbidden from running in elections, Padre Jorge had been singled out as someone who could save the town. Interests gathering in opposition to the incumbent mayor had invited him to run for the post, but he was yet to accept the invitation.

The regional bishop was on a rolling mission to prevent Padre Jorge from abandoning his religious ministry for a political career. When attempting to dissuade him through discussion had failed, he forbade him from visiting the town itself. When that failed to dull rumors about

Padre Jorge's intentions, he visited the town's parish and gave a sermon on the sinfulness of soliciting priests for political candidacy. Further unsuccessful attempts by the bishop to halt the process followed, including conferences at his palace, to which all the mayors and clergy of the region were invited, and ecclesiastical letters exhorting the People of God to renounce any involvement with political priests.

Finally, as rumors of Padre Jorge's imminent candidacy intensified and the bishop came to know of several more priests from his diocese intending to run for mayoral offices, a mandate was sent out to all clergy declaring that any priest who candidated himself for the next election would be permanently excluded from ministry.

The bishop was desperate—but so were the people of Iati. Padre Jorge was the last resort of a populace who felt trapped by the power of an old regime and wanted a new leader.

By seeking an audience with Padre Jorge, I hoped to learn more about his specific intentions and to gain some insight into the increasing popularity of mayor-priests across the region. That day, however, Padre Jorge had prior commitments and was unable to make time for me. Wondering if my friend had got it wrong about Padre Jorge's willingness to speak about the situation, I thanked the priest and turned to leave. But as I did, he called after me: "Saturday night there should be time. Find me after Mass, around 10 P.M."

It felt unseemly knocking on a priest's door so late at night. The housekeeper who let me in was clearly on her way out, having left the rectory gleaming. She looked at me a little suspiciously but pointed me down the corridor to the visitors' area, where the padre would receive me. This area of the rectory comprised a squared-off section of hallway that fed onto a staircase at one end and a dark passageway at the other.

I took a seat on one of the small sofas arranged around a glass coffee table and waited. A photograph of the erstwhile bishop hung on the wall before me, and a meter-high statue of the folk saint Padre Cícero loomed in the corner. Not knowing who else was in the rectory, I waited on the edge of my seat, poised to explain myself should anyone wander past. But the passage stayed quiet, and after a while I started to wonder if Padre Jorge was even aware that I was in the building.

Eventually he emerged, shuffling into the hallway, wearing shorts and a half-buttoned shirt. Evidently, he had come from the upstairs part of the house and looked somewhat as though he'd just woken up. I stood to greet him, and we shook hands.

He was a tall, broad-shouldered man with dark hair and blinking, wide-set eyes. I looked around; the area we were in did not offer much privacy, but we sat back down together, and, after a round of polite chatting, I braced myself and asked, as tactfully as I could, about his political ambitions.

To my relief, Padre Jorge did not flinch at my question; he merely fixed his gaze on my face and smiled very slightly. He opened his mouth to respond, then closed it again and looked hesitantly toward the passageway. Lowering his voice, he indicated that it would be best if we moved somewhere more private. I stood and followed him up the staircase.

If knocking on the rectory door at 10 P.M. had felt unseemly, following a priest into a part of the house that presumably contained his bedroom felt even more so. The inappropriateness of it all made my mind spin and my face flush red.

"This way," said Padre Jorge upon reaching the top.

Across the tiled landing were two rooms: one with a bed in it, the other arranged like a small sitting room with a television, some chairs, and a frayed green sofa. We made our way into the sitting room and sat down. The weirdness of the situation propelled the conversation in the only direction that could justify it, and I asked Padre Jorge about the invitation he had supposedly been issued to run for mayor.

Yes, he answered, the invitation had come to him in several stages: by word of mouth, via old acquaintances, and more recently in the form of a letter that had been typed up by a local schoolteacher on behalf of the town's inhabitants.

"I have been in a terrible state," he confessed, rubbing his palm back and forth across his head. "For months now, I have been wrestling with this decision of whether or not to accept the invitation."

"What would happen if you declined it?" I asked.

"The people would call me *mole* [soft]," he replied. "They would not say it to my face, but I would be labeled a coward. The reputation would stick."

Padre Jorge looked suddenly fragile, his black hair now pointing in odd directions like the fur of an animal stroked the wrong way. He went on to describe his troubles with the bishop, a man whom he believed was intent on punishing him—not for having yet broken any ecclesiastical rules but merely for the possibility that he might. He explained that his current situation as parish priest of Jupi was a demotion from his previous parish, which had been larger and somewhat more affluent. Here in Jupi, he could only afford domestic help for half the day, and there was no money to refurbish the rectory. He pulled at the frayed edges of the green sofa he was sitting on. On the other side of the equation, he went on, were his potential political adversaries, trying to bribe and intimidate him to stay out of the race.

Nonetheless, Padre Jorge could not get the idea of being a mayor out of his head.

"I just can't stop thinking about it," he sighed; then, following some thought of his own, he said, "You know, it's not a power thing. I'm not obsessed with power. It's just I can't help thinking that, as mayor, I could make a real difference. Actually change things. . . ." His voice trailed off as he lost himself in thoughts of the difference he could make.

"What would you change?" I tentatively probed, unsure how far the conversation would travel.

Padre Jorge arched his eyebrows in thought, then slowly refocused his gaze on my face. "Infrastructure," he said, and then, "The roads need mending. . . . And, well, I have this dream that all schoolchildren will receive a decent meal. I cannot bear the thought of hunger."

I wondered what advice the predecessor of Padre Jorge's current parish in Jupi, Padre Ivo, would have offered him, for only eight years earlier he had sat in the very same room weighing up his own invitation to run for mayor. Maybe he too had been transfixed by the possibility of making a difference, and it was this that had driven him to become mayor. But Padre Ivo's political career had ended in disaster.

On winning his first election he had filled his cabinet with individuals who were not from the area, and had distributed many coveted jobs among his own siblings. Accusations of incompetence and corruption had followed, such that, by the next election, Padre Ivo was unanimously voted out of office - spurned by the very same people who had invited him to run for mayor in the first place. Wondering how that scene might have played out, I couldn't help picturing him packing his bags in a bedroom somewhere, gazing mournfully at the wall-mounted crucifix above the bed; his political odyssey over, his religious career in tatters.

"Are you not afraid that what happened to Padre Ivo could happen to you?" I asked.

"Yes, very much so," he said. "What happened to Ivo was a terrible thing. But he, at least, did his penance and was eventually allowed back into ministry. For me the risk is greater. Under the current bishop, if I lost the election, there would be no returning to the church."

That meeting took place in 2011 in the rural interior of Pernambuco state, a region of Brazil known to scholars for its history of religious and political vitality. Such vitality has famously taken two forms: millenarian movements and liberation theology.

The former is perhaps best exemplified by the dramatic rise and fall of Canudos, a large community founded by the charismatic Antonio Conselheiro at the end of the nineteenth century. Conselheiro's Christian messianic vision of a "New Jerusalem"—in which the harsh realities of the drought-ravaged backlands would be inverted—was one of the most spectacular of a series of millenarian movements that have continued up to the present day. The latter, the explosion of liberation theology from the 1970s onward, sought to apply religious faith by aiding the poor and oppressed through involvement in political and civic affairs. Both messianic movements and liberation theology were political manifestations of a Catholicism that sought to critique rather than sustain hegemonic hierarchies and forms of capitalism.

My initial decade of research on kinship and popular religion had been strongly guided by people who were the heirs of a strong liberation theology tradition and whose struggles for social justice were guided by a different, almost utopian vision of how society could be. It was this group of people—radical in their dreams, survivors of jail and torture during the dictatorship (1964–85)—who had molded my perception of what religious politics in Brazil could mean, and upon whom I thought my research might focus when, in 2011, I returned to the field to study the intersection of politics and religion.

By that time, I was already aware that recent gains of converts to evangelical Christianity in the rural interior would perhaps be marking a shift in configurations of the political, as they were elsewhere in Brazil (Dodson 1997; Freston 1994; Machado 2003; Steil and Toniol 2013). I was also aware of shifts across the liberationist landscape toward more secular forms of political discourse (Dullo 2013), as well as a growing conservative turn at the level of national politics (Hatzikidi and Dullo 2021; Shapiro 2021). What I did not predict, however, was the markedly different nature of political involvement I would find among ordinary parish priests.

The people on whom this book is based were neither the founders of new social movements nor the leaders of breakaway religious groups—they were secular diocesan priests who had swapped their cassocks for a turn at political governance—men who did not seek to change the world in any radical way but who appeared, on many levels, resigned to its imperfections.[1]

Given that the church is officially against priests running in elections, a significant level of controversy surrounds the mayor-priest. For all his popularity, he is nonetheless a figure who, on some level, has betrayed God, not for the romance of a utopian vision but for the ambiguous glory of party politics. As Padre Ivo's story suggests, mayor-priests don't necessarily come with a great track record, but people continue to believe in them. It is paradoxes like this that make the regular appearance of mayor-priests in rural areas of Brazil something of an ethnographic curiosity.

This is a book about Brazilian Catholic priests as men, fathers, lovers, and politicians and the people who oppose and support them. On one level, it is a story about the mutually constitutive relationship between Catholicism and secular power; at a broader level, it is about sexuality, kinship, and human desire—forces both divine and immanent that bind the religious and the political together.

Although the histories of power explored in this book are unique to a particular region of Brazil, the themes concerned have broader import. Mayor-priests, I argue, embody particular responses to democracy in its guise as a "failed" or existentially imperfect system—one that aims to address or mitigate the problems of existential lack and social division but ends up reinforcing those very problems.

The response priests offer is rooted not just in their status as men of Christian authority but in their performance of a unique form of sexual sterility that in turn embodies principles of abundance and unity. In order to effect such a solution, however, priests must immerse themselves in practices that are highly divisive and sexually fecund. The failures and contradictions that result are uniquely clarifying, for they show us both how the religiously produced body of the priest shapes the nature of the political and, conversely, how the political constitutes the power of the Catholic Church.

From this particular space we gain a view on the Roman Catholic Church as an enduring institution that is still important at a time when it seems to be losing ground to other religious and secular imaginaries, both within Brazil and more globally. In sum, this book moves toward an understanding of how Catholicism continues to promote itself as a political force not through ideas alone, but at a more visceral level, through faith and desire and the psychosexual dynamics that animate them.

The Secular and the Sacred in Brazilian Political History

Secularism, formally conceived, is a political idea that describes the separation of religion and state.[2] In the Brazilian context, a formal concept of "the secular sphere" emerged in 1889 with the proclamation of the republic and the first constitution in 1890, which aimed to make politics more autonomous from the Catholic Church. Catholicism played a key role in the development of this ideology, initially, through the collaboration of priests as leaders and intellectuals in founding the Republic and, later, through the Brazilian church's centralized opposition to the dictatorship and its subsequent campaigns to strengthen civil society (Oliveira 1992; Pang 1974; Serbin 2006; Silva 2012).

Given this particular history, it is debatable whether secularism in its purest sense has been a consistently defining force in the Brazilian political context (Giumbelli 2002, 2013; Montero 2006). At the very least, the secular in Brazil must be seen not so much as a sphere that has been emptied of Catholicism as one in which Catholicism has been frequently allowed to stand for a kind of neutrality, therefore giving it an important if unmarked role in political life (Dullo 2016; Mayblin, Norget, and Napolitano 2017). As Elayne Oliphant (2021, 25) has argued in the case of France, the scale of Catholicism's artistic and architectural heritage renders it both "banal" and "privileged" at the same time. Such forms of privilege may be common to historically rooted and powerful institutions whose ubiquity allows them to "stand above reproach, while others are forced to endure the oppressive surveillance that shapes the experience of the marked."

The various shades of "Catholic" that colour Brazilian secularism point to the fact that Brazilian priests have always been political, not only in the broad Foucauldian sense of the word that encompasses the entire field of power relations, but in a more prosaic sense that defines the political as a sphere of worldly action (apart from the transcendent) directly connected with the organization and distribution of material resources.[3] During the colonial era (1500–1822) and the empire (1822–89), when the church was bound to the Portuguese crown, priests largely collaborated in state projects of capitalist expansion and control through diverse roles as bureaucrats, deputies, and rural oligarchs. They also played a key role in the transition to independence in 1889, helping to populate the provisional government and continuing to occupy roles in the legislative and executive chambers well after the 1890 decree that separated church from state.[4]

The prevalence of mayor-priests in Brazil during this era was largely a result of the priest's (often) superior level of literacy and administrative experience in small-town contexts and his connection to elite circles. As political doctrines of secularization started to crystalize, however, the Brazilian church rebuilt itself as a powerful religious institution in its own right, and priests found new ways to lead and participate in politics.

By the 1970s, priests were less active on legislative and executive bodies but played an instrumental role as pressure-group lobbyists against the dictatorship. From the start of Brazil's *abertura* ("opening" to political democracy) in 1974 to the 1988 signing of Brazil's new constitution, priests continued being political, but more as activists than as party politicians, with many going on to become founders of new civil organizations and social movements (Serbin 2006).[5]

During the 1990s, the Brazilian church's relationship with the political began to change once again. Following a movement of restoration that began in the 1980s under the papacy of Pope John Paul II, continuing through the 1990s with Pope Benedict XVI, which all but eradicated the liberationist agenda, a new generation of priests emerged who were more conservative and less politically active. Social action under this generation became increasingly contained to pastoral commissions, and the discourse that accompanied it was increasingly framed as a neo-charismatic call to *caridade* (charity) rather than *luta* (struggle).

The proliferation of parish-based charitable initiatives and church-wide pastoral commissions from the 1990s onward was often pointed out to me by Catholic Brazilians as evidence of the church's continued engagement in politics. But this perspective did not convince all within the fold, particularly priests who came of age during a liberationist era and who entered ministry as a means of holding the state directly accountable to its citizens. It could be said, therefore, that the slightly higher flow of priests leaving the church to take on roles in local government throughout the 1990s and early 2000s was partially caused by the church's broad-cale retrenchment from civic and political *struggle*.[6]

The church's response to the participation of priests in politics remains complex. Historically, Catholic priests were able to hold public office with the permission of church officials, but in 1983, the Vatican officially revised canon law to state that "clerics are prohibited from assuming public office, which implies participation in the exercise of civil power" (CCC 285, §3). Nonetheless, canon law also states that "clerics cannot take an active part in political parties and in the direction of trade union associations, *unless, in the judgement of the competent ecclesiastical authority, the defence of the rights of the Church or the promotion of the common good demand it*" (CCC 287, §2).

The "competent ecclesiastical authority" responsible for enforcing or interpreting this law is, in most instances, a bishop. Throughout Brazilian history and up until the present day, therefore, secular priests who wish to candidate themselves in an election must come to some sort of arrangement with their bishop. The details of such arrangements have always been variable, reflecting the needs of the place, the sensibilities of the time, and the quality of relationship that the priest has with his superior.

Since the 1980s, the Brazilian church has dealt with this situation mainly by allowing the priest to take a sabbatical from ministry for an agreed period of time (normally one that matches the expected period of political office). Such a sabbatical effectively suspends a priest's ministerial income and prohibits him from the performance of ministerial duties within the territory where he has become a political representative. Whether or not that prohibition on conducting ministerial duties also extends to neighboring territories where, technically speaking, he has no political jurisdiction depends largely on the individual outlook of the bishop.

Some priests never return from sabbatical. Either they get married or decide to pursue a different career. For those who wish to return, however, a bishop's approval must be sought, and a curious process of political "de-roling" and spiritual renewal must be effected. As with the allowing (or prohibiting) of sabbaticals, the particular form this process takes is ultimately down to the bishop in charge but in practice tends to be negotiated with the priest in question. What it must involve is a distancing the priest from the region where he served as a politician for at least one year. Frequently this achieved by sending him to Rome to complete a course in theology, or by relocating him to a distant parish where he must work under the authority of another priest as a visiting curate. Whatever the method, an ex-mayor-priest can only be allowed back into the diocese where he took political office once he has completed such a period of absence.

The way bishops interpret regulations around priests who take on political offices can tell us as much about how mayor-priests are perceived by local publics as they can about canon law. Even among non-Catholics, the idea that the mayor-priest has privileged access to a more potent source of power than the ordinary politician remains an influential one. As one evangelical supporter of a prospective mayor-priest explained it to me, a Catholic priest is still someone who "lives in the presence of God every day." That, she reasoned, put him above other candidates for the position.[7]

A point that runs parallel to all this, important for the pages to follow, is that a concept of public space as religiously neutral, or "secular" in the liberal sense of the term, was not salient for the average voter. Or at least, among those for whom it was salient, mayor-priests were believed to pose little if any risk to secular values because they already came from an institution (the Catholic church) that embodied them.[8]

In this book, I argue that to truly comprehend the contemporary mayor-priest, it is necessary to look beyond formal debates about Brazilian secularism toward theories of ritual, kinship, and gender. Mayorship, in this context, is less about political ideology and more about how the priest stands in relation to the sacred via his own and others' bodies. To some extent, this is true of any Brazilian politician who seeks to bolster their standing in the eyes of the electorate by seasoning their political speech with idioms of paternal love and spiritual solidarity. What makes the mayor-priest special is that he does not need speech to tap into such Christian ideals because he is already the living embodiment of them. His status as a spiritual "father" and his gendered capacity to mediate the

Eucharist contribute in vital ways toward his m(M)ass appeal—a phenomenon reinforced by the nature of his sexuality and the subterranean desires around masculinity and power it gives rise to.

The potent desires that collect around mayor-priests are famously exemplified in the case of Padre Cícero Romão Batista (1844–1934), a renegade priest of the drought-ravaged Cariri Valley, who acquired a mass following on the back of miracles he was believed to have performed in 1889. Padre Cícero's fame rests not only on the power of his miracles but on the fact that he helped to found the municipal region of Juazeiro do Norte, serving as its mayor for many years before becoming a federal deputy and eventually vice president of the state of Ceará (Braga 2008; Neto 2009). In his lifetime, he was many things to many factions: to the rural poor, he was *Padim Cícero* ("Godfather Cícero"), a miracle worker, a living saint; to the landed elite, he was both a potential adversary and potent ally; to secular urban elites, he was, at best, a religious fanatic, at worst, a political charlatan exploiting an impoverished and illiterate populace. To the republican-leaning ecclesiastical hierarchy of the time, he represented a dangerous and defiant form of ultramontanism and messianic religiosity.

Today, he remains a central figure of Catholic devotion in the Northeast: black cassocked images of him leaning hunched upon his walking cane stand prominent in homes, and in every small town, supermarkets and pharmacies carry his name. Every year, some 2.5 million people make a pilgrimage to his shrine in Juazeiro do Norte—in the words of Lira Neto (2009, 12, *translation my own*) "like half the population of a metropolis the size of Rome relocating en masse, annually, to revere a priest banished from the Church."[9] And yet, Padre Cícero's importance for contemporary society is more than just religious, for he is also widely remembered for "secular" attributes such as his rational intelligence and sheer political skill. This paradigmatic framing of Padre Cícero as a "both and" figure (both miracle worker and skilled political mover) is part of his complex, powerful legacy—one that served as an inspiration for many of the mayor-priests I worked with.

What Is a Mayor?

Being the mayor of a "small town" in rural Brazil is no small thing. It can involve having jurisdiction over a vast geographic territory, ranging anywhere from 500,000 to two million square kilometers and being responsible to anywhere between 15,000 and 70,000 inhabitants. Voters of interior municipalities care passionately about mayors. In fact, they often care more about their mayors than they do about their presidents, not least because in rural areas, municipal bodies are among the biggest employers, sometimes providing salaries for anywhere up to 30 percent of the local population.[10] Mayors are the focus for personal and aspirational projects; they have the capacity to distribute incomes that allow people to "advance" economically or simply remain rooted with dignity to the territories of their birth. In other words, mayors are key to survival.[11]

The research on which this book is based was carried out in the *agreste*, a narrow zone of land that crosses several Northeastern states and sits between the humid climes of the coast and the desert-like backlands of the western *sertão*. The term *agreste*—meaning "countryside"—describes what is, in fact, a climatically diverse but fertile region: semi-arid for large tracts but generally more suited to mixed agriculture than the sugar-dominated coast or the cattle-dominated *sertão*. Because of its more temperate climate, it has long functioned as the dominant food-producing region, generating enough manioc, beans, and maize to feed the inhabitants of the mono-cropped coast and the cattle ranchers further inland. Despite this productivity, however, it is also heavily drought-prone and bears the legacy of many historic and devastating droughts.

Nestled in Brazil's oldest state, the Pernambucan *agreste* has been shaped since the earliest years of Portuguese conquest by slavery, violence, and extractive economies and has served as home to various indigenous peoples, runaway slaves, and the mixed-race descendants of colonial settlers. The brutal legacies of the colonial era—its rapacious transatlantic slave trade, its near genocide of indigenous peoples, and its imposition of a system of land tenure known as captaincies—are still clearly evident in the region, burdened as it is with some of the highest rates of poverty, illiteracy, and social inequality in the whole of Brazil.[12] Today, the area retains a small number of autonomous indigenous groups and quilombo communities, but the overwhelming majority of people identify simply as *Nordestinos* (Northeasterners) or as *povo do interior* (people of the interior).

Unlike Afro-Brazilian communities of the coast, people of the interior go out of their way to minimize racial difference as a source of identity, emphasizing that they are *um só povo* (one people). This, however, belies the continuation of a covert racial ordering rooted in a past of slavery, wherein appearance and skin tone continue to correlate with relative wealth. Such racial inequality is usually downplayed in local understandings, however, and does not tend to coalesce into discrete racialized identities as it does elsewhere in Brazil.[13]

A mayor, in this context, is the executive head of a municipal body comprising an executive council and a *câmara municipal* (legislative body) made up of elected *vereadors* (councilors).[14] Brazilian municipalities receive most of their funds from state and federal budgets, which make up, on average, 75 percent of municipal revenues. In sparsely populated and economically underdeveloped municipalities, however, these budgets may account for as much as 99 percent of the municipality's income.[15]

Across the rural Northeast, poverty is a persistent problem, and basic services remain perennially underfunded (Mota 2020). In small towns such as those discussed in this book, fiscal emergencies at the administrative level tend to impact directly and dramatically on local inhabitants. During such episodes, there may be delays, sometimes of months, to the payment of municipal workers' salaries. The chaos and despair that ensue quickly become palpable as electricity supplies are cut, food must be purchased via informal systems of credit, and money must be borrowed. The cause of such crises is normally some combination of corrupt leadership, failed revenue transfers, and inherited debts, but in the eyes of the people, the fault lies invariably with the mayor.

In the rural interior of Pernambuco, where civic structures are weak and nongovernmental organizations rare, mayors therefore carry a heavy load as problem-solvers, but they also loom large among their subjects, as problems in their own right.

Although mayors must belong to a political party to run for election, they are not strongly associated with national parties or their particular positions. On the surface, this makes them appear typical of populist, "anti-political" type leaders who come to power on the strength of their ordinary relatability. However, to classify rural Brazilian mayors in this way would be to overlook that which marks them out as distinct from the ordinary person. For one thing, the small-town mayor is typically a local figure who is already well known to inhabitants for his possession of a substantial degree of personal wealth. Although he (for most mayors are men) may not need to appeal to partisan ideologies for votes, he must nevertheless appeal to ideologies of normative masculinity and power.

Aaron Ansell, who writes about political cultures in Northeast Brazil, argues that male politicians are judged successful if they can embody and perform the moral virtues of an ideal father:

> A politician's successful channeling, begetting, and nourishing depends on his embodiment of the virtues of fatherhood: love (*amor*), vitality (*força*), and presence (*presença*). These virtues are also thought to vary across generations, that is to say, the degree to which a person inhabits these virtues corresponds to their proximity to the source of these virtues (God). (Ansell n.d.)

This is not to say that mayors do not possess formal political ideologies of their own or that partisan schemas have no influence over their municipal policies. Rather, what voters give precedence to are skills and qualities that befit the job of mayor—a role understood principally in connection with the management and redistribution of material resources. Politics in such a context conforms to the densely transactional logic of patron–clientelism.

Anthropologists of Latin America have written extensively about patronage as a practical adaptation to poverty and structural marginalization (Gay 1998) and as a system of morality based on the values of friendship, alliance, and reciprocity (Ansell 2014; Palmeira 1996; Villela 2012). Local politicians prefer to describe such transactions under the rubric of *assistencialismo*, a term that evokes a system of political administration exercised through dyadic relations of help and care. Today, all such designations come with a pejorative edge, associated as they are in contemporary Brazil with discourses of corruption and illegal forms of vote-buying.

Over the past two decades, corruption discourse has developed at pace in Brazil, producing shifts in the way politics is practiced and spoken about.[16] But concern over political corruption is also nothing new. As Roberto da Matta (1991b, 62–63) once put it, politics in the Brazilian imagination is "fundamentally dirty . . . a game in which anything goes but ethics." Such a view is premised on the notion that people are innately selfish and politics part of the human condition. As one local councilor put it, tracing a finger down the underside of his arm, "politics is blood, it runs in the veins." In short, we are born political.

Metaphors of blood and inheritance cast politics in a complex light as a substance or set of dispositions both intrinsic and exterior to the person. This is why, as Marcio Goldman (2006, 250) observes, politics in Brazil is invariably encountered by the ethnographer as "multiple mixtures of belief and suspicion—of the system and of the people within it."

What Is a Priest?

Although diocesan priests (also known as regular or secular clegy) are central to any understanding of Catholicism, we know relatively little about them anthropologically. The dearth of in-depth studies of such priests may be put down to a number of factors, among which has to be included Christianity's status as "the repressed" of anthropology over the period of the discipline's formation (Cannell 2006, 4).

The irony is that for much of the discipline's history, anthropologists have worked in close proximity to priests (from religious orders in particular), relying upon their hospitality in distant outposts and benefitting from their knowledge of local people, languages, and customs. And yet priests themselves and the ecclesiastical worlds they move in have rarely gained anthropologists' attention, perhaps for being, as Cannell once put it, "at once the most tediously familiar and the most threatening of subjects" for a social science whose heritage of European philosophy already draws deeply from Christian thought (3).

With few exceptions, most of the literature on the anthropology of Catholicism eschews any focus on the world of diocesan priests but focuses instead on lay Catholics and vernacular religion.[17] When priests appear in ethnographies, they usually only do so as peripheral or unsympathetic characters: delivering sermons or correcting "folk practices." Such depictions may serve as excellent counterpoints for broader anthropological arguments concerning the way laypeople (as opposed to clergy) live or reason in relation to divine principles, but they bring us no closer to understanding the peculiar world of the priest.[18] This poses something of an obstacle to any understanding of Catholicism as a lived religion, for not only are diocesan priests essential critics, influencers, and mediators of everyday Christian practices, as religious leaders go, they come with a fairly unique set of markers that illuminate how power, in Catholicism, flows.

The priest is pastor, preacher, and spiritual leader of the religious community. In many ways, his role is not unlike that of other religious leaders, particularly other Christian leaders. But what makes Catholic priesthood different from other institutions of leadership? And what is it about those differences that makes Roman Catholicism a political form with unique characteristics?

The answer to these questions is grounded in two sociological dimensions of Catholicism. The first concerns its elaboration through kinship and sexuality—an aspect that will become evident over the chapters to come; the second concerns its relation to authority. In the Roman Catholic tradition, access to divine power (via the sacraments) and religious belonging (remaining within the fold of the church) ultimately revolves around acquiescence to the tiered authority of the priesthood, the bishopric, and the pope. The priest is a figure of authority who, in turn, lives subject to a higher authority. Regardless of the personal wealth he might possess or the degree of freedom he might carve out for himself, it is deference to that higher authority that connects him to the church as a global institution.

The priest's uniqueness among Christian leaders is largely based on the ontological change that he is held to undergo through the ritual of ordination. The *Catechism of the Catholic Church* describes ordination as conferring "a sacramental character or 'seal' by which the Christian shares in Christ's priesthood," and that "brought about by the Spirit, is indelible; it remains forever in the Christian" (*CCC*, §1121). In other words, the Roman Catholic priest is a human like any other but simultaneously an *alter Christus* (another Christ), who through having received the "seal" at ordination has been divinely and permanently enabled to represent Christ to the faithful and to deliver the sacraments.[19] Moreover, the supernatural power this bestows upon him to turn Communion bread and wine into the body and blood of Christ is not impeded by the individuating circumstances of his life but remains "the fruit of grace" (*CCC*, §1550).[20] In other words, while priests are meant to live lives of Christian exemplarity, their "seal" is held to be unconditional.

The mysterious transformations conferred by the seven sacraments are key to any understanding of Catholicism, but they are also central to any understanding of the person of the priest. According to the *Catechism of the Catholic Church*, sacraments are "signs of grace, instituted by Christ and entrusted to the Church, through which Divine life is given" (CCC, §1131). There is nothing figurative about sacramental grace—the Mass is a mysterious event that in the words of the catechism is "efficacious" and that the priest "makes visible" by his person (CCC, §1549).

This mysterious divinity gives the priest a special charisma, or magical capacity, that marks him out from other Catholics in terms of power.[21] Such a capacity does not obviate his humanity but is, rather, said to *animate* it. Technically, this makes him different from other spiritual prophets or mediums in Christianity whose bodies simply become temporary channels for a divinity that resides, essentially, elsewhere. In other words, a priest's charisma is a permanent and unquestioned part of him because it has been stabilized by the rational-legal authority of the church. As a form of power, it unusually combines all three of Weber's categories of authority: traditional, rational-legal, and charismatic (Weber 2013 [1922]).

A priest's identity finds concrete expression in the special rules that govern his life, determining everything from who he may live with and how he must dress to how he is addressed and the authority he answers to. Parish priests are unique among church leaders for their constant contact with ordinary parishioners keeps them rooted to the world. As pastors who live in the midst of lay communities communities, they are called upon as wordly problem-solvers and as gatekeepers to the sacraments.[22]

In Catholicism the office of priest is only licit (binding in canon law) if the candidate conferred is male, and men admitted to the priesthood are expected to remain celibate.[23] While celibacy as a spiritual discipline can be found in other religious traditions, no other religious institution demands celibacy from its specialists to quite the same degree as the Catholic Church. The chastity demanded of priests is a lifetime commitment, one that binds the priest to the institution of the church and to Christ "in such a way that [he is] able to act in the person of Christ the Head" [CCC, §1563]. This particular bond gives rise to a series of oppositional combinations, for although the "seal" of ordination is unconditional, it is nevertheless founded on promises of obedience to authority and submission to discipline. According to Pope Paul VI's famous encyclical on the celibacy of the priest, the promise of chastity an ordinand makes at the moment of his ordination is simultaneously a charism to be received "with interior joy," a "total gift of himself to the Lord and his Church," and a bodily discipline he must work hard at. Celibacy, therefore will be proved by the firmness of the spirit with which he accepts the personal and community type of discipline demanded by the priestly life . . . it demands clear understanding, careful self-control, and a wise elevation of the mind to higher realities. (Paul VI, *Sacerdotalis Caelibatus*)

Clerical celibacy is therefore, at once, a gift received, a sacrifice offered, and an ongoing skill to be mastered through discipline. The potential contradictions in this flow of logic (why does the "gift" of celibacy spontaneously bestowed upon the priest require such sacrifice and discipline?) belong to a form of Catholic reasoning premised on centripetal elasticity. Such reasoning proliferates across documents issued from the magisterium, and its effect is both centralizing and elastic, reaching toward oppositional possibilities and logics while continually returning to an authoritative center.[24]

A final feature of the diocesan priest, then, concerns his doubleness (Mayblin 2019b) or the specific manner by which he is configured in social life through a panoply of oppositions: the priest is chaste and virile, human and God-like, equal and superior, universal and specific, servant and leader.

The notion that the priest's body is made in the model of the church to be a container of opposites finds echoes in theoretical articulations of Catholicism as a formidable political form based on Roman imperialism, in which a central authority constitutes itself as hegemonic by encompassing and thereby cannibalizing all diversity. The political thinker Carl Schmitt used this articulation of Catholicism to attack Protestant forms of liberalism and democracy, arguing that the great political virtue of the medieval church was to have understood itself as a *complexio oppositorum*—a complex of doctrinal and social opposites brought into a single formation. As Schmitt characterizes it,

> [The Catholic Church] has long and proudly claimed to have united within itself all forms of state and government; to be an autocratic monarchy whose head is elected by the aristocracy of cardinals but in which there is nevertheless so much democracy that, as Dupanloup put it, even the least shepherd of Abruzzi, regardless of his birth and station, has the possibility to become this autocratic sovereign. Its history knows examples of astounding accommodation as well as stubborn

intransigence, the manly ability to resist and womanly compliance—a curious mixture of arrogance and humility. (Schmitt 1996, 7)

The *complexio oppositorum* is a unity that specifically resists the resolution of opposites. Rather than capitulating to a higher Hegelian third, it permits oppositions to clash and derives political energy from the tension generated. In this way, the church can encompass vast differences almost impossible to reconcile. For Schmitt, this capacity to contain opposites in tension did not signal collusion or compromise but strength, as embodied by the maxim that what makes the imperial imperial is its capacity to entail its own negations (Muehlebach 2009, 499).[25]

The priest's body is a site of such political energy, for it is sexually and theologically configured to act as a symbol of a transcendent universalism yet belongs to a culturally and historically situated person whose individuating circumstances give his mission a certain uniqueness. Through the stories of Padre Jorge (described at the start) and other priests, I argue that the political energy of Catholicism is not the product of abstract antimonies held in tension (as Schmitt might have it) but antimonies that are continually being resolved and reconstituted via networks of relations articulated by desire.

Desire is both transcendent and transgressive. People desire what is just beyond them, and that which they are forbidden from desiring. To speak of the priest as an inherently transgressive figure seems odd when we think about the church as such a bastion of order and authority, but the transgressive possibility is a necessary dimension of Catholic priesthood. As one priest theologian elaborates:

> The Catholic priesthood can and cannot fail, each in important ways. It can fail because the image of Christ that is meant to be impressed on the soul of each priest can be obscured, in more minor or extremely serious ways, by the absence of justice, chastity, wisdom, holiness, or zeal in the life of the given person. But by another measure it also cannot fail, since Christ sustains the mystery of the sacramental priesthood in every age.... Peter is archetypal, crucified upside down, a paradoxical inversion of Christ, unworthy to imitate him but still bearing witness to his Master mediating truth to the world. (White 2020, 13)

Put differently, priests represent the virtue of the church but in a motile way that is inherently unstable. This is not necessarily to the detriment of the church for as Massumi (1993, 27–31) stresses, boundaries are set in the process of passage. It is only through their constant journeying through the profane world that a scared stillness at the heart of the church can be properly established. In continually moving toward or away from that sacred center, priests enable the church to heave into view as a magisterial entity that transcends their humanity.[26]

By accompanying some mayor-priests for part of their passage into the turbulent world of party politics, this book illuminates specific instances of Catholic centripetal elasticity in action and contributes toward a more general theory of Catholic institutionalism. For it is only through such movement and elasticity that the church constitutes itself as an exceptionally enduring institution.

Vital Concepts: Faith and Desire

This book traces a relationship between politics and religion: two locally salient categories that, in formal terms, should not mix—or should only mix in carefully controlled ways. In that sense, it traces the cultural construction of categorical boundaries and their continual renegotiation. But in the unfolding of that story, what really comes to the surface are certain recurrent forces that work across both categories, dissolving and reconstructing them.

The social construction of the priest as male and celibate is central to this story. It cascades outward, making this very much a book about love, desire, gender, and sexuality. This focus on sexuality shores up a peculiar collaboration between two kinds of patriarchal institution: the organized homosocial core of the church and a male-dominated world of local politics. In the following pages, faith and desire traverse the borderlines between the religious and the political, weaving together practical yearnings for a fairer society with more existential desires for recognition and self-worth.

Like other ethnographers, I have found desire a useful analytic for grasping certain elements of the human experience that have to do with needs and wants and examining the peculiar (sometimes latent, often irrational) charges that needs and wants generate.

Like the anthropologist Holly High, who employs a revised Lacanian model of desire to draw attention to "the holes: the missing or hidden parts where meaning fails, is contradictory or incomplete, but nonetheless compelling" in Laotian political culture, I, too, have found desire helpful to think within a context where needs are great, silence is pointed, and ambiguities are formative (High 2014, 15). Theoretically, this has involved triangulating psychoanalytical and vitalist philosophical (or Deleuzian) languages of desire with ethnographic material to produce a fundamentally anthropological understanding of desire as "culture work"—what Henrietta Moore sees as the productive translation between the cultural specificity of psychoanalytical constructs and the full diversity of human experience (Moore 2007).

A central challenge when weaving psychoanalytical and Deleuzian concepts of desire together concerns the quite different sets of imagery they give rise to and their oppositional stances on the question of lack. Rather than pinning my colors to either theoretical mast, I follow my interlocutors in their own negotiations of desire's variegated flows, and in the rest of this section, I outline these opposed conceptions of desire—both as lack and as presence—and suggest how they combine in people's own understandings of religion and politics in Northeast Brazil.

Desire as Lack and Presence

In the psychoanalytical tradition that traces back to Freud, desire emerges at the point of castration complex that leads to the separation between males and females and so, in part, to the notion of human identity itself. For Freud, the process through which we emerge as individuals is fundamentally associated with a sense of loss that manifests as neuroses and in the setting up of symbolic surrogates for the "lost object."

Lacan would later develop this notion of loss into a notion of "lack" generated from the subject's relation to the symbolic order of language. In a Lacanian perspective, lack is not tied to any one specific object but is rather an innate and essential part of one's being derived from the human inability to think, want, or express anything outside of the symbolic order. In Lacan's famous line, desire for recognition can be no other than "the desire of the other" (Lacan 2004). Subjectivity is nothing more than a permanent extension of the famous "mirror stage," marking a fundamental alienation between the self and the world.

In contrast to the psychoanalytical emphasis on lack and alienation, the tendency emerging from continental philosophy and, in particular, the work of Deleuze and Guattari is to construct desire as a positive force of production. Desire in their model is neither the product of a lack nor something trapped in an endless, melancholy relationship to it. Rather, it is an "engine of becoming," actively producing more of itself—more sensation, more horizon. To use their phrase, it is "desiring production." Herein lies a critique of philosophical and psychoanalytical traditions of thought that establish connections in a "top down" manner through vertical relations and transcendent principles. Deleuze and Guattari's tracing of desire is, by contrast, horizontal and takes place only on a plane of immanence. Desire as they imagine it is diverse and multiple—"the synthesis of heterogeneity as such" (Deleuze and Guattari 2004 [1987], 330)—and "machinic" in the sense that it forms connections between human and nonhuman things.

One of the key contributions of this alternate tradition for thinking about desire—indeed, of Deleuzian thinking in general—is its capacity to be as unexpected and liberating as it is predictable and imprisoning. If thought in the style of Foucault and Lacan would appear to lock people into cages from which there is no possible angle for escape, in Deleuzian philosophy, the social field "leaks out on all sides" (Deleuze 2006, 127). In other words, desiring production—with its inventions, escapes, and sublimations—is a motivational force, constantly undoing power and opening up alternate forms of subjectivity.

As Biehl and Locke argue, there is important potential here for anthropology:

> Deleuze's cartographic approach makes space for possibility, *what could be*, as a crucial dimension of what is or what was. It brings crossroads—places where other choices might be made, other paths taken—out of the shadow of deterministic analytics. It brings alternatives within closer reach. Ethnography, at its best, strives for the same achievements, and Deleuze's approach has obvious potential to inform and inspire new partnerships and methods. (Biehl and Locke 2010, 323)

For my interlocutors, such potentiality is important, but for them, social fields do not simply "leak out on all sides"; transcendent forces compel them to. One of the problems anthropologists of Christianity confront, then, particularly when working with a vitalist philosophy of the Deleuzian sort, is one of incommensurability. As Bruno Reinhardt points out, Deleuzian concepts were crafted with the aim of subverting transcendentalist strategies of absolute definition and control of the human. . . . But Christianity comprises its own multiplicities, the most fundamental of them being the mystery of a triune God, a source of both theological specificity and heretic imperatives. (Reinhardt 2015, 406)

The "difference Christianity makes" to thought and action at the ethnographic and philosophical level needs to be retained (Haynes 2014). Following Reinhardt (2015, 406–7), my approach in this book is "contrapuntal" in the sense that it seeks to embrace "moments of resonance" as well as "dissonance" between native and academic concepts.[27]

In the first part of the book, I therefore trace a familiarly biblical and hence vertical notion of desire deriving from the origin story of the Fall. With this event, God retreats from the world, leaving humans in the lamentable condition that St Augustine was so astute in establishing. This melancholic situation—well articulated among my interlocutors—belongs to a broader poetics of lack-desire in the Brazilian imagination that finds ample expression in the "Biblical culture" of Northeast Brazil (Velho 1995) and its various traditions of moral and penitential suffering (Campos 2013; Mayblin 2010).[28] Focusing on priests as gendered and sexualized agents of lack and desire, I utilize concepts of fantasy, Eros, and the unconscious in an effort to render people's connections to priests and to glimpse how Catholic Eros exceeds associations with "politics" or "religion."

Clearly any discussion of clerical sexuality must acknowledge the church's long history of sexual abuse and clerical crimes against minors (Keenan 2011). Given this reality, my discussion of priests as "agents of desire" could easily be taken as romanticizing. This is certainly not my intention. Indeed—and as I hope is fairly obvious to the reader—there is no sense in which the desire I explore precludes the potential for clerical abuse; if anything, it illuminates dimensions of the clerical-lay relationship that make people, and especially minors, more vulnerable to such violence. While this book does not deal with questions of Catholic clerical abuse directly, there is a growing literature that addresses the tragic complexities of this topic (see Ballano 2019; Keenan 2011; Renzetti and Yocum 2013; Rodrigues 2017).

In the final two chapters of the book, I take a more horizontal approach to desire in exploring rituals of elections and their aftermath.

Fé (faith), the ethnographic concept enervating these chapters, was considered relevant in any sphere of life, and the political was no exception. The "vote of faith" in the title of this book refers not only to the mixing of politics and religion but also to the basic phenomenology of small-town elections that are held to depend upon a complex of forces, immanent and transcendent. Every vote, it was variously explained to me, constituted a "vote of *fé*" regardless of religion.

"A person trusts in their chosen candidate—it's a trust thing," said a young lorry driver on the topic, "but everyone knows that trust can be broken. Without *fé*, no intelligent person would ever vote."

Fé is imagined as a driving force and compunction toward goodness. It is commonly associated with the category of "religion" and is believed to become stronger though prayer and good works. *Fé*, in this traditional sense, aligns with desire for God. Such desire is human and therefore based on lack and imperfection, but with proper training, it becomes closer in type to God's desire, which, by definition, cannot be based upon lack because God is plenitude. In everyday life, however, *fé* is not necessarily a conscious expression of trust in God; it may simply be the embodiment of a vital energy, intrinsic to all worldly matter. *Fé* therefore differs from its English cognate "faith" in the sense that while it may become dormant, it can never be said to be lost or absent.

Fé runs through mayor-priest discourse in connection with electoral practice, rituals, and miracles. In its broad articulation of the human, the nonhuman, and the more-than-human, I view it in a Deleuzian sense as "horizontal" and "machinic." As a mode of desire that is so often experienced as spontaneous and that serves to open people up to miraculous events, I find it to be, in Deleuze's terms, "productive." But *fé* does contain a fundamental relationship to lack-based desire in the fact that it both precedes and responds to needs and yearnings. As a divine spark or vitalist force that is simultaneously inside and outside the person and, for that matter, inside and outside the Fall, it is not "either/or" but "both/and" in nature.

"A Form of Devotion to This World"

The ethnographic research that makes up this book emerges from almost twenty years of engagement with the region and its people during trips of differing lengths. My two most sustained periods of fieldwork happened in 2001–3 (eighteen months) and in 2011 (six months), and the data on the mayor-priests was collected mostly between 2011 and 2017. The period of research and writing of this book has therefore spanned a rather large section of my life and weathered changes both personal and global.

In Brazil, I have come and gone between the houses of my original host family in the village of Santa Lucia (the site of my first research, 2000–2005) and friends in the neighboring market towns. From these close contacts I came to know a diverse cross-section of the population, from small-holding producers and landless sharecroppers to doctors, mayors, and state deputies.

As the research on mayor-priests intensified, I ended up traveling deeper inland to interview people living in the *sertão* region, as well as in neighbouring states. Between 2010 and 2014, I observed and participated in many forms of public and religious life: church services, Bible study groups, civic processions, political rallies, and local council meetings. I also had countless serendipitous conversations with local inhabitants about politics and religion and conducted dozens of interviews with parish priests, lay leaders, local politicians, and mayor-priests.

While the book is broadly about a particular region and its people, the specific focus for this research was a cohort of six priests who all knew one another and who were at the time, or had been in the past, municipal mayors. Out of that particular cohort, three had left the church to marry and assume families, one had returned to the priesthood, another intended to return to the church as soon as his political term was over, and the last intended to continue living a secular life. All six of these men were at the time and still are, to my knowledge, fully ordained priests. Over the course of my research, I increasingly came to see these men as a unique collective: a group of peers who had made similar choices in life and who, for all their individual differences, were bound together by a common understanding of what those choices had cost them.

The mayor-priests had many things in common. They were all proud *Nordestinos*, had been born in the late 1950s to 1960s to poor or lower-middle-income agricultural families and, prior to entering the church, had been involved in religious, youth-led political and civil movements. All described their attraction to ministry as an extension of their desire to "serve the people" and spoke of their vocations in connection with the political commitments of liberation theology. At the same time, they almost all recognized that, given their backgrounds, the church had been one of the only routes available to higher education and to eventual economic stability.[29] These mayor-priests were trained for the priesthood at one of two seminaries located, respectively, in Olinda and João Pessoa, which were, at the time of training, fading bastions of liberation theology.

A final significant point of convergence was the fact that all openly identified as heterosexual and tended to be more liberal in their interpretation of Catholic pronouncements on gender and sexuality. As clergy they were therefore representative of a particularly progressive epoch in Brazilian church history. Nonetheless, their trajectories can show us something broader.

As with all fieldwork, my positionality in Brazil as a foreign researcher has shaped the form this book has taken, from the nature of the data gathered through to its final analysis. Most interlocutors, on coming to know me, categorized me as a white, middle-class, "doutora", and this probably facilitated my access to certain circles of people. Such affordances weren't always forthcoming, however, as being a woman made it difficult to gain access to masculine spheres—and to the worlds of priests especially.

The mayor-priests who feature in this book eventually came to know me as the *Inglesa* (Englishwoman) who was conducting research on *padres na política* (priests in politics) and participated willingly in the study. The lives of diocesan priests can be hard to research, for they are beholden to secretive ecclesiastic worlds, and may be cautious of secular researchers. With time and some effort on my part, however, most of the mayor-priests I contacted became interested in my project and were happy to be interviewed.

Through chains of conversations—some occurring in municipal or home offices, others in rectory parlors or on car journeys—I was able to put together the trajectories of these men's lives and to understand what had led them to where they were. As the fieldwork months passed, I was given permission to research one priest's electoral campaign and to shadow some of the mayor-priests as they carried out their public duties traveling around their municipalities, visiting local amenities, and attending to people in their offices.

Starting out, I had no idea how ethically challenging researching the mayor-priests would turn out to be. But I quickly realized that the two local institutions I had chosen for objects of study—local politics and the church—functioned in a collaborative sort of tension with one another through sexual taboos and shared ideas about the status of women. The mayor-priests may have been outside the church, but they remained to differing degrees beholden to the patriarchal "culture of secrecy" that governs it (Jordon 2000; Mayblin 2019b). Part of my research process therefore involved learning how to decode pointed silences, how to read the double meanings embedded in jokes, allusions, and gestures.

That said, this book would not have been possible were it not based on some very open and honest conversations with the mayor-priests. The level of working connection I achieved with this small cohort of men was undoubtedly down to the fact that, at the time of my research, they were not in active ministry and therefore had a level of professional and psychological distance from the church that allowed them to speak to me freely. But I also believe that their willingness to put their stories on record stemmed, in part, from their own curiosity. In talking about their unusual trajectories, they were better able to understand their complex identities.

Given the delicate nature of some of this research, I have taken care to anonymise as much as possible. The names of the mayor-priest protagonists and certain place-names could not be changed because they are already connected in the public domain, but in most other instances I have employed pseudonyms, and in one or two places, have filtered data through composite characters.

As Bhrigupati Singh (2015, 2) once wrote, "An anthropologist may strive for expressive knowledge, not as a subject mastering an object but rather as a form of devotion to this world." While the writing of this book has posed some ethical challenges, the final product is very much "a form of devotion to this world"; an attempt to pay tribute to the honesty of my many interlocutors by bringing their reflections into conversation with honest reflections of my own. Such a book would not have been possible had I opted to participate in the institutional church's culture of silence around priests' sex lives or on matters of sexuality, but neither could it have been based on full disclosure. I hope the reader will see that, throughout this book, my principal interest has been in the public discourse that already exists in relation to the sexual and private lives of priests rather than the facts of any individual's life.

Other caveats should also be noted, connected to the onward march of time. During the protracted writing of this book, key events rocked and recomposed the country. Among these were Operation Carwash and the impeachment of Dilma Rousseff, the coming to power of far-right president Jair Bolsonaro, the Amazonian Synod (which debated and ultimately rejected the possibility of a select, non-celibate Amazonian priesthood), and the global pandemic of COVID-19. As the effects of these events concatenate outward, shaping Brazilian lives as I write these very words, it is right to suppose that they will have some influence on the cultural patterns discussed here and the trajectories of future priest politicians. While this book cannot possibly do more than mention the fact of these events, my hope is that it will nevertheless open windows onto the important work currently being done on those events by other scholars.

An incontrovertible truth about the anthropological process is that it never ends. Books get written, but they cannot put a stop to things. John Collins (2015, 43), in the opening pages of his ethnographic account of life in Bahia's Pelourinho, puts it pithily: "I must admit that this book is an artefact of a story that has gotten, and will continue to get away from me."

The Chapters

The first two chapters set up some of the key issues that bring mayor-priests into existence and animate discussion about them.

Chapter One establishes the setting of "small-town" politics in the rural *agreste* and explores the laments and critiques that circulate among people in relation to the practice of patronage. Focusing on recurring tropes of addiction, suffocation, and vice, I ask what productive work such tropes perform when it comes to imagining other political worlds.

In Chapter Two, I explore how clerical celibacy models a concept of divine kinship that is offered up as a radical alternative to the corruption of democratic party politics. By tracing celibacy's history in Brazil and connecting it to the lived histories of the mayor-priest cohort, I locate it within a wider libidinal ecology of desire, promise, and secular passage. Celibacy as a *theopolitical performance* is key, I argue, not only to understanding the nature and appeal of the mayor-priest as a figure, but for understanding the Catholic Church as a political actor whose power and influence derive not from its rejection of the human sexual body but from its capacity to inhabit and discipline it.

Chapters Three and Four explore politics and religion as a libidinous cartography.

In Chapter Three, I focus on a Catholic gender paradox: why do women make up the majority of the active Catholic faithful? Rather than asking what benefits organized religion brings to women's lives, I use the lenses of gender, sexuality, fantasy, and desire to examine how women negotiate cultures of machismo and situate themselves in relation to priests, in particular. What social goods are produced by female-priest encounters? And why does women's desire entail both collaboration in and resistance to patriarchal violence? Starting with the carnality that structures the relationship between priests and laywomen, I explore the priest's (dis)connection from secular heteronormative masculinity and hazard some answers.

Chapter Four examines how queer, celibate, and heteronormative concepts of gender and sexuality are held in tension in the making of mayor-priests through a delicate performance of what I call "virile celibacy." Using the metaphor of "passage" and the priest as a transgressor of boundaries (between the church and the world, the religious and political), I explore the situations of three mayor-priests at different points in their political careers to show how private choices and public performances in connection with women have concrete effects on political trajectories. I ask what this might reveal about the conflicted nature of a church that enshrines sterility but depends, for its continued reproduction, on the fecundity of the female body.

In Chapters Five and Six, I examine how *fé*, understood in the "machinic" sense described by Deleuze and Guattari, manifests as a political and economic method.

Chapter Five centers on the final week of a mayor-priest's electoral campaign, detailing, from a personal perspective, the ritual mechanics, overall sensorium, and affective materiality of rural Brazilian elections. The story of what happens to me, the ethnographer, that week provides context for a deeper discussion on the nature of *fé* (faith) and of its constitutive role in local political process. Why, I ask, do highly cynical people who are not particularly religious and do not believe that morality has the chance to prevail in party politics because corruption is the unwritten "rule" of the game repeatedly throw themselves into political campaigns with such gusto? And how does small-town factionalism, coupled with the intense and extraordinary quality that temporality takes on in the run-up to voting, thicken the role of faith, making it productive?

Chapter Six concerns the trials and tribulations of a mayor-priest as he takes up office and compares and contrasts the two divergent models of economy—"miraculous" and "mundane"—that trailed in his wake. The chapter explores how questions of political ideology, and even questions of faith, eventually find themselves subsumed in the simple question of who gives what to whom and on what grounds.

Layered into such questions are fundamental differences between resources that are infinite and those that aren't, resources freely gifted and those that form part of an exchange. Through an intimate examination of the challenges confronting a single mayor-priest, the chapter illuminates key differences between Catholic and democratic forms of authority and reveals something of the enervating yet oppressive potentiality of the mayor-priest's journey.

I conclude by drawing lessons from the preceding chapters that can be applied more widely to the formation of a broader anthropology of Catholicism and, more precisely, to our understanding of Catholicism as a political form.

Combining Schmitt's notion of the *complexio*, Giorgio Agamben's notion of *oikonomia*, and Valentina Napolitano's notion of the church as "passionate machine," I propose we think of the Catholic Church as a desirous and agentive being whose strategy for reproducing itself over the *longue durée* is both political and erotic. What looks at first like an enduring form of authority (i.e., religion) being put into the service of a more transient form of power (i.e., politics) is, in fact, just as likely to be the other way around. The Catholic institution has always been deeply *served by* erotic drives and secular constructions of power.

1 Politics
Endless and Addictive

No one could tell me what it was. It looked like some sort of public art, badly conceived or not quite finished: a thick cement trunk, slanting thirty meters into the air, topped by an outstretched hand, palm flat to the sky. A colossal begging hand? The hand was poised above a gigantic cement bowl—a begging bowl?—which was empty.

Turning away from the hand, I retrieved my old red suitcase from the bowels of the bus and set off to see Dora. Dora and I had met ten years ago when I was a student looking for a base from which to carry out research. As people inexplicably do with young anthropologists, she took me under her wing and allowed me to stay in her house. So it was that I had come to spend my first few months in the interior of Pernambuco, shadowing Dora as she went about her work as the director of a community crèche, trying—with limited success—to make myself useful in ways beyond being a source of curiosity for the neighbors.

Dora was a giver: whatever she had she shared with no expectation of return. When I lived with her, she refused to take rent from me, so I had to find alternative ways of paying for my up-keep, like overpaying for the phone bill, shopping for groceries, or purchasing occasional items for the crèche. Of course, all such efforts paled in comparison with the immense kindness Dora showed me during my first difficult months in Brazil and the support she continued to provide as the years passed.

Dora was born in 1943 in the small market town of Lajedo. Her father was an agricultural trader who bought and sold produce from the surrounding cultivators. The family weren't poor, but their low to middling income was never quite enough for a comfortable existence, so Dora had grown up mired in domestic labor of various sorts. In her mid-teens, she traveled to Recife, the state capital, and joined the Salesian order. Her vocation, as she explained it, was partly motivated by a desire to escape the tyranny of caring for her younger siblings, but the convent turned out to be "just a different kind of tyranny." By the early 1970s, she had become impassioned with liberation theology and left her religious order. She did not see this as leaving her religious life behind but simply as taking her vow of poverty out into the real world.

In 1978, Dora moved into a swampy *favela* on the outskirts of Recife where the houses stood on stilts and the mosquitoes hovered in clouds. There she busied herself with various social projects—bread-making workshops, weekly soup kitchens, prayer meetings—until, one night, a young woman with a drug problem called at Dora's front door, placed a new-born baby in her arms, and walked away into the darkness. Dora took the baby into her hammock for the night, intending to seek a solution in the morning, but by break of dawn had fallen in love with the little girl. She named the baby Rigoberta and, once the formal adoption process had been completed, returned to Lajedo, the small interior city of her birth, to raise her.

The house I'd lived in with Dora and young Rigoberta was on the edge of that small interior city, next to the *bairro novo*, a neighborhood populated by landless migrants from the rural surrounds. The bairro was a place in constant evolution: newly cobbled streets lined with rows of small colorful houses morphing into corrugated metal shelters and twisting dirt tracks. The neighborhood had few civic amenities apart from a modest chapel and an underfunded state school, and it was there that, after a few years, Dora decided to open a crèche.

By the time of my first arrival in Brazil, Dora's life had become synonymous with the crèche, which she had worked hard to build up with the help of local volunteers, charitable funding from a French church, and regular donations of food and other items from local business owners. The vibrancy of the crèche was something of a wonder in the greater global scheme of things, given its peculiar location in the world. The town of Lajedo was hardly Recife, and the *bairro* had none of the sensationalist appeal of a large urban *favela*. This was a part of Brazil that foreign aid never seemed to reach and where locally funded NGOs were scarce on the ground.

Yet even from its earliest days, when the crèche was little more than a bare brick building, women from the surrounding region had arrived in streams. They came in various states of dignity and disarray, pleading in voices—timid, polite, desperate—for Dora to take their children in so they could find work. Word had got around that the crèche was a place where the children of the poor were treated with affection (*carinho*) and better fed even than the children of the private nurseries. And it was true. Dora was obsessed with nutrition and child development. She planned the menus meticulously and encouraged her volunteer helpers to engage the children in play rather than sitting on chairs watching over them like security guards. There was an optimistic energy about the crèche that buoyed us all, and Dora was the source of it.

In the many years since my first arrival in Brazil and my return to Lajedo, a lot had occurred: the crèche had doubled in size, Rigoberta had grown up and left home to study in Recife, and I'd had two children of my own. That evening, as my battered red suitcase sat unopened, blocking the entranceway, Dora and I settled down at her kitchen table to catch up. Dora spoke, I spoke, and Dora listened carefully to my explanations of what it was I was hoping to do next. I was back for new research, I told her; I was interested in the curious intersection of politics and religion.

Dora's apparent interest in my new project boosted my confidence. Her encouraging gaze seemed to make up for the gaps in my rusty Portuguese, giving my speech an unusual feeling of eloquence—an illusion, I was aware, that only she could create in me. Spurred on by Dora's presence, I found myself branching on to the topic of liberation theology and from there on to the contradictions embedded in the notion of "secularism." "A curious example," I explained, "are these mayor-priests: the region, as you know, is filled with them, and one of my aims is to interview some of them."

Dora listened and nodded. She then shifted the conversation over to the topic of the last municipal elections and, in particular, to the subject of the town's previous mayor—a man who had helped the crèche significantly, but who had lost the most recent election. Erivaldo, the new mayor, had a "more complicated" attitude toward the crèche, and this was a source of worry for Dora. She was phrasing things tactfully, but I could tell from her expression that she regarded Erivaldo as she did most municipal politicians, as an untrustworthy species.

I asked about the giant hand at the town's entrance, and Dora rolled her eyes. "An absurd waste of public money," she exclaimed. "Pure vanity."

"But what even is it?" I asked.

She laughed. "Who knows? We call it 'the Mayor's begging hand.'"

I noted the irony. Erivaldo was a wealthy man, but everyone knew that his wealth depended on his skill at extracting resources from the people who surrounded him—first by promise, then by persuasion, and finally by petitioning those higher up the political ladder.

A mustached youth stepped over my suitcase and into Dora's kitchen. I didn't recognize him at first because the last time I'd seen him he was still a *nenê* (baby), or rather, a small boy called Nenê, with a winsome smile whose appearance lined up better with his nickname.

"Nenê!" cried Dora, her face lighting up. "Join us for coffee!"

Nenê had been one of Dora's original crèche children and had even lived with her on and off following various calamities in his young life, including the murder of his father in a bar brawl. It was good to see him after so many years, all grown up and, despite being only eighteen, supporting his young wife with a job Dora had arranged for him.

Nenê greeted me with his renowned smile but didn't appear to remember me.

"It's Maya, boy. You must remember our friend Maya, our visiting Inglesa! . . ." said Dora.

Nenê furrowed his brow, reaching back into childhood memory, but his brain had evidently overwritten any eight-year-old memories it might once have held of me. He laughed apologetically and explained that he wasn't stopping anyhow; he was only there to pick up a horse's saddle he'd left in Dora's backyard. But Dora persuaded him to stay for coffee, and while I went to fill the kettle, she told him why I was back: to interview the mayor-priests of the district.

Nenê grinned and immediately reeled off a long list of mayor-priests' names. "The padres are cunning; they're running the show, aren't they, Dora?" he said, laughing.

"The padres of this region aren't as cunning as the people who keep putting them there," replied Dora drolly, but with a spark of amusement in her eyes.

"Boy, that's true," said Nenê. "This mayor-priest business, it's a strange thing!"

As the evening wore on, Nenê picked up his saddle and left, and Dora and I remained at the kitchen table, our faces fading to silhouettes. I wondered if Dora was being mindful of electricity or if she'd simply not noticed how dark it now was.

Thinking quietly, she suddenly said, "This thing about the mayor-priests, this little project of yours is fine, but the thing I really wish someone would decide to study is the *politicagem* in our politics. It's so destructive. This factionalism we live with is ruining all our lives. That's what really needs to be looked at."

I'd forgotten this aspect of my relationship with Dora: how intensely I needed her approval and how disoriented I felt whenever she failed to find worth in my projects. By *politicagem*, Dora meant something akin to politicking—the small, everyday actions that functioned to persuade or coerce others into voting for a particular side. But she was speaking about a highly localized situation.

"The *politicagem* in *our* politics," she stressed, by which she meant a specific mood of factional warfare common to small-town municipal politics, as opposed to the misdemeanors of politics occurring at a national level. Yet, Dora also used the word *politicagem* to express something about her understanding of politics as a category of behavior in a more ontological sense: that politics was a manifestation of human imperfection, a doomed and futile exercise in itself. In the thickening silence that followed Dora's statement, I sensed her frustration with me for apparently failing to perceive this most perturbing problem. What use was a study of mayor-priests when politics itself was the problem, not the solution?

Something I did not yet know, but was soon to discover, was that the crèche was in a state of crisis, and *politicagem* was the cause. In time, I would also come to see that Dora's point about *politicagem* would turn out to be a crucial one for my own research, or rather, that *politicagem* was the very malaise that mayor-priests were uniquely placed to address. In order to understand the mayor-priests appeal, therefore, this chapter will look more closely at political relationships via the laments, suspicions, and frustrations they provoke.

The crèche had run on a voluntary capacity for years. A small group of committed women had put in the labor necessary to run it. The two minimum salaries Dora had secured from a pool of regular donors were split between them according to a system of relative need and the number of hours each volunteer put in. Sometimes Dora even used her own personal pension to help support the crèche, and while none of the crèche workers lived in abject poverty, making ends meet was always a struggle.

Every other month at least one of the volunteers would suffer some sort of financial crisis: a relative would fall ill, debts would have to be paid, a member of someone's household would suddenly lose a job, and the stress this caused would pull at the seams of the crèche's capacity to function. Whenever this happened, Dora would maneuver in whatever ways she could find, funneling small amounts of money to wherever it was most needed, hosting emergency gatherings around lit candles, brewing coffee, and generating solidarity. Energy levels would recover, work would continue, and, somehow or other, the crèche's volunteers remained committed.

By my return in 2010, Dora had started to have some success with federal sources of funding. The mayors had come and gone in the intervening years, and along the way there had been one in particular who had attracted a federal grant for primary-level education and channeled some of it into the crèche. But there was a catch: federal resources could not be used to provide any of the original volunteers with a living wage because none of those women had any formal qualifications. So a new cadre of recently qualified nursery teachers joined the crèche—not as volunteers but as salaried workers. Unlike the volunteers, they came mostly from middle-class backgrounds.

In 2010, the crèche had become, to all intents and purposes, a hybrid organization running on a mixture of voluntary and paid labor, local charity, and federal resources. And yet it was at this point, when the crèche was richer than it had ever been, that it seemed to be facing collapse.

The new mayor, Erivaldo, had continued channeling funds toward the crèche but was trying, in return, to claim its good reputation for himself. In a coup d'état of media and marketing, he had produced a glossy magazine advertising his various achievements. On the cover was a photo of smiling crèche children and, inside, an article claiming that "the administration" had "assumed care of the crèche."

This enraged the volunteers, not merely because Erivaldo's administration was not paying them for their labor, but because they now risked becoming identified as supporters of the mayor's faction. For several of the volunteers, this was a disaster, as they were, in fact, long-time supporters of the mayor's opposition, bound up in political allegiances rooted in complex webs of kinship and long-standing chains of reciprocity. In short, it was not so much that the *prefeitura* (municipal office) had given money to the crèche that was the problem; it was the fact that Erivaldo had boasted about it in public, thereby appropriating their free labor for his own political advancement.

Politics had certain rules, and the only way to survive was to play by them. "Here in the interior of Brazil," said Mery, one of the volunteers, "in a *town like this*, this is how it is."

In laying emphasis on the words "town like this," Mery sought to convey to me the common perception that things could be otherwise. She was also keen to stress how working for politicians and working for the "common good" were not, in her opinion, the same thing. Gifting one's labor to a charitable organization like the crèche was not politics; politics was a direct exchange relation—with politicians there were no free gifts.

In the days that followed my return to the region, Dora grew ever more desperate. The core of volunteers who had been devoted to the project for so many years was threatening to leave it, posing a risk to welfare of the children. An emergency meeting was called, which I attended.

Arriving in twos and threes, the volunteers sat themselves down in various states of despondence and anger. Once Dora had opened the circle by lighting a candle and saying a prayer, the gathered women began explaining to Dora that they resented becoming *escravos da prefeitura* (slaves of the municipal office). Dora responded by reminding the volunteers that their gifts of free labor were for the poor children of the community, not for the mayor.

"The crèche does not belong to any political faction," she clarified. "And you are not slaves," she insisted.

But the volunteers couldn't see it that way. When politicians got involved, there had to follow a series of personal, dyadic exchanges, but all that Mayor Erivaldo had done was to take from them.

Dora changed tack and stressed that if the *prefeitura* had indeed entered a sort of exchange, it had done so with the crèche as a collective and not with each person individually. "You *are* the crèche," she emphasized. "You own it!"

But this was met with stony silence. The volunteers' ability to identify with the organization, to feel a sense of pride and ownership, had begun to atrophy the moment certain people within it had started earning salaries. It was hardly fair, they complained, that some of the team were getting paid when everyone could see it was the volunteers who did most of the work. After all, it was the volunteers, not the salaried workers, who cleaned, fed, and cuddled the infants. It was the volunteers, not the salaried workers, who waited after hours for the late straggling mothers. The salaried girls clock-watched with their handbags on their shoulders, ready to leave the second their shift was over.

Dora, now wondering if money was the real issue, offered to divide more of her personal pension among them. She would draw from her own pocket, she would go in search of charity, she would try to match the salaries of the paid workers. No one had any doubt that Dora could make this money appear in an emergency—they all knew that charity was always, in the end, forthcoming. The problem was the logic by which the money circulated. Even if charitable donations for volunteers suddenly began outstripping the salaries of the contracted workers, the volunteers would continue, under Erivaldo's political boasting, to feel like "slaves."

Rosa, one of the founding members of the crèche and a long-standing friend, intervened with an argument that was astute, if a little idealistic. She suggested they reject all funding from the government and return to subsisting 100 percent as a charity. "Before the *prefeitura* got involved, we worked well; we never had such problems. We were poor, yes, but we thrived—we were united," she said.

The volunteers nodded in agreement. All except Dora, who pointed out that the crèche was in fact better off because of the federal grants. Since the *prefeitura's* engagement, resources had stabilized, the food was better, the infants now had access to doctors and education specialists, and the number of children they could take on had increased dramatically. Returning to charity status would involve turning away half the children—an impossible task. No, they simply could not go back.

The discussion continued into the night, but no solution could be found. Finally, three of the volunteers expressed their respect for Dora but confirmed their decision to leave.

A Famous Essay on the Gift

As Marcel Mauss (2002 [1950], 16) said in his famous essay on the gift, "To make a gift of something to someone is to make a present of some part of oneself." Mauss's study of gift exchange in various so-called "archaic" societies has given us a deeply human theory of obligation in which the giving of our time, wealth, and labor is the means by which we receive and in turn bond ourselves to, or gain influence over, or fall under the spell of, others. We offer, bequeath, presage, demand, and in return receive all the things we need and desire—above all sociality.

Gift systems come in different configurations, including that which anthropologists have called "patronage" (or patron-client systems), in which patrons, higher in the pecking order, hand out resources to clients lower down the social line in return for loyalty and prestige. Because the exchanges in such systems tend to occur between actors of unequal wealth, status, or influence, inequalities between people are ultimately reinscribed. Over the years, writes Anastasia Piliavsky (2014, 10), "whatever role patronage has played in the literature—whether a means of exploitation, a vestige of feudalism, a governmental pathology, a politics of the poor or an ancillary institution—it has never been a site of positive value in its own right." This may be because patronage routinely appears in places it supposedly should not: in modern institutions where principles of equality and transparency are meant to hold sway. To liberal commentators the world over, patronage is problematic because it appears to work against the very ideals of a particular form of liberal democracy in being personalistic and individualizing. Such exchanges, often subsumed under the rubric of "vote-buying," are said to inhibit collective forms of organization and to therefore work against the whole idea of a "conscientious vote."

"No other concept," writes Aaron Ansell (2014, 6), "has been more frequently invoked to explain the deficits of democracy and social justice in Latin America, and Brazil specifically." And yet, anthropologists have been among those "more open to the possible synergy between clientelism and democratic modes of political participation" (Ansell 2014, 13). At least since the 1990s, there have been significant counter-critiques of the liberal condemnation in circulation, pointing to the ritualized nature and moral complexity of vote-buying in different contexts. In these works, vote-buying has been shown to be far more nuanced, far more "Maussian" in its logics and achievements than its liberal-minded critics could ever appreciate.

As Ansell's (2014) work on politics in the Northeast Brazilian state of Piauí reveals, ordinary people's exchanges with patrons are not altogether oppressive or degrading, nor do they necessarily reinforce power imbalances. The system Ansell observes is more accurately described as an "intimate hierarchy" in which, although hierarchies remain central, transactions occur because both parties adopt a posture of mutual vulnerability. Political practice of this sort is based upon a "fellowship of the flawed," and the intimacy this generates can have an equalizing effect of sorts (67–90).

The Brazilian anthropologist Marcio Goldman (2006) takes the ethnographic defense against liberal critique of vote-buying even further, observing how the tendency to compare Brazilian institutions with Western institutions of any kind is not simply the preserve of liberal-minded political scientists but a trend throughout Brazilian society. In a monumental critique of mainstream perceptions of Brazilian democracy, Goldman takes aim not only at political scientists and their dependence on inappropriately universalizing concepts but also at cosmopolitan middle-class Brazilians who share, with political scientists, the belief that Brazil's political institutions are weak and its representative democracy "backwards."

Goldman's study (2006, 90) of an Afro-Brazilian political block in the state of Bahia shows that politics is a complex "native category" in its own right: not a discrete domain of human activity and judgment set apart from other areas of life but a disruptive set of behaviors (favors, accusations, disputes) that seduces people into "its own space and time." In this way, Goldman is able to present aspects of political process, such as clientelism and vote-buying, not as deviations from a universal model of politics but as a vital dynamic that constitutes an equally valid understanding of "politics."

Brazil is not the only place where anthropologists have tacked such a course, reassessing patronage relations on their own terms through detailed ethnographic work. As the number of the world's countries claiming to be representative democracies steadily rises, anthropologists have turned to the multiplicities of the nominally singular phenomenon of democracy, exploring the interconnections and contradictions between "normative democracy" and actually existing democracies (Nugent 2008; Paley 2008). This is a classically redemptive anthropological register in which local, non-Western systems are shown to triumph according to intricate logics of their own, rather than being simple corruptions of foreign logics.[1]

Written discourse about patronage displays a particularly marked division of this intellectual labor: whereas political scientists tend to view patronage as a kind of problem for democracy, the anthropologists who study it up close frequently see a more complex picture and seek to define patronage as a different but equally valid form of political practice. What I want to suggest in the remainder of this chapter is that beyond the liberal critique of patronage as broken democracy, and beyond the anthropological redemption of patronage as simply an alternative means of doing democracy, there is space for a third take on patronage, an emic critique, which Dora pressed upon me that first night in her darkening kitchen and which I would encounter with ever greater frequency as I began inquiring into the role of mayor-priests and the broader intersection of politics and religion.

The emic critique I encountered in 2010 was unanimously negative about the possibilities and the moral correctness of municipal politics, whether based on older forms of patron-clientelism or on more contemporaneous notions of political friendship. In many ways, it was reflective of a very particular moment, for at that time the national mood was a critical one reflecting a faltering economy and numerous anti-corruption campaigns.[2] Yet some of its elements transcended such campaigns in pointing toward older, enduring regrets about the nature of human being in the world and the impossibility of trusting in any but God. Within that emic view of politics were the voices of those caught up, like Dora, in interminable cycles of *politicagem*.

As we shall see, emic critiques of this kind differ in important ways from both liberal attacks on patronage as corruption and anthropological defenses of politics as a "native category" because they express themselves as structures of feeling: laments rather than fully defined arguments. In other words, the emic critiques I encountered on a day-to-day basis all revolved around sense perceptions of puzzling impossibility and the complicity and claustrophobia that politics entails. They repeatedly implied feelings of frustration within a system that appeared to drag all but the luckiest participants down with it.

Exploitative People

A few days after my return to the region, I traveled to the village of Santa Lucia in the foothills near Lajedo to visit Dida and Amauri, the married couple who, alongside Dora, had hosted me for the duration of my earlier research. I had wanted to surprise them, but as usual, Dida had got wind of my return from somewhere and was waiting for me when I pulled up outside her house on the back of a motorbike taxi. She observed me with a teasing look as I disentangled myself and my various bags from the vehicle, and then laughed out loud: "So the English *cabrita* [nanny goat] is back for more, is she?"

Embarrassed by this greeting, but excited to see her, I dropped my bags and swept her into an embrace, lifting her feet off the ground and spinning her around until we were both weak with laughter.

I had heard on the grapevine that the village had seen some interesting political developments. Tonio, Dida's brother, who, during my doctoral research, had worked mainly as an agricultural worker, was now the head of the local town council. In other words, he'd made it to *vereador* (town councilor), and although he remained, in regional and national terms, a politician of modest resources from a cultivator background, in village terms he was everyone's "friend."[3] That night, I stayed with Dida and Amauri, and the following evening, after supper, I asked Dida about her brother's new role.

Dida took a while to answer me. I watched expectantly as she placed the dirtied crockery into the large maroon washing tub and covered it over with a tea towel, as though tucking it into bed for the night. She would tackle the washing of it in the morning. Finally, she sank down onto the pale rock that protruded like a whale's back from the sand of her backyard and lit a cigarette.

Tonio had become a victim of his own success, she said. She went on to tell me that the family had been worried about him ever since he became a councilor. Since that time, he'd left his wife for another woman and had stopped living in the village with his family. Financial stress and separation had accompanied his political rise. Today, he might have an apartment in town and be president of the chamber of councilors, but he no longer seemed in control of his life. As Dida explained it, debt was the most urgent problem. Tonio owed his lenders everything, even the "shirt on his back." The problem was such that the whole family had been forced to pool resources to help him stay afloat.

We sat in silence and watched the moths working single-mindedly at the only bulb. Eventually I asked Dida why Tonio's debts had become so bad.

"It's the people," she said. "They are too exploitative."

As was her way, Dida used the common phrase *o povo* ("the people") to indicate something between a Rawlsian voting public and a rowdy mass of rural petitioners. Dida's *povo* encompassed all the nameless people in the market, mere acquaintances in town, the familiar faces in church every Sunday, friends, neighbors, and multiple shades of kin. All, to her—in the context of that particular conversation—heartless exploiters.

But then the noun *povo* is rarely employed neutrally. Where sometimes it denotes an immoral rabble composed of endless individuals, each thinking only of themselves, other times it denotes a more deserving if oppressed collective, as in liberationist discourse where the phrase is sometimes used interchangeably with *os pobres* (the poor), who are also, in biblical terms, *os escolhidos* (God's chosen).[4]

Dida's *povo*, in this instance, was the immoral rabble. The problem, she said, was that Tonio did not know how to say no to their constant demands.

"He only wants to help . . . ," she said, her intonation drifting upward, together with the smoke from her cigarette, "because he's too proud to ask the mayor for help like the other councilors. He assumes the expense himself. But he's not rich. We're not rich people. He doesn't have the resources to do this work."

Dida's concerns were, I would learn in the coming months, typical of close female kin of male politicians. In interviews with councilors and their families, I noted that mothers, wives, daughters, and sisters commonly expressed mixed feelings about their male kin's political activities. Wives frequently described themselves as reluctant participants in their husband's political careers, drawing attention to the costs incurred: the inevitable loss of privacy within the home and outside of it and the increased absence of the husband. Some described the drain on household resources ("half the town arrives for lunch," "groceries that would do for one week now last only two days"). Although in theory such women now had greater access to municipal resources, in actual fact, they remained in competition for these with the "exploitative" *povo*.

"And how are things for you?" I asked Dida. I meant the small but steady minimum wage she received from being the village health-post cleaner.

"I'm counting the days until I retire, but my situation is OK for now. The mayors of this region can't mess with me, even though I know they want to.[5] I have no respect for any of them."

Speaking now from the point of view of an ordinary voter rather than from her brother-politician's perspective, Dida changed moral perspective: "They promise you things; they break those promises."

Her complaint had a well-worn tone about it. I wanted to ask whether she, herself, had ever exploited a politician, but stopped myself. "Yes," she would probably have said, laughing, forcing me to recognize the stupidity of my question. Given the opportunity, why would a poor woman like her not ask a politician for things?

"What do you mean 'politicians don't do as they promise'?" I asked instead.

Dida glanced at me with a flicker of incredulity, perhaps irritated by my apparent naivete. But a second later her expression changed, as though she had decided to take my question seriously and was thinking of how to respond. She finished her cigarette, then flicked the butt high over her backyard fence and said, "I mean *politicagem*."

It was that term again. Dora had used it; now Dida was using it, so the next day I brought out my recorder and asked Dida to explain it.

> *Politicagem* is like this: people like me, we the poor, we play the game but never go forward. I have been playing it for years now; my family has. We go back with the politicians of this area for many years. But it's like the saying: a river runs always to sea. Money follows money. The rich get richer, and the poor, like me, get nowhere.

I had known Dida and Amauri for almost as long as I had known Dora. Through my research, I had watched their meager fortunes dip, plateau, but never rise or fully stabilize. Returning after ten years, it was heartening to find their small house freshly painted and still well cared for, but, apart from the small flat-screen television mounted on the wall and the fact that everyone had a mobile phone, nothing else had changed.

The small patch of land out back that had been Dida's inheritance was no good for planting but could support small quantities of livestock. Amauri had continued to combine raising goats and pigs—an occupation that, over the years, seemed to have cost him more than it had earned him—with other small business ventures like making *palmonha* (corn-based cakes) and selling gas canisters, which had done little to ease their precarity. It was thanks to Dida's job as a state-contracted cleaner of the village health post that the couple were able to pay their utility bills and consume meat.

Dida didn't entertain the dream that her life would one day turn around dramatically so she might find herself living in luxury like a character in a Brazilian soap opera. But she recognized herself clearly in the greater scheme of things as a "poor woman"; that is, as someone whose life, though far from abject, was a life that no modern Brazilian aspired to have. What Dida dreamed of was, like most ordinary cultivators and townsfolk across the region, another dependable source of income in the form of a better-salaried position for herself or a close family member. This was the only way she recognized that the poor could *andar pra frente* (get ahead), by which she meant make small improvements to one's house and one's lifestyle, albeit through access to greater credit that could facilitate the purchase of a second-hand motorbike, a new sofa, or a fridge.

"People like me, we the poor, we play the game but never go forward."

Dida had said this several times over the years I had known her, but in that moment, I perceived the shadow cast by Tonio's debts and felt ripples of Dora's desperation. The crèche volunteer's words also came back to me: "Here, in this place, *politics is like this*." For even if, as Goldman (2006) has documented, politics is pervasively understood in Brazil as a "disruptive technology," a game that anyone can be seduced by or taught to "play at," many still recognize it as one in which the decks are unevenly stacked.

In the literature on gift and commodity exchange, it is generally accepted that generalized forms of exchange based on long-term intimate alliances in which gifts are exchanged but not immediately returned have a moral dimension that short-term exchanges and one-time transactions do not (Bloch and Parry 1989). This point has been turned over by anthropologists of Northeast Brazil, who find that long-term exchanges of a political nature work to sustain the moral structure underlying the world, while short-term exchanges, in contrast, "stifle the circulation of objects, prevent a person's renown from spreading over space and time, and generally contract the scales on which the dramas of social life play out" (Ansell 2014, 79).[6]

How do Dida's expressions of unfairness and exploitation intersect with what anthropologists habitually claim about the "moral" nature of longer-term cycles of gifting and counter-gifting? From Dida's perspective, politics becomes *politicagem*, despite the enduring presence of long-term exchanges with "friends" and "patrons" with whom she and her family went back many years, and this was connected to the increasing monetization of the local political system.

Two points have relevance here. The first concerns the fact that electoral politics in this region is rooted in an irremediably complicated system of exchanges between actors motivated by different objects at different points in the electoral cycle. As such, political exchange is neither exclusively long- nor short-term (Villela 2005). The second point concerns the kinds of force that diverse types of "gifts" command. What voters of all classes most often want in exchange for their votes are municipal salaries, but these are limited in number and expensive to procure. A single vote, or a handful of votes, is rarely enough to secure such a coveted dividend.[7] Cash-poor voters like Dida, who have nothing else to gift (besides their votes) but their time and labor cannot compete with richer voters from the landed and commercial elites who are able to capture the same politicians with votes plus cash.

The irony is, of course, that the political gifts poorer voters give to their candidates tend to take much more visible forms: hours of campaign trail work, endless running of small but essential errands. As will be shown in the pages to come, at every step of a political campaign, the cash-strapped poor are visibly present: rigging up stages, driving speaker-cars, knocking on doors, and making up the political crowd. But these myriad small gifts of time and presence can easily be lost, dissolving into the collective vortex of activity that leads up to polling day. In other words, poor people's gifts to political candidates don't always pay dividends.

By contrast, the cash gifts given to political candidates by wealthier elites remain curiously invisible as they are proffered in private and quickly put to purpose. Despite the relative invisibility of these gifts, however, everyone knows that large cash gifts exert a more immediate pressure to be paid back than small gifts of time and labor.

The Suffering Politician

In the weeks and months that followed, I spent more and more time among the region's municipal politicians, and the story was always the same: *politicagem* was an overwhelming concern, but it was not entirely clear whether there was any clear solution because, as a condition, it was so dispersed. Politics, it was emphasized, was ultimately a shared responsibility. Blame for *politicagem* lay upward, with friends and patrons higher up the political ladder, but it also lay downward with the *povo* themselves. "The people exploit. Keep asking for things—it's an addiction they have," said Vitor in 2010.

Vitor was a veteran municipal politician, having worked as councilor for the previous fifteen years. His baritone voice, jet-black hair, and liking for deep purple shirts gave him something of vampiric air, but Vitor was no Dracula. If anything, he perceived himself the victim of a bloodhungry populace.

"I'm a verea*dor* (councilor)," he once let out with a stylized sigh. "This explains why my life is nothing but suffering. Just take out the *verea* and all you have is *dor* [pain]." He leaned back and smiled at me languidly after he said this, watching expectantly for my reaction. I smiled back, wondering how well-worn that particular pun was, and asked him to elaborate.

"Ah . . . ," he carried on in his deep barrel of a voice, "to be a councilor is to have people in your house all day, all night, every day of the week. Never a mealtime in peace. Always someone arriving, someone at the table asking for something. You solve one problem, and another pops up. It's a life of misery."

"How do you cope?" I asked.

"Well, let's just say my mobile doesn't 'pick up' signal when I'm at my farm," he replied.

Vitor's performance was paradigmatic of the load that municipal politicians commonly felt themselves to be carrying. Among local councilors in particular, but also among mayors and municipal ministers, I heard frequent complaints that politics was a brute activity—nothing if not exploitative of resources, goodwill, energy, and relationships. Complainants tended to concede that this negative state of affairs was mostly a result of *assistencialismo*, the preferred local term for patron-client relations that, while referencing a system of hierarchically ordered exchanges, casts it more in the light of "assistance," "friendship," or "charity."

In one interview, Potó, a young president of the chamber of councilors, tried to convey how it felt:

> For example, here I am speaking to you, and in a couple of hours we will all be going to sleep [we are speaking in the evening], which is just when someone will come who needs a lift to the city because they are

ill. I see it as an act of goodwill, but it is *assistencialismo*. Now, I am not going to say it is an exchange, but one knows the people that want to exploit you. You get to recognize the difference after a while. I've never refused to help anyone, but there are situations where, well, I'm human after all, and there are situations when I reach my limit. Sometimes I am rude, I slam the door shut, I don't want to know about it.

Under the first government of Lula, words like *assistencialismo* and *clientelismo* went from being analytical terms used by social scientists to describe particular forms of patronage relationship to concepts reported in the Brazilian media as "political syndromes" in need of redress (Ansell 2014). And it is true that in 2010, patronage (whether under the rubric of *politicagem* or *assistencialismo*) was subject to constant objectification in public and media debates, affording politicians like Potó and Vitor the opportunity of seeing themselves from different angles as both victims and perpetrators in a broader system.

Whenever politicians lamented the weight of their roles, however, I took the opportunity to ask whether they could ever see themselves doing politics without recourse to *assistencialismo*, and the answer was always, "No, that would be political suicide."

As Potó put it, "You can't run away from it. My ideology was always contra *assistencialismo*, but if you don't do it, you just don't get elected."[8]

Potó's words, like those of other politicians I spoke to, point back to the common and—at that time—widely unquestioned difference in Brazil between efficacious and idealistic politicians. Efficacious politicians are Machiavellian; according to the common saying *robou mas fez* ("robbed but got the job done"), their moral compromises are legitimate because they get the job done. The irony of the idealist politician whose exacting moral standards make him a "bad" politician in practice derives from a deeper assumption about the nature of municipal-level democracy, which is imagined as a pragmatic method for the circulation and production of resources and not as a relevant context for the expression of abstract political ideologies (Villela 2005).

All the same, even democracy as a pragmatic mode of action is based on codes of loyalty and honor, and this leaves it open to criticism. As Jorge Villela and Ana Claudia Marques (2006) once noted, politicians feel exploited by the *povo* when these codes are shattered; when, for example, a town councilor works to support a client all year around with hospital trips and baskets of food only to discover they have "lost" their investment, on the eve of an election because the client accepted a bundle of notes from an opposing candidate. Complaints of this kind are common, particularly among politicians who have failed, by these rules, to get ahead. But the complaints related to me all came from political representatives in relative positions of success.

Vitor and Potó were, at the time of those conversations, highly regarded heads of council, potential candidates for vice-mayorships and therefore, one could say, at the top of their games. In describing themselves as "exploited," they were alluding not so much to individual transactions that had failed to provide the desired return but more to a generalized state of affairs: a collective experience of worn-downness (*desgaste*) within a system of constant and unending demand.

There remained a charged awareness among all the politicians I spoke to that the line between an exploitative *povo* and a needy *povo* was a blurred one. No politician I spoke to ever denied this, and many expressed sadness and some embarrassment about the sorts of things they had been asked to provide ("a mattress to sleep on"; "a new pair of shoes"; "I gave her a rusty old stove I had lying out the back and from that moment on, it was like I was a saint"). The notion of exploitation, when used in these kinds of narrative contexts, has a complex semiotics: it gestures to the unfairness of broader state structures influencing those encounters but reaches, also, beyond the contemporaneity of those structures toward a more enduring assessment of the human condition in which needs and desires, victims and perpetrators are often one and the same.

Ontological Mistrust, Suffocation, and Entrapment

Complaints about the moral fiber of politicians (and people in power more generally) may be familiar to anthropologists the world over, but in the literature on Brazil, such lamentations form part of a broader perspective on personhood. For Otávio Velho (1991, 1995), the presence of what he calls a "Biblical culture" in rural communities across the North and Northeast gives rise to an "ontological mistrust" of others and a concern with the presence of evil.

Ashley Lebner (2012, 506) elaborates upon Velho's point, arguing that complaints about politics cannot be separated from lamentations about human nature in general. The impossibility of trusting in others (or in human systems of sociality in general) is ultimately connected to the impossibility, within a Christian ontology, of truly knowing the human mind. In other words, the fact that humans are porous to supernatural influences both divine and diabolical means that true intentions are often opaque, and this makes constant benevolent "giving" and therefore "friendship"— especially in its political form—"nigh on impossible."

One does not have to look far for evidence that constancy and harmony are "nigh on impossible." The ethnographic record on Brazil is replete with accounts of mistrust and disunity, not only among friends but also among family. Despite the sacrality of the family in Brazil, much has been written about the impossibility of full trust between couples (Dainese 2017; Mayblin 2010; Shapiro 2016), family blood feuds (Villela 2004), and the role that factionalism plays in the creation of kin-based political lineages (Marques 2002, 2013; Goldman 2006; Palmeira 1996).

The emic critique of politics I encountered in those first few weeks of the mayor-priest project is contiguous within this broader tradition of lament and conveys a frustrated sense of entrapment.

As an ex-nun and social worker, Dora's discourse was laced with frustration at people's inability to adopt correct political behaviors, yet her assessment that "*politicagem* is ruining all our lives" clearly came from a place of personal anguish in relation to the crèche she had dedicated half her life to building. Like Dora, Potó and Vitor's discourse also contained elements of liberal critiques of patronage. As politicians, they were familiar with ideological arguments that opposed gifts to rights and that categorized acts of "help" as political corruption; nonetheless, their complaints grew mainly from the desperation of their everyday existence: constellations of spiraling debt, political uncertainty, and constant exhaustion. Dida's lament came, in a similar vein, from the intensity of personal circumstance: on the one hand, from watching her politician brother suffer, and on the other, from her own apparent failure to progress economically.

Borne from the frustration of lived, material reality, what united those laments was a troubling sense of inevitability. Dora could not see a way to keep the crèche funded without *politicagem*, Dida could not see her family's circumstances improving under the rules of give and take that structured municipal politics, and local politicians like Vitor and Potó could not see anything other than a slide back into poverty unless they played the exhausting role of patron to keep resources circulating.

When people spoke of politics in a way that was partly self-accusing, what they so often fell to emphasizing was the endless and systemic nature of political exchanges. Once inside such an exchange system, a person cannot get out of it—even if they can see beyond, or perhaps behind, it. Reflecting on this conundrum generated an immense sense of exasperation. Even the very language used to convey it reiterated a sense of entrapment. The *povo*, for its part, was said to be "addicted" to asking, but politicians acknowledged that they fed such addictions—indeed, that they could not imagine politics without doing so. Politicians, for their part, regarded their own acts of giving as a vice and admitted that they were addicted to the influence it brought them.

"Here in Brazil, this business of *assistencialismo* is an addiction for everyone," said Tonio, Dida's brother, before continuing:

> Unfortunately, in our town—in every small town—it is like this. The *povo* don't understand the role of the councilor, no. They think the councilor's job is to give them things. They think the councilor's salary is to be divided with them. My own salary is not my own. Sometimes I stop and think to myself: *Hell, Friday was pay day and where did it all go?* A trip to the pharmacy here, a stop for petrol there and before you know it, there is nothing left. This is an addiction for lots of people. It's a vice. My first four years as a councilor of the opposition was when I really learned about this. I'm still suffering for it today. I was in opposition to the mayor and wanted to assist people using my own salary. I wanted to be mayor of the village; I wanted to be mayor to the *povo*! Until today I am suffering the consequences.

Neither voters nor politicians, it appeared, could muster the willpower to break such chains of gifts or promises. I heard this collective critique from councilors, mayors, and ordinary voters time and again: "We're addicted to *assistencialismo*"; "we're too deep into this stuff"; "politics is a vice"; "corruption is an addiction." What addiction conveys is a kind of desire that can only be made sense of in terms that are both intrinsic and extrinsic to the self. Powerful desires have an externality about them—they seem to derive from an outside force, even as we recognize our own complicity in them. To speak in such terms is to reflect on what it is to be part of a system, to sense one's powerlessness in the face of a force that is fundamentally greater than oneself, whether it be divine, diabolical, or immanent in nature.

That sense of compulsion and inevitability was contagious. It consumed me over those first few weeks, putting me in a plaintive mood along with everyone else. Perhaps, being an anthropologist, I was far too sensitized to the problem. Since Mauss's founding essay on the nature of the gift, anthropologists have recognized gift exchange as a powerful vector for sociality in part because it is so difficult—in some contexts impossible—a system to break out of.

So it was that after some weeks of research, I returned to thinking about Dora's initial comments about *politicagem* and started wondering what role the mayor-priest played in that never-ending political cycle.

It was easy to adduce that priests, as religious symbols, represented some sort of solution to this intractable problem, but it was not yet clear to me how they did this. The mayor-priests I was coming to know were not charismatic political leaders and had little interest in grand eschatological narratives. In fact, and as far as I could tell, they rarely engaged any religious language in their public-facing speech. Whatever sense of hope they might have brought to the problem of *politicagem*, it did not, on the surface of it, involve them making miraculous promises or even overt appeals to Christian values. Yet, and as the chapters to come will detail, mayor-priests still differed markedly from ordinary secular politicians. They differed not only in terms of the work they performed, but also in terms of what they represented, and—most importantly—how they represented it.

2   Celibacy as Theopolitics

In 2002, I sat next to a young man on a bus. He was headed from the countryside to the state capital, Recife, returning to his work as a kitchen hand in a restaurant. His eyes were puffy, and his nose was red with what I took to be a cold. But it was not just a cold.

The young man was doleful because, as he was quick to disclose once we started talking, he hated Recife. Cities were lonely places, he lamented—places where it was "every man for himself." Life in a city meant "buying every single thing you need, even all your food." Unlike the village he came from, where beans could be grown and neighbors shared what they had, in cities "no one helps anyone." On the other hand, he reflected, there was no future for him in the village as, since his father's death, his married older brothers had taken over working his father's land.

"I'm sorry to hear that," I said, and after some time, as conversation had reached a hiatus, I returned to reading my book.

The man stared in interest at my English-language book for a while, which made me assume he had placed me as a foreigner. But after a few moments he asked how my father's bean crop had turned out. Surprised, I explained that my father was not a cultivator and that, for work-related reasons, I was, in fact, a traveler in those lands.

The young man considered this for a bit then offered me his condolences. He said he felt sorry for me, so far from my family. In a perfect world, he continued, we'd never have to leave home and lose the protection of our fathers. "Perhaps," he added as an afterthought, "there would be no need for marriage."

I remember thinking this a little strange. What pleasure could there possibly be in never leaving our parents' laps? Never establishing affinal connections? And yet, all these years later, it strikes me that for one possible answer, we could look to the Catholic Church itself, which, for a great part of its own history, has promoted a form of kinship based on mandatory priestly celibacy that is both patriarchal and generationally constricted: one asexual father and many equally loved children stretching horizontally in perpetuity.

The logic reproduces itself at different scales: all the laity children of the priest; all priests children of the bishop; all the clergy children of the pope; all humanity children of God. Whichever scale we look at it from, such a divinely structured family acknowledges only one degree of separation and two kinds of kin relation: that between parent and child and that between siblings. Within this system, humans are related as "brothers," and there are no grandchildren, nor cousins, nephews, aunts, or stepparents.

This shallow, patriarchal model of a family is certainly not the only model of kinship Catholicism elaborates, but it has certain political implications for the way society can be imagined. Based on the Catholic notion of agape (divine, unconditional love), it posits a world in which a father's love flows equally among his children and in which submission to that loving authority brings with it absolute equality among siblings despite differences of age, race, class, or gender.

The priest/father is not the only figure around whom agape imaginaries collect; the mother is, too, and it is the mother who, in many ways, represents the paramount icon for thinking through tropes of sociality based on unconditional love (Mayblin 2012). But whereas women are thought to be capable of loving their children unconditionally as a result of their biology, the capacity of a priest to love his parishioners equally is attributed to his celibacy.

The idealization of the mother-child and father-child or priest-parishioner relationship recapitulates a harmonious Christian origins story in which life proceeds without fissure or competition, thanks to the loving omnipotence of a single, benevolent creator. Such a story has continuity with other love-centered stories of Catholic distributive justice in which the obligation of the person in a superior position is discharged with utmost equanimity, ensuring "that the burdens and benefits are distributed among subordinates in equal or proportionate fashion" (O'Boyle 1998, 18). By replicating God's inaugural and life-constituting gift to humanity, the love of the father does not simply attend to everybody's needs; it generates a sense of unity by eradicating competition and hierarchy among children.[1]

Worldly kinship based on sex and marriage is acknowledged, by contrast, as a deviation from this harmonious model, as is society, writ large with its diverse and overlapping forms of division and segmentation.[2] Ordinary lives belong to a Fallen state ontology in which unity is at best a faltering and provisional achievement and competition is the default state. In this world, people are forced to leave home to look for work, families divide, parents die, and competition reigns.

In addition to this, there is democracy to deal with, problematic insofar as it is based on elections that, in local terms, translate every four years into a bitterly divisive war of sides. As discussed in Chapter One, the fact that people value democracy does not prevent them lamenting the fact that it foments *politicagem* (greed, factionalism, corruption, favoritism). In light of this, the idealized desire of the young man on the bus for a world in which one never has to leave the warmth of the parental home may not have comprised a rejection of affinity so much as a lament about the competitiveness and fissure that worldly kinship entails.

Mandatory priestly celibacy is perhaps one of the most radical political experiments in all of Christian history because it suggests a solution, at both a practical and conceptual level, to the problem of social division. This chapter considers this radical solution through a more detailed exploration of celibacy as a total social complex—that is, by tracing its historical and theological contours in the Brazilian context, up to and including the more contemporary context of the mayor-priests of this study. Doing so raises both the question of the priest's symbolic power (his capacity to represent concepts and ideas that he does not necessarily live by) and the question of how such power is managed and enacted.

In exploring these questions, this chapter places celibacy within a wider social cartography of struggle, desire, and political imagination and shows it to be crucial, not only for our understanding of the nature and appeal of the mayor-priest's authority, but—and perhaps counter-intuitively—for understanding the Catholic Church as a political actor whose power and influence derive not from its rejection of the human sexual body but from its celebrated capacity to inhabit and harness it.

Celibacy as the "Jewel in the Crown" of the Priesthood

The most common justification for clerical celibacy one hears among Brazilian Catholics today is that it frees the priest for complete service to God. Unshackled by the social and economic demands of a wife and children (and undistracted by the pleasures of the flesh), the priest, in theory, has more time and energy to dedicate to prayer and good works.[3] Clerical celibacy is, in this sense, like a radical political movement—its goal revolutionary, its example extreme. In the words of Richard Sipe:

> A priest's statement that "I am so convinced of the Message and my mission that even my sexuality is unimportant in the face of this reality" is startling and strong proof of his convictions, if nothing else. And this strength of conviction is what makes revolutions. (Sipe 1990, 48)

In the 1967 encyclical *Sacerdotalis Caelibatus*, Pope Paul VI officially rejected calls to reassess mandatory celibacy for priests by opening his address with the following lines:

> To the Bishops, Priests and Faithful of the Whole Catholic World. Priestly celibacy has been guarded by the Church for centuries as a brilliant jewel, and retains its value undiminished even in our time when the outlook of men and the state of the world have undergone such profound changes.

This famous depiction of celibacy as the most "brilliant jewel" in the crown of the priesthood has been echoed in addresses and encyclicals ever since and continues to function as a thought-provoking metaphor in theological debates. For Vatican theologian Max Thurian, celibacy is:

> one of those signs that reminds us of Christ's absolute demands, of his liberating return, of the economy of the kingdom of heaven, of the need to be vigilant, to break with the world. (Thurian 1993)

In Thurian's argument, celibacy is necessary not because, as is the way in other cultural traditions of abstinence, it preserves a man's life-force or is good for his health, or even because, in being a sacrifice, it is good for his soul; rather, celibacy is a sign for the non-celibate masses, a "reminder of Christ's absolute demands" and of the eventual end of the world. As Thurian puts it,

> No one who wants to obey Christ can go on wanting this world and the order of creation and the natural order to last forever; we look forward to the end. (Thurian 1993)

The "end," in this formulation, is a heaven where the frustrations of natural existence are no more: an end to poverty and social division, and perhaps even to economy itself. The divinely ordained end Thurian speaks of is radical in its negativity; as a suspension of all "natural order" including labor, exchange, and reproduction, it signals a stillness and sterility that mark the end of the world. Celibacy hereby gestures toward that which Giorgio Agamben defines as "the supreme theological problem" for Christian thought: How can we think or imagine a dimension most appropriate to God? (Agamben 2011, 241).

Augustine explored this supreme theological problem through the motif of "the eternal Saturday" (*sabbatum non habenas vesperam*), making the counterintuitive supposition that it is not the work of creation that is most sacred but the day on which all work ceases.

Agamben (2011, 166) imagines this moment of ceasing as one of "final inoperativity," wherein "the ultimate and glorious telos of the law and of the angelic powers, as well as of the profane powers, is . . . deactivated."[4] According to Agamben, the quintessential representation of the inoperative is the angel who, once God's work is done, has nothing left to do, no messages left to convey, so floats around blowing a trumpet in acclamation of God's glory.

Glory and acclamation, here, cannot be categorized as forms of work, for their purpose is not to produce anything. The celibate priest who does not beget new humans through the "work" of sex or marriage also acclaims, but via his body; like the asexual angel with "nothing left to do," he points toward a state of "final inoperativity." From this perspective, celibacy is not simply a technology of the self with disciplinary purpose (as Foucault would have it); it is a theological sign for the end of the world.

All the same, as an institution that reinforces the operativity of patriarchy, it might be argued that celibacy is nothing if not productive. As celibacy laws solidified across the twelfth century, resulting in the forbidding of inheritance to the wives of priests, a theology of sex was sacrificed and women became increasingly associated with lust, sin, and witchcraft (Malone 1993; Schüssler Fiorenza 1988; Sipe 1990; Torjesen 1995; Walker 2004).

Today, it is not just women whose lives and possibilities for flourishing within the church are tangibly constrained by the institution of mandatory clerical celibacy; it is anyone whose gender or sexuality falls outside the traditional binary. The celibate priesthood is, at its core, a homosocial institution that formally denies the validity of any form of sexual activity between people of the same sex. In subsequent chapters, I shall explore some of the exceptions to this exclusion, but in the sections to follow, it is the productivity of celibacy I want to draw attention to, first via a brief history of its trajectory in Brazil in relation to broader political movements and, second, by turning to my own ethnography to explore how celibacy is lived (or assumed) through everyday forms of ritual interaction, thus reproducing itself as a powerful religious symbol.

Celibacy in the Brazilian Priesthood: A Brief History

In his *History of Sexuality*, Foucault (1998 [1976], 155) describes a cultural network embracing canonical law, Christian pastoral practice, civil law, pornography, and psychiatry, all of which work to codify the "forces, energies, sensations, and pleasures" of the body. Foucault's observations on the history of sexuality in the West suggest that sexuality, far from being something separate from the deployment of power, is in fact the product of it. The historian Kenneth Serbin describes how the Luso-Brazilian Catholicism of the colonial era was pervaded by its own erotic forms that enabled the development of a particular kind of Brazilian Catholic subject:

> The faithful might bless a saint's penis or pray to the famed Saint Anthony for help in finding a marriageable man—a practice still widespread in Brazil. During coitus women pronounced in Latin the words of the Eucharistic transubstantiation in order to guarantee the affection of their mates. In the 1730s a Carmelite father in Salvador used his semen to "cure" women suffering from melancholy or illness. (Serbin 2006, 39)

Within this atmosphere, the confessional provided ample opportunities for arranging trysts:

> Nuns, prostitutes, slaves, poor women both white and black, and *donas* and *donzelas* of the elite all had romantic encounters with priests starting in the confessional. At times priests and women engaged in sexual foreplay or masturbation in the confessional. Preachers offered women money or absolution from sin in return for sex. (Serbin 2006, 41)

Such forms of Catholic eroticism were also undoubtedly entangled with the production of a racist colonial body politic (Aidoo 2018), generating particular challenges (and affordances) where clerical celibacy was concerned.[5] In the early days of empire, for example, entry to the priesthood was denied to Amerindians and Afro-Brazilians on the assumption that such races were unable to stay celibate. This, as Serbin (2006, 38) writes, was paradoxical because "to be a priest in Brazil was to be noncelibate."

From conquest until the birth of the Republic in 1889, the church was technically a bureaucratic arm of the Portuguese crown, and its clergy came more under the direction of the state than the Roman ecclesiastical hierarchy. In Northeastern territories—socially and geographically distant from the centers of religious and political power[6]—priests engaged, as did other colonials, in the sexual exploitation of the slaves they kept. Some kept concubines, and it was fairly common for priests to live openly in consensual union with a woman and to father her children. The degree to which priests informally recognized such offspring probably varied—as it did for all children born out of wedlock—nonetheless, it was generally the case that during the early colonial period, the sexual indiscretions of priests were socially tolerated in a manner quite different from today.

Although clerical flouting of celibacy rules had always presented a problem for the church, it was not until after the Council of Trent (1545–63) that concerns about the quality of the Brazilian clergy, in particular, started being voiced in Europe and movements to "clean up" Brazilian Catholicism gathered pace. However, as pressure for greater autonomy in regional affairs mounted, many sought a more radical reform of the Brazilian church. As the old colonial system started being dismantled, the celibacy question became explicitly connected to broader debates about the abolition of slavery, freedom of press, and the nature of Brazilian citizenship. Like slavery, celibacy came to be viewed as a foreign and imperial imposition that needed to be shrugged off in pursuit of an authentic, national Brazilian identity.

Priests, who were more likely to have access to large libraries and thus to new ideas, were frequently at the forefront of such reformist movements, and many became luminaries of Brazilian Independence (Silva and Coelho 2013). One of the most widely celebrated figures of this time was Padre Feijó, a priest-politician who fought for Brazilian Independence and who in 1834 was appointed both bishop and regent of the empire, all while keeping a mistress and fathering five children. In 1827, the General Council of the Province of Sao Paulo dominated by Padre Feijó and his faction asked the General Assembly to abolish the celibacy law. The proposal was blocked by the ultramontane camp who sought to maintain a centralized Catholic authority.[7]

As the example of Padre Feijó illustrates, it was more often men at the top of the Brazilian church hierarchy than those lower down its ranks who were outspoken critics of clerical celibacy. Such outspoken opposition, moreover, was never isolated but always part of a wider picture of political change, as occurred once more in the 1930s and 1940s during the establishment of the Estado Novo under Getúlio Vargas.

In that era, the Brazilian bishop Dom Carlos Duarte Costa publicly criticized the doctrine of papal infallibility and Vatican positions on divorce and clerical celibacy. The bishop's opposition to the Vatican was interwoven with his opposition to both the Vargas regime and to fascism more generally. Having publicly accused Rome of aiding and abetting Hitler, in 1945 he broke from the Roman Catholic Church and set up his own branch of Brazilian Apostolic Catholicism. The church he established, the Igreja Católica Apostólica Brasileira (ICAB), allows its priests to marry and hold regular jobs in the lay world and elects its bishops by popular vote (de Freitas 1987; Serbin 2006).[8]

The Sexual Revolution and the Negotiation of Discipline

By the middle of the twentieth century, landslide changes in sexual morality were occurring across Europe and the Americas, triggered by advances in contraceptive methods and a new questioning of forms of authority. Under the rational auspices of a post–Vatican II church, Brazilian seminaries started embracing liberation theology and offering broader forms of higher education than ever before, even including courses on anthropology and psychology (Serbin 2006). Priests were also becoming better traveled and connected with foreign clergy and religious and therefore increasingly exposed to liberal forms of reasoning.

Such cultural changes contributed, in the 1970s, to a dramatic decline in vocations to the priesthood and an increase in cases of laicization (Serbin 2006). The unresolved celibacy question remained at the heart of such trends, and, in 1979, the Movimento dos Padres Casados do Brasil (Movement of Married Priests of Brazil, or MPC) was formed (Silva 2008). At its third national congress in 1981, which was attended by the cardinal archbishop of Sao Paulo, Dom Paulo Evaristo Arns, the MPC defined its aims as being

> (a) to provide a welcoming and mutually supportive space for married priests, (b) [to] remain in dialogue with the hierarchy about a more open and inclusive church; and (c) to be active in Christian communities and engage in struggles to create a more just and liberated human society. (Boletim do MPC 1981)[9]

In advocating for a progressive agenda very much in keeping with liberationist goals, the priests of the MPC clarified that, for them, celibacy was just as much an outward-looking political issue as an inward-looking theological one.

As indicated in the Introduction, the mayor-priest cohort of this book were ordained during a progressive time in Brazilian church history, and those who spoke frankly to me about the sexual relationships that had animated their lives as seminarians framed these as normative in relation to the radical liberation theologies in circulation at the time. Moreover, the formal introduction of proportionalism into Catholic moral theology during this era reflected a turn away from deontological forms of reasoning in moral theology and made it easier for priests to relativize the harm caused by their sexual indiscretions. The mayor-priests, for their part, found little comparison to be had between the harm caused by breaking their celibacy vows and the harm caused by drought, poverty, and the military regime.[10] As one mayor-priest put it, "We were impassioned with social causes. We didn't waste energy fighting our libidos when there was justice to be won." By breaking their celibacy vows, therefore, many priests of this era did not see themselves as sinning so much as participating in broader forms of spiritual and political awakening.

All the same, the morally conservative culture of the broader rural populations they had to serve dictated that the sexual relationships of parish priests remain an "open secret"—a situation most young men in training for the priesthood accepted without too much question. As another of the mayor-priests explained:

> For many of us, priests of the Northeast, marriage was not a big sacrifice because we could have a relationship if we wanted to, so long as we were discreet about it. The context—inside and outside the

Church—was agreeable (*agradável*) . . . we were allowed to be priests *and* to take lovers.

Here it seems important to mention that what may have counted, from Vatican II onward, as an "agreeable" context for Brazilian priests themselves was not necessarily so for those with whom they entered into sexual relationships, or for any offspring that resulted from such unions. This is a point I shall return to in Chapter Four. Here it is enough to note that despite an increasingly liberal and permissive society on the one hand and a network of progressive movements within the church on the other, being a priest continued to involve a certain level of submission to an essentially conservative Vatican.

As such, those entering ministry in the 1970s and early 1980s found themselves having to carefully mediate the Vatican's teachings about "natural law" for an increasingly liberal society. Among the mayor-priests, this was managed in a variety of ways, from incorporating proportional forms of reasoning into the counsel offered to parishioners seeking instruction on the use of contraception ("*Senhora*, it is permissible if both husband and wife are in agreement on the matter") to simple, outright avoidance ("I made it a point never to touch on sex in my sermons"). Again, the confessional was the space where much of this negotiating took place ("my child, masturbation is not a sin; we know it is necessary for healthy development"; "sex before marriage is not a sin if your relationship with him is exclusive and committed").

By the late 1980s, the number of radical Christian base communities in action had greatly dwindled, many of the more progressive seminaries had been closed, and the most vocal followers of liberation theology had been silenced.[11] The Brazilian church could not afford to replace its entire clergy, however, particularly at the level of the priests who maintained parishes. Career-minded bishops striving to run large dioceses therefore continued with business as usual by employing the time-honored strategy of willful ignorance when faced with evidence of clerical sexual (mis)conduct. Such strategies have contributed to the tragic cover-up of pedophile priests in Catholicism worldwide, but it is important to recognize that it was not just pedophile priests who were overlooked in this way: priests who deviated from orthodox teachings on sex and contraception or those in consenting adult sexual relationships were overlooked just the same.

The mayor-priest cohort, for their part, belonged very much to that particular generation who witnessed the end of the military dictatorship and received their training post–Vatican II, in the fading rays of a once-brilliant liberationist movement. This was a generation who had always viewed the church as a political vehicle and a means of mobilization. But the mayor-priests also belonged to a generation who had been forced to negotiate a large conservative shift during the course of their sacerdotal careers.

As Rome under the papacy of John Paul II became increasingly inward-looking, the possibilities for open flouting of sacerdotal discipline in other parts of the world became much narrower—even under willfully ignorant bishops. From the 1980s onward, progressive priests who valued their jobs were faced with a simple choice: leave the church or strive to keep up appearances. In other words, remain theologically progressive but make certain outward concessions to moral conservatism in public, such as wearing a clerical collar and living *as if* one were celibate.

Although there was never a period when Brazilian priests could comport themselves with complete disregard for canonical legislation, what changed over time—first, in response to nineteenth-century Romanization, and second, in response to the twentieth-century conservatism of John Paul II and Benedict XVI—was the manner in which particular social, spatial, and theological separations were cultivated and maintained (Mayblin 2019b). So long as priests maintained a celibate veneer in public spaces where they needed to be recognizable, at a glance, as "men of God," many adduced that, in private, they could do as they pleased.

Thanks to modern technology like telephones and increased access to cars of their own, a clear public/private professionalism became easier to maintain. Sexual relations suddenly became "proportionately" permissible in the intermissions of the sacred play: on days off, for example, or in sex motels situated far from parishes on the edge of highways, or even in the parish itself but in spaces that counted as "backstage" to the sacred theatre.[12]

In summary, for the mayor-priests' generation, sexual experimentation was partly an embodied response to the "agreeable" ignorance of parishioners and superiors and partly a conscious adherence to alternative theological principles. While some priests would undoubtedly have interpreted their own sexual compulsions and indiscretions as signs of sin and moral failure, others interpreted their celibacy in more pragmatic terms, not as a prohibition on sex itself, but merely on marriage or cohabitation. Among the latter, some at the more progressive end of the spectrum may even have consciously sought sexual exploration out as a means of spiritual and psychological development. In other words, although there was no official change to the rule of mandatory celibacy, Vatican II opened a gamut of new possibilities for clerical sexuality to affirm itself.

Within this history of challenge and exploration, however, it remains important to recognize how the institution of celibacy, in its core aspects, endured unchanged. The second part of this chapter is dedicated to addressing a major ethnographic paradox that emerges from this—the question of how celibacy, at once such a historically fragile and contested part of the Brazilian priesthood, manages to remain such a central and enduring part of the church institution.[13] In order to address this question, I shall return to Catholic imaginaries about unity and spiritual fatherhood, exploring its symbolic status and its affective power over people in the course of ordinary priestly ministry and interaction.

"Politics Divides, Church Unites"

About a month into my research on priests in politics, I called into a local church office and booked myself a meeting with the parish priest, Padre Ednaldo. Several people had urged me to present myself to him because he was a learned man who openly disapproved of mayor-priests but would speak knowledgeably to me about the situation. Accessing Padre Ednaldo, however, was trickier than anticipated.

Upon arrival at the rectory, I was intercepted by two young men: one a teenager, the other in his twenties. Did I have an appointment? The teenager speaking to me was neatly turned out, with side-parted hair and carefully pressed clothes—even his "distressed look" jeans had been crisply ironed.

"Yes, I have an appointment to interview the padre," I replied, hoping that the word "interview" might speed up my entry. It did not.

The elder of the two sat with his arms spread proprietorially across the row of chairs opposite me. "I was not aware of any interview," he said. "Didn't the padre have plans to travel tonight?" he asked the immaculately pressed teenager.

There followed some discussion, and then I had to wait while they took it in turns to come and go through a beaded curtain that led into the rectory's inner sanctum. Their disappearing and reappearing went on for what seemed like an extended period, like a puppet show with no discernible plot line.

"Padre Ednaldo will see you now," came the words at last. I looked at my watch. It had been almost an hour.

Leading the way through a series of passages, the teenager informed me that the delay had been a result of the padre forgetting about my scheduled visit—because, as mentioned, he was "about to travel." I was lucky, however, he'd very kindly made time for me.

"Oh, we have lots of them," said Padre Ednaldo on the topic of mayor-priests.

> In Brazil we have had various priest politicians, even federal deputies, even our celebrated popular saint Padre Cícero, he was a politician, a vice-governor, a federal deputy . . . the lot. The story of this diocese is punctuated by priests running for mayor and winning elections. The current mayor of São Bento is a priest, my predecessor left this parish to become mayor of Jupi. There's Padre Djalma who served as mayor *twice* in Quipapá. There is Padre Daniel who was vice-mayor of São João. There's been Padre Marcos, mayor of Ibimirim and Padre Kazuza, mayor of Poção . . . too many if you ask me!

Dusk was falling, and we were sitting on an L-shaped sofa with my digital recorder propped up between us. The rectory, a strange warren of dark rooms with ceramic-tiled walls and framed pictures of popes, was attached to the church, which stood tall and proud in the center of the market town. Padre Ednaldo, animated by the turn our conversation had taken, was leaning forward as he spoke. "Why have there been so many mayor-priests?" he asked rhetorically. "Because the priest, whether one likes it or not, is still a great symbol."

"How so?" I asked him.

> If you're a priest in this region, it is not difficult to win an election! If you are a priest, you establish good relationships, people generally trust you. So if you already have a certain—as our friend Friedrich

Nietzsche once said—"will to power" then it is not difficult. I say this again: it is not difficult for any priest to be a mayor!

Intrigued by Padre Ednaldo's ironic reference to Nietzsche, I asked whether he approved of priests taking up politics. He shook his head.

I'm afraid I don't look kindly on priests who leave their ministry to take up politics because, whether they like it or not, the danger is so immense, so absurdly immense that—unless you are a person of profound and unshakable ethics—you will end up being corrupted. Politics is a game of interests, one of the most absurd games possible! When you enter politics to be a mayor, it's not enough to be liked by people; you have to organize employment for every single person. Even the ones who want to exploit, who want only to rob the government! That's why I say this business of mayor-priests is controversial!

Padre Ednaldo's disapproval of "this business of mayor-priests" was based not simply on the classical notion that politics is polluted but on a more specific concern about the impossibility of organizing employment for "every single person," and therefore on the failure of patronal politics to care fairly and equally for everyone. The role of the priest, he emphasized, was not to take up political office himself but to prepare the laity for political office.

At this point our conversation took the following turn:

MAYA: Why is it wrong for a priest to be a mayor, when it is acceptable for him to be political in other ways? For example, many priests of this region have been active leaders in movements like the Landless People's Movement, and the Church has never objected.

PADRE EDNALDO: Yes, activism is politics, but not in the same way as party politics. For example, if I were to candidate myself for mayor here, I'd have to join a political party. At present, this municipality has a population of some 50,000 inhabitants, most of whom are, in theory, Catholic. So as a priest, I represent 50,000 people, but as a member of a political party, I represent only half of them. A people within the church are one; outside the church they become two; two sides—one over here, one over there. As a politician, I stand only for one of those sides. Do you see the divisiveness? As a padre, I promote a beautiful idea, I promote unity. What do I promote as a politician? Division!

MAYA: So it is electoral politics that damages the Church, not politics in the form of social activism?
PADRE EDNALDO: Electoral politics does radical damage. Tremendous, horrible, terrible damage!
MAYA: But what if the ideals of the political party are Christian ones? What if the ideology is to unite?
PADRE EDNALDO: Yes, your thesis is, in ideological terms, possible. But even if it is the best political system in the world, it does not work in practice. Because wherever men go, they always produce havoc, create divisions, create problems. That is self-interest. Behind it, all our interests do not correlate with the principles of the gospel; our motivations do not correlate.
MAYA: Would you say Jesus was a political man?
PADRE EDNALDO: jesus's politics was to defend the poor—this has a political dimension. But he never aligned himself with a political party. On the contrary, he was beyond all such groupings. All the groups of that time had a political dimension. Either they were tied to Roman power, or more attached to the Jewish power, but Jesus transcended all this; his politics was beyond the inferior vision of that society. Where politics divides, the Church unites.

The phrase "where politics divides, the Church unites" is a common claim across Christian denominations in Brazil, but Padre Ednaldo's use of these words did not simply refer to Christianity's power to unify people in a broad ecumenical sense; it referred, quite specifically, to the Roman Catholic Church as the one and only unifier. As such, even though he was not contra-democracy per se, his conviction that democracy was inevitably divisive and claim that electoral politics did "radical, tremendous, horrible, terrible damage" stemmed from a view of the world that was characteristically Catholic.

Symbol and Practice: The Publicness of the Priestly Body

What is it about the Catholic Church in particular that allows it to stand for unity in the way Padre Ednaldo had asserted? The answer, as I will argue here, is not simply in the universality of the Christian message, in fellowship through faith, or the fact that any person might walk into a church and partake in a service. Rather, it is in the configuration of the priestly body.

The parish priest belongs to everyone: Catholics are united through their common claim to him. However, the business of belonging to everyone isn't entirely given. A certain amount of work goes into reinforcing such perception: work that is uniquely premised not only on linguistic and ritual practices (to which I shall shortly turn) but on the priest's assumed sexual abstinence. By sexually belonging to no one, the priestly body becomes, in principle, a crucible for human unity.

Recall the lament of the man on the bus featured at the start of this chapter: in particular, his longing for a world in which one never has to leave the aegis of a loving father. In such a world, runs this idea, the father's benevolence allows kin to remain united. Such an idea is merely a variation of the model of kinship that the church seeks to reproduce under the banner of celibate fatherhood, which in turn gives rise to nested sets of equally valued "children" in the form of congregations, fraternities, and other bodies of faithful. All Catholics are herein of "one blood," equally entitled and protected by the father.

In light of this, we might well ask how it is that the priest, as an ordinary human being with a natal family of his own, manages to reproduce such a unifying ideology. In seeking some sort of answer to this question, it is worth pausing to unpack one of Padre Ednaldo's central assertions: "The priest, whether one likes it or not, is still a great symbol." Throughout my research, I was often surprised by the reflective stance many priests took when asked to speak about their roles as representatives of the church and Catholic ideals (such as love and unity). As Padre Ednaldo explained:

> The Church is a respected institution: she inspires respect, attracts respect. The priest, too, inspires respect, but he has to deal with the great expectations that come with it.

Expanding on the subject, he said:

> The priest represents the Church wherever he goes, which is to say that he symbolizes many beautiful ideas and feelings; so many, in fact, that he personally may not even be aware of them all!

Padre Ednaldo was pointing to the fact that priests are as likely to be respected for what they symbolize as for who they are. Like many priests I spoke to, he resisted any suggestion that priests were intrinsically exemplary individuals, insisting, instead, that the "beautiful ideas and feelings" they represented had nothing to do with them as individuals, but were simply accorded to all priests, automatically.[14]

His assertions on this matter were much like those of other priests I interviewed, revealing something important about the public nature of the priest's body in this ethnographic context: how it comes to stand for the transcendent, and in particular for notions of harmonious kinship and unity that almost anyone, regardless of religion, can identify with. In order to understand the priest as a public figure brimming with political potential, we need first to know a bit more about the origins and reproduction of his symbolic capital.

Through the sacrament of ordination, the priest is formed into a type of exemplar almost instantaneously. This is somewhat in opposition to the saint or religious charismatic who earns the status of exemplar gradually over time through the performance of miracles and the amassment of repeated signs and evidence (cf. Bandak 2022, 115–35). Here, it is worth noting that while saintliness in itself is not ordination's primary function, symbolism—a kind of exemplarity that saints also partake in—is.

The theology of the priesthood is fundamental to the establishment of the priest-as-symbol, for while priests as servants (and representatives) of Christ are meant to live lives of Christian exemplarity, the "seal" they receive through the sacrament of ordination is unconditional. Unlike the saint whose supernatural reputation is built around the amassment of evidence and whose power to exemplify can be easily impeded or undone by the instability of such evidence, the supernatural power ordination confers on priests (to turn communion bread and wine into the body and blood of Christ) cannot be impeded (CCC, §1550). In other words, a priest's "seal" depends on a vital disconnection between his universal status as an *alter Christus* and the individuating circumstances of his life. Such disconnection is not dissimilar to that held to exist between the modern "public figure" and the "private self" in the idealized secular public sphere (see Warner 2002).[15]

The nature of the priest's disconnection from his supernatural power remains, nonetheless, ambiguous. For one thing, the priest is still meant, in ideal terms, to be an intrinsically good person with a vocation for ministry—not just a symbol but an exemplary individual.[16] For another thing, his gender determines his capacity to symbolize, for he is only a priest so long as he is male. Above all, however, it is a priest's day-to-day interactions with people—his *performance* as priest—that cement the social respect he is routinely accorded. To understand the status of the priest as a living symbol, therefore, it is necessary to understand symbolism in a double sense, as a kind of doing as well as a kind of being. This emphasis on the symbolic quality of practice and the practical nature of symbolism is most clearly evident in the priest's performance of sacraments at key stages of a person's life.

A priest who spends a long time in one parish is likely witness to numerous major life-crisis events, any single one of which may generate a vital connection with those concerned. One does not even have to be denominationally Catholic to be affected by a priest's centrality at a life-crisis event, as was the case when Dona Irene died.

Dona Irene was a devout Catholic, catechist, and composer of hymns and religious poems. As she was nearing the end of a terminal illness, her daughter Josefa—a long-time convert to the Protestant Assembleia de Deus—returned from São Paulo to look after her. The day came when Josefa telephoned the parish and requested the priest to come as a matter of urgency to administer the last rites to her mother. The priest took a while to arrive, however, and as the hours passed, the atmosphere grew anxious. A serious air descended over the village as neighbors came out of their houses to sit on steps and lean in doorways.

Eventually, to everyone's relief, the priest turned up. A while later, I spotted him as he left Dona Irene's house and returned to his car, accompanied by Josefa, whose voice carried clearly through the still, flat night. "Thank you, Padre," she kept repeating, "Thank you, Padre. Thank you."

The priest told Josefa to have courage and blessed her.

"With faith in God, Padre, I will find strength," she replied.

Something struck me about the intimate tone of Josefa's words and her repeated use of the term of address "padre." It was more than just respectful—it was familiar, almost proprietorial. Josefa did not know the priest personally, nor was she denominationally a Catholic anymore, but she clearly recognized the priest's importance to her mother as she transitioned from one world to the next. Given such a context, Josefa was prepared, through her tone of voice and choice of words, to acclaim the priest as spiritual father—to avail herself of that fatherly potential.

The mediating presence of the priest at specific moments of life crisis (a birth, a baptism, a marriage, a death) can create a zone of emotional intimacy between the individual experiencing the crisis and the church. Such a connection works in turn to engender or intensify the notion of spiritual paternity, contributing to the symbolic capital of the priest.

These kinds of intimacies are concatenating, for they have a tendency to spill out of the dialogical framework that exists between the priest and the individual parishioner, traveling outward through networks of kin who care for one another. As in the passing of Dona Irene, the priest's power to perform a crucial sacrament makes him a figure of importance to all those who care about the individual receiving the sacrament. In other words, one does not have to possess an unshakable belief in the power of the sacraments to appreciate the importance of a priest to someone who does. Hereby, the notion of spiritual paternity is already somewhat in abundance as a "beautiful idea," one that is continually reinforced through specific priests and specific encounters in societies densely networked by kinship.

"Who could even count the number of fetuses I have blessed?" said Padre Aldo. I had been asking him to describe what being a spiritual father entailed. He explained:

> The sheer number of pregnant bellies I've touched! The women request it—they say, "Padre, bless the baby!" And then I will baptize the same child, and watch them grow. Some of those children, would you believe, I have also married. Some I have even buried. Let's just say I have been more present for some children than their actual fathers!

Across the Catholic community, a priest becomes intimately connected with a broad cross-section of families, and particularly with babies, both in and out of utero. Padre Aldo explained how this sense of kinship rooted in touch, blessings, and sacraments was a given ("a very natural thing in the life of the priest") and something that had to be carefully managed lest it develop into "cases of favoritism" that could interfere with the experience of equality among siblings. Illustrating his point, Padre Aldo referred both to the diocesan policy of capping the number of years a priest spends in the same parish, lest he become too attached to particular families, and to the practice of parents asking priests to become official godparents to particular children, which, he clarified, was canonically permitted but not particularly encouraged by the church.[17]

> I, for example, have many, many godchildren, but I try to avoid this happening because in theory it makes me more obligated to some than others, and this is not the principle of the Church.

However, it is in the linguistic practice of addressing the priest as "father" that intimate relations concatenate, for even in the simple act of that address, the possibility of filial connection jumps into frame. I sensed this in conversations between priests and parishioners, but also in my own experience of addressing as "father" men to whom I had no such social or religious connection. In such moments, I could not help but notice that using such a term, even as a routine formality, produced a definite sort of relation—or *potential* for a relation—to occur between myself and any such man addressed. Such a potential had the capacity to evaporate almost as immediately as it had come into being or, given certain affective conditions (a life-crisis event, perhaps), crystallize into something more enduring.

The mayor-priests I spoke to on the topic were well aware of the illocutionary power of the title "Padre" and reflected both on its positive and negative potential. Padre Daniel, for example, had never forgotten the psychological shock he experienced the first time he was addressed as "Padre" following his ordination. "No one can understand this shock unless they have gone through it," he told me.

Recounting his early days as a priest, Padre Daniel explained how ordination brings about an abrupt change in a seminarian's status. The young man goes from a conditioning in which he has been taught to regard himself as "nobody and nothing" to suddenly being addressed as "father," even by older men who, prior to his ordination, would have been considered his senior. "The impact of that first address by an older man is something you never forget," he said.

The symbolic quality of the priest (and his relation to unity) is not, therefore, an entirely fixed or spontaneously occurring phenomenon; it is continually produced—in some senses commanded—through ritual, touch, and language itself. And it is through this mixture of doing and being that the Catholic priest in small-town Brazil is able to plug into the affective ties that bind people together within and beyond the sacramental life of the church.

Celibacy and Unity: A Total Social Complex

Before concluding, it is worth casting back to Chapter One, where I considered people's complaints about the tiresome and inescapable character of party politics as a system of constant exchange. I ended that chapter by asking what role the mayor-priest may (or may not) play in such a never-ending cycle, and in this chapter, I have started to answer that question through an examination of the priest's celibate status.

Celibacy, I have argued, continues to play a critical role in the church's self-image as an institution that—contrary to party politics—unifies. The mantra "where politics divides, the church unites" is not a generalized claim about the power of Christianity as a religious option, but one about Catholicism in particular and the positioning of its celibate priests as fathers to all. The priest father promises equality and gestures, symbolically, toward a utopian state of "final inoperativity" beyond the interminable and divisive exchanges exacted by the world. This makes him life-giving in ways that other kinds of fathers (including lay politicians) and other kinds of institutions (including the sex-based family) can only ever fail to be; and in a rural Catholic society that is densely networked by the complexities of kinship and "impossibilities" of social relations (Lebner 2012), priests can easily capitalize on this divine possibility.

All the same, and as many priests themselves acknowledge, the "beautiful ideas" their celibate, gendered bodies stand for are enduring precisely because as symbols they are conveniently detachable from the troublesome materiality of their actual lives.

This chapter has explored priestly celibacy not simply as a theological counterpoint to *politicagem* but as a total social complex whose cultural and historical contours have, over the centuries, served the church at different levels and in diverse ways. A curious issue in the Brazilian context examined concerns the power and resilience of clerical celibacy as an idea, given the Brazilian church's history of ideologically contesting the rule or creatively circumventing it (Serbin 2006).

Here, as in other parts of the Catholic world, clerical celibacy can be viewed as an essentially discontinuous aspect of the priesthood—one that has endured over time only because it has been able to feed off the disjunctions and separations between public and private forms of practice. In other words, clerical celibacy is none other than a stable instability at the heart of the institution (Mayblin 2019b). For the priesthood to exist in this public sense, it is what is conveyed (or "acted out") in public that counts. Public action builds the priest-as-religious-symbol, thus working to reinforce a notion of the priest as "sacramentally altered" and therefore as different from everyone else. Like all great symbols, celibacy endures as an ideal, thanks to its strategic detachability from the cut-and-thrust of actual lives. But in the chapters that follow, we will see how well that symbol manages when thrust into the materially demanding context of real-world politics.

3 Faith, Desire, and Machismo

One market day, some weeks after my first-ever meeting with Padre Jorge, I found myself outside his church and decided to look in on him. By that point, I was still no wiser about whether he intended to run for mayor and hoped that a serendipitous meeting between us might reveal his decision.

The market in the square outside the church was in full flow, with Forró music blaring at ear-splitting decibels and people, carts, and motorbikes weaving chaotically around one another. At the church's reception, an acne-faced young man attended the people, screening Padre Jorge from the excesses of the street: the market-day opportunists, foreign anthropologists, and streams of parishioners with various requests.

Catching the young man's attention, I asked for a meeting with Padre Jorge and was pointed through the church to the sacristy, where I joined a group of combed and scented women, mainly middle-aged and older, dressed in best market-day clothes. Through a side door in the sacristy that led to the garage I spotted Padre Jorge and an elderly woman in a white lace headscarf. They were seated facing a wall, on plastic chairs, in a makeshift confession. The parish car was parked beside them.

A stout woman in a yellow dress observed the scene with me. Arms crossed above her protruding stomach, she rolled her eyes and muttered drily, "All the world is queuing here for the padre, and then one woman decides to confess. God give us patience!"

The elderly woman confessing was leaning into Padre Jorge, rocking back and forth with her head facing down. Padre Jorge was sitting bolt upright, his face in profile. He placed his hand on the woman's bowed head and uttered something. She grabbed for his hand and held it. Stiffly, Padre Jorge arose, his left hand still in the woman's grip. With his free hand, he kept patting the woman on her shoulder while gently pulling his other hand away. She stood up and followed him.

As he entered the sacristy, the other waiting women encircled him. He was an exceptionally tall man; some of the women reached only to his waist. The woman who had just confessed followed close on his heels and shuffled up beside him, tears running down her cheeks.

"Don't cry, don't cry," he said, patting her on the head, but with a flatness in his voice that indicated the ritual-like nature of the situation. The crying woman was then guided away by another woman, while Padre Jorge turned his attention to the gathered group.

A mother and her adult daughter stepped up to shake his hand, and Padre Jorge's assistant from the front desk introduced them: "Padre, these are the people who have come about the man with the cancer in his leg."

A conversation ensued about how the man with the cancer in his leg needed to confess; could the padre do it tomorrow?

Yes, after Mass he would go to the house, but was it far?

No, just beyond the town, in the village of Salobre.

Padre Jorge noticed me, smiled in greeting, then turned to someone else who had been waiting to ask him a question. I felt like an imposter. I too had a question, but it was not of a spiritual nature, and it was clear that this was not the right moment to ask it.

As ministers, confessors, and pastors, priests have privileged access to people. Ritual techniques connect them emotionally to individuals, and performing the sacraments binds them to families and gives them access to intimate spaces of the home. Distilled to an essence, a priest's whole business is solace and hope. Add to this his indelible status as holier than other men, and it is not hard to intuit why it is so common to see priests followed around by groups of people as they try to go about their everyday business. It was a constant problem for me when seeking interactions with priests; there was never a moment for sustained conversation.

Rural parish priests worked incredibly hard celebrating Masses, running Bible study classes, and carrying out baptisms, confirmations, and weddings, as well as overseeing the many religious lay groups that came under their jurisdiction. When not in town, much of their time was taken up traveling the semi-arid plains to out-of-the-way communities, performing outreach work, and participating in saints' day festivities. Because of these schedules, priests had to be chased—caught by the hems of their robes as they passed through corridors and paused in sacristies.

The ones who overwhelmingly do this chasing are women—a fact so banal it rarely merits comment, except occasionally in the form of joking. A male friend once compared women who flock around priests to *urubus* (vultures) gathering around a carcass. "Wherever there's a cluster of women, you know a priest must be somewhere in the middle!" His ironic comment tapped into a typical and somewhat anti-clerical joking tradition that casts priests as effeminate "half men" and devout older women as pitiful figures motivated by obsessive faith and repressed sexual longing. But the image he evoked—that "cluster of women"—rang true all the same. This chapter is about the maleness of the priest who sweeps through vestries, pausing in passages to bless and confess, and the desiring nature of those who flock after him. In this sense, it opens a window onto long-standing feminist debates about the apparently paradoxical way that women, in patriarchal religions such as Christianity, make up the pious majority.[1]

Within the anthropology of Christianity, the question of why women tend to be more churchgoing than men has been addressed mainly in the case of Pentecostalism, following Bernice Martin's (2003) discussion of what she called "the Pentecostal gender paradox." For the multitudes of women joining Pentecostal churches back in the 1990s, the paradox that presented itself to researchers was all the more prominent, as women's enthusiasm for those conservative churches was clearly not connected to ethnic identity or part of an inherited tradition unquestioningly adhered to: it was a conscious choice, individually motivated and demanding in its rules and disciplines.[2]

The intensity of women's enthusiasm for these more rigidly patriarchal churches has been partly understood in Christian terms as an effect of intense, emotional conversion experiences and the sense of eschatological urgency that Pentecostalism brings about. It has also been explained by the various economic advantages that reportedly accrue to poorer households when women encourage their husbands to convert and embrace sobriety. As Martin (2003, 54) puts it, "women have used the Pentecostal religious discourse to rewrite the moral mandate on which sexual relations and family life rest. . . . In an entirely literal sense, Pentecostal men have been 'domesticated.'"

Similar arguments could be made for women who participate in other kinds of Protestant churches, but do the same arguments hold for Catholic women? In seeking to answer this question, it is necessary to recognize that in places where Catholicism has been the dominant religion for centuries, women's greater participation in religious activities is not necessarily a result of the energy generated by their recent conversion or their belief in a near and present eschaton. Neither can it be put down to the fact that—as might be the case in Pentecostal contexts—the church helps them to curb male drinking, adultery, and wasteful spending.

Belief aside, this is not to say that women's greater participation in Catholicism is necessarily all that mysterious. It is widely recognized, for example, that much of the devotional labor women carry out is both for their own and others' benefits, functioning in some ways as an extension of their gendered roles as primary caregivers and domestic heads of households (Mayblin, Norget, and Napolitano 2017; Mayblin 2010; Peña 2011; Kaell 2012; Malara 2018). In other words, by cultivating piety, one also performs being a good woman—or more specifically, a good wife/mother/daughter.

It has also been shown how ritual and ascetic practices can empower women by allowing them to embrace and elevate the feminine above the masculine (Bynum 2011), critique patriarchy (Mayblin 2017b, 2019b), and even transcend binary conceptions of gender entirely (Mayblin 2014).[3] Given all this, it would be wrong to assume that, much like their Pentecostal counterparts, pious Catholic women are not creatively empowered by their faith.

All the same, it might be recognized that the Catholic gender paradox differs in certain ways from the Pentecostal one, for as far as I am aware, there is no established discourse about the effeminacy of Pentecostal pastors or the repressed sexual desire of pious female congregants. This kind of discourse is uniquely Catholic and therefore uniquely significant— particularly for any understanding of mayor-priests.

Returning, for a moment, to that figurative cluster of women on the horizon who signal the proximity of a priest, I am reminded of a conversation I witnessed between a young female friend, Emiliana, a group of seminarians, and a priest.

Emiliana and I were visiting the town she grew up in and had been invited to dinner at the rectory. During the meal, conversation had unfolded in a relaxed but spirited manner, as Emiliana knew some of the visiting seminarians well from childhood. At one point, two seminarians started exchanging stories about the gifts, meals, and attentions they had received from a particular coterie of faithful women, jokily competing to see who among them was most popular.

"It's the old *beata* you have to look out for," one of them quipped. "If she takes a shine to you, there is no escaping her!"

Laughter followed, and the conversation turned into a series of questions: Why, when it came to religion, were women the more "faithful" sex? And why were priests and seminarians so often the object of womens' attentions?

The priest who was present offered his opinion: women were the more faithful sex, he reasoned, because they were naturally more loving. And Christianity was a religion of love. Priests were invariably the focus for that nature.

Later that same evening, as Emiliana and I walked back to her grandmother's, I found myself reflecting on the kinds of questions I had witnessed the seminarians asking themselves, about priestly masculinity and womanly desire—and, in particular, about women's emotional and psychological attraction to priests.[4] Curious, I asked Emiliana if the husbands of priest-liking women ever got jealous. Emiliana looked at me, her eyes shining like pebbles in the moonlight; "All the time," she replied, matter of factly.

How does desire of this kind figure into our understanding of Catholicism as a political form? In the rest of this chapter, I want to explore some of the libidinous undercurrents that make up the Catholic gender paradox in order to gain a fuller understanding of the priest as a figure whom voters do not simply support, but whom they might also desire in ways that are, partially, erotic. In doing so, my aim is to look afresh, perhaps more critically, at received understandings of Christian patriarchy as a set of rules and institutional structures. By approaching the Catholic Church as "passionate machine" rather than as a set of legal codes and consciously elaborated practices, I seek to uncover its nature as an assemblage powered, in important ways, by desires, inversions, and unconscious wanderings. Desire of this kind is not inconsequential—it has measurable, sociological consequences. It is no less important for understanding Catholicism's success as a "political form" than its theological definition or economic infrastructure.

Desire and the Person

The concept of desire—at least in the term's basic sense of vital striving—has a foundational yet troubled role in Western thinking. In Roman Catholic theology, desire's connection to the flesh makes it problematic but also, potentially, a great mobilizer toward divine union. As the theologian Sarah Coakley (2013) argues, desire is central to Christian theological models of the person; God's trinitarian nature being both "the source and goal of human desires, as God intends them" (6). Human desire, however, is "misdirected" and must be forged by stages, into "incorporative, transformative, *divine* desire" (310).

A key aspect of this Christian conception of divine desire is the potential for its fulfillment. Unlike certain secular philosophies of desire that start from a primordial condition of lack and deny the possibility of fulfillment, divine desire emerges from God's original plenitude. True desire, in this sense, is nothing more than "that plenitude of longing love that God has for God's own creation and for its full and ecstatic participation in the divine, trinitarian, life" (Coakley 2013, 10). Lack, need, and impossibility are only features of humanity's inferior form of desire.

In secular psychoanalytical theory, by contrast, desire is never fulfilled. For Lacan (2004), desire is the product of a gap that emerges at the intersection of language and experience, at a point where the subject—who is defined and inscribed by language—perceives that she can only ever relate to the world via language and is therefore trapped within the symbolic order. In this understanding, language is our basic condition, and yet we experience it as a barrier preventing us from merging with the world, from truly understanding the other. The sense of lack and unfulfillment this creates is what Lacan calls desire.

Desire, in this sense, is a social phenomenon, for what is fundamentally desired is not so much this or that random object but to "complete the other," to desire what they lack, or, in other words, *to desire what they desire*. Desire, in this conception, is about our existential relationship not only with other people but with something more abstract: the social structure through which we experience and construct ourselves as living subjects.

Among my Catholic interlocutors, lack and fulfillment are not mutually exclusive concepts but combine in the twinned concepts of *fé* (faith) and *desejo* (desire). Desire, in this ethnographic conception, is simultaneously the grounding condition for and result of *fé* (faith) in God and therefore offers the possibility of fulfillment, as it is rooted in an existential sense of lack, and hence, as one encounters it in the tumult of living, is the root of all suffering.

Lack is expressed in desire's common synonyms *sede* (thirst) and *carência* (neediness), which can be used to convey deprivations of either a material or spiritual nature. Desire, in this context, is somewhat related to the famously untranslatable Brazilian concept of *saudades*, which denotes the pleasurable sense of "absent presence" felt when missing someone or something, accompanied by an optimistic expectation of eventual reunion. This celebrated appreciation of "absent presences" is also echoed in the idea that a person's moral worth emerges through *luta* (struggle) in the face of suffering (Mayblin 2010). In this context, therefore, lack is essential to local Christian concepts of the morally striving person.

With these theoretical models in mind, I shall continue my ethnographic exploration of desire through the stories of four different women whose relationships with priests have framed my understanding of the Catholic gender paradox. Working from the premise that a priest's appeal lies not only in his sacramental privilege but in his sexuality and in the particular brand of masculinity that this represents, the ethnography presented will trace desire's emergence in the wake of women's negotiations of machismo and through the tension that exists between heteronormativity and the "silent" queerness of the Catholic priesthood.

The Demands of Men

By my last period of research in Brazil, public discourse surrounding male-female sexual politics (and its intersectional points of contest) had become more visible and politicized, but levels of gender-based violence were much the same.[5] Most women regarded male violence as an ordinary if regrettable fact of life, and femicide remained commonplace (see Portella 2014). Machismo, the catch-all term sometimes attributed to this reality, was present for women as the diffuse threat of a partner's jealousy. Sexual jealousy swirled about at low densities within most relationships, but sometimes it crystalized into something more sinister, spiraling into terrible brutality.

The reality of this fact was reinforced for me in 2017 when I was shown the photograph of a young woman's decapitated head circulating on social media. The murder victim, who had been killed in the next town over, had been the victim of a jealous boyfriend. I still don't know if it was the shock of the image itself or the casual manner in which it was shown to me that caused me, shortly afterward, to throw up in the toilet.

Remaining safe from men's jealousy required wits and, as my friend Milene consistently modeled for me, a certain amount of emotional and intellectual skill in the handling of desire.[6] Milene was a witty and vivacious woman and a close friend of mine. Like other middle-class women of the town, she cared expertly for her appearance. Her closet was filled with an endless supply of platform heels and colorful, off-the-shoulder blouses, her hair was meticulously cared for, and she was always well presented. She lived with an older sister, and, although neither of them was married or had children of their own, their house was constantly full of friends, kin, and various nephews and nieces whom they helped to raise.

Early on in my friendship with Milene, she told me how much she loved the romances of the English author Barbara Cartland. As a teenager, she had read every single translated Cartland book she could find until there were no more left to get her hands on. When Milene discovered that I was from the same country as Barbara Cartland, her eyes lit up with excitement. I was asked a great many questions about England and then about Barbara Cartland's novels, none of which I was able to answer, having never actually read any. However, the more I got to know Milene, the more curious her love for Cartland's old-fashioned, sentimental novels came to appear to me. That passion seemed to hint at an interior landscape of fantasy and longing, strangely at odds with her habitual skepticism toward romance and her fierce independence.

Milene's own love life was complicated: lovers and potential lovers seemed to be constantly circling her, but no man was ever allowed to take center stage. "Who has time for jealous men?" she said to me irritably one day. "If he's the sort of man who gets angry over the phone when he hears a male voice coming from the TV, I tell him to get lost!" Milene was clear about what she wanted from life. She enjoyed her job as a schoolteacher and valued her autonomy; her commitment to independence seemed to emanate less from any discourse about women's rights than a sense of tedium and irritation with men's jealousies.

Milene had mastered the art of keeping men present—of harnessing their capacities without sacrificing either her independence or her standing within the wider community. This was no small feat in a context where older unmarried women had to tread a fine path to avoid being labeled as *sem vergonha* ("shameless/promiscuous"). In this sense, she was rare, perhaps unique in her ability to have lovers in her life while holding the accompanying machismo at bay, but for most women, machismo seemed an inevitable part of any relationship with men.

Nail Varnish and Fishing Nets

If the subtle and sometimes not-so-subtle presence of jealousy and machismo was part of everyday life for most women, some men provided exceptions, and priests were among them.

Milene and I were circling the town, looking for the rectory where Padre Adilson would apparently receive us. Milene had the afternoon off and had joined me on that interview quest, more for the distraction of a car drive than any interest she had in priests or my research. We had found ourselves pulling up outside a spacious, detached, one-story house. The front door was firmly shut, something unusual for those parts, where doors were often left open to let in air and light. Furthermore, all the windows onto the veranda were shuttered closed, as though whoever lived there had gone away.

We knocked and waited, and waited some more. A man walked by on the dirt track below, and we asked him if this was the house of the padre. "Yes," came the reply.

We knocked again, but nothing happened. I sighed loudly into the silence, and Milene was about to light a cigarette when suddenly there was a rummaging sound behind one of the windows. A moment later, the shutter burst open and out popped the face of an irritated, middle-aged man.

"What do you want?" he asked, grimacing, whether from anger or the sudden glare of light. His nails, clutching the shutter, flashed with the unusual brilliance of what I thought could only be clear nail varnish.

"I'm sorry to bother you, *senhor*," I replied. "We're here because we had an appointment with Padre Adilson."

The face disappeared, the shutter closed behind it, and, once again, we were left to wait.

Just as we were giving up hope, the front door rattled back and forth and finally swung open. The same man, now in a crisp white shirt and glasses, stood in the doorway.

"Padre Adilson, the one you seek, is I," he announced in a formal voice laced with amusement at having been caught out of role, then gestured gracefully for us to enter the house.

Immediately inside the doorway was a set of large armchairs arranged around a glass coffee table, where we were invited to sit down. Padre Adilson, now transformed into an endearing host, took a seat opposite us and crossed his legs, his face fixed into a broad, if somewhat inscrutable, smile. He gave nothing much away about the mayor-priests he had encountered, except, that is, for praise for the good works they'd performed.

"Thanks be to God, there were never any difficulties between me and the mayor-priest. Each padre always kept to his own work," he said, swiveling a palm upward before slapping it down, as though shutting the cover of a book.

I asked Padre Adilson if he had ever witnessed confusion among parishioners and citizens about the towns where there were mayor-priests.

> Sometimes people confuse the padre and the mayor, the mayor and the padre. I was only young, a curate in those days, but I remember many people would come to the parish house to ask for things: medicine, a clinical exam, employment of some sort. Many of these things they'd ask for because the padre is a father, right? Many people aren't that involved in parish life and assume that the padre is like a mayor as well. The church is a source of charity so we had an account at the local pharmacy to fund medicine for the really needy, but the padre had to say to many people all the time, "Look, I'm a parish priest, not a mayor! There is a mayor for this city, who is also a priest, but he attends to people in the municipal office, in that building over there! That is the municipal office, so you, madam, should go there and speak to the receptionist!"

As the conversation flowed, Padre Adilson revealed how he had, indeed, had plenty of occasion to reflect deeply on the topics we wanted to speak to him about. Nothing about the rise of mayor-priests across the region was, from his perspective, particularly strange. The padre is a highly visible figure throughout the community, he explained. Parishes are large, sometimes spanning hundreds and hundreds of square kilometers. Like a giant fishing net, one parish was capable of encompassing over a hundred communities. The priest circulates that vast territory:

> Celebrations, meetings, baptisms, weddings . . . our day-to-day lives enable us to really penetrate the community, to be in the middle of the people. . . . We know the problems, as we travel the highways, we see the kind of state they are in. We hear it when people complain about the schools, the health system, when there is no work. We know when the price of milk is up or down, when eggs go down too much, when poultry is good for sale, when it is not . . . with all this, the padre ends up whether he likes it or not, with that uncomfortable knowledge. Wanting to help *more* but unable to. . . .

Padre Adilson told us about various ongoing outreach projects that he was involved with: in schools, hospitals, and with the local prison. He described episodes of horror—open sewers running through prison cells, old people entirely forgotten about in isolated rural houses, starving to death—and told us of his organizational efforts to address such issues. It was understandable, he mused, that in such circumstances, people ended up *olhando o padre* ("eyeing up" the priest) as a possible mayor. Padre Adilson roughened his accent in imitation of an agricultural laborer: "Hey, Padre, you're the one, you're the one!"

Had Padre Adilson ever felt tempted to run for mayor?

Yes, he replied, he had certainly thought about it. But he had never lost himself in such a thought for fear that it would ruin his life.

> Were I to start working in a political vein, I would ruin my image, ruin everything. I perceive that once a priest enters into that world of politics, he's never the same again. Politics is a very corrupt system, very two-faced, very addictive! . . . In a tiny space of time, your whole life is stained. You'll never get back that . . .

He paused, searching for the right word.

"That respect?" I offered.

"Exactly," he said, "that respect."

By the time we finished conversing, the sun was starting to set. Padre Adilson invited us deeper into the rectory for a drink. We were taken through several dimly lit rooms, each connected to the other, and into the kitchen, where a woman with her back to us was shyly washing pans.

We shifted back into small-talk mode. When had I arrived in the interior? How long would I be staying?

Padre Adilson, smiling hospitably, pulled out chairs and wiped crumbs off the table. Moving cups and saucers around, he urged us to have some coffee. He grabbed a tin off a shelf, pulled off its lid, and peered inside it. "Zenilda!" he called to the pan-washing woman. "Where are the biscuits? They seem to have all been eaten!"

Driving home later, Milene and I basked for a little in silence. Overall, I thought, it had been an odd encounter, not in its content but in its sudden changes of register.

Sandy scrubland whizzed past as we left the town behind and drove westward into the setting sun.

"That was a good interview," I said. "But I felt bad waking the poor guy up from his siesta."

Milene narrowed her eyes and lit a cigarette. Blowing smoke out of the open window, she glanced at me sideways and chuckled. "What do you mean 'siesta'?" she said.

"There's no way he was sleeping. Did you not see him? His clothes? That nail-varnish? If you ask me, he couldn't answer the door because he was otherwise occupied—busy with his mouth full!"

I had to replay Milene's comment in my head a couple of times; at first it didn't make sense to me. It was only when I glanced over and noted her mischievous expression that I realized what she was getting at.

Queer Vitals: Celibacy, Homosexuality, and Clerical Power

Being the lover of a priest is not a good prospect. There is a well-known expression for this in the region: *a mulher do padre* (the priest's wife). The expression describes a person who is a loser or a situation that is hopeless and plays into an established tradition of joking about the sexual incontinence of priests.[7] While Milene's comment about Padre Adilson was delivered with mocking irony, in line with that established tradition, it also challenged its heteronormative contours. This, I contend, is not insignificant for our understanding of the Catholic gender paradox.

There are no reliable statistics on just how many priests in the Catholic Church worldwide identify as homosexual, but a growing body of literature, derived mainly from research conducted in Western Europe and

North America, projects the rate to be well above the 10 percent average one would expect to find distributed throughout the ordinary population.[8] According to some journalistic research carried out for Brazil, "dozens of priests and priest-educators" have informally estimated percentages of between 30 percent and 80 percent (Brandalaise 2020). Brandalaise's research echoes the informal estimates of some of the mayor-priest cohort I questioned on the topic, all of whom put the figure at 60–80 percent and, in one estimate, 90 percent.

Whatever the (in)accuracy of these estimates, collectively they indicate that homosexuality is fairly common among Catholic priests for the obvious reason that by joining the priesthood, homosexual men in homophobic societies are exempted from heterosexual activity while having their sexual purity certified. It is not hard to intuit the emotional damage this coping pattern has wreaked on generations of clergy destined to identify with an institution that conceives their own nature as "objectively disordered" and inherently disposed toward "intrinsic moral evil" (Kappler, Hancock, and Plante 2013).[9]

Even so, the last forty years have seen a flowering of LGBTQ+-affirming Catholic theologies that has made it possible to talk in Catholic terms of same-sex love as a "created good." Such discourse, notes Kelby Harrison, is "miraculous" and "a kind of speaking in tongues." That queer people—Catholic and many religious others—learn to articulate new sexual identities is peculiar, they note, because the religious discourses that have most strongly shaped those subjectivities "have offered next to nothing in terms of language to shape the articulation of sexual subjectivity" (Harrison 2014, 26). Here, my intention is not to summarize LGBTQ+-affirming theology, only to note its existence on the margins of a broader Catholic discourse about sexuality in which the subject of homosexuality within the priesthood remains particularly taboo.[10]

According to the journalist Frédéric Martel (2019), the contemporary church is an "empire of closets" that operates along the lines of don't ask, don't tell. Within this system, some homosexual priests choose to suffer the church's pronouncements on their "disordered" nature in secrecy and isolation, while others keep conversations about homosexuality off the record, choosing carefully to whom they reveal themselves.

Brandalaise (2020) offers the example of a Brazilian seminarian who confides to his clerical superior about his homosexuality during a conversation on the beach and finds his superior accepting and supportive. When a seminary form that he later must fill in asks for his sexual orientation, he remembers that positive conversation and puts down "homosexual," only to be made to erase it by his previously supportive superior.

In another case, this one related to me by one of the mayor-priests, there was a young parish priest who quickly became famed for throwing large, noisy rectory parties frequented by the local gay crowd. His homosexuality was often the subject of gossip, but it never caused any consternation for the bishop because he was otherwise diligent about his priestly duties.

The prevalence of homosexuality in the priesthood is widely recognized and often accepted, but as social knowledge it remains a "public secret," shrouded in silence. The overarching "economy of restraint" (Foucault 1998 [1978]) that governs discourse about this topic involves principles of doubleness (Mayblin 2019b) and the creation of social subjects who "know what not to know" through the skilled practice of silence, concealment, and revelation (Taussig 1999, 49).[11]

For some scholars, however, the relative silence that shrouds the existence of homosexuality in the priesthood is itself an instrument of power. According to Mark Jordan, the priesthood is a homosocial institution that trades felicitously (if unintentionally) on the silences, lacks, and desires that feed homosexual fantasies. Desire, he argues, works as "charge or energy that circulates" (Jordan 2000, 43), maintaining the profoundly homophobic/homoerotic duality of a priesthood based on the exclusion of women. Jordan's analysis centers priests not so much as the objects of Catholic desire but as desiring subjects who themselves desire power. It is this desire, he argues, the desire for "all male power," that propels the priesthood as a system (50).

For the theologian Mary Hunt (2002, 14), likewise, homosexuality and the Catholic priesthood cannot be understood apart from one another, but for Hunt, the desire that powers the system is less existential and more economic, leading her to the stark conclusion that:

> the Catholic priesthood and its theological arm is really a large system of gay male prostitution, perhaps more economic even than sexual. Catholic seminaries and religious orders are tax-exempt institutions that discriminate legally against women and non-homoconforming men.

Jordan and Hunt's interventions point, each in their own ways, to the intertwined roles of silence, desire, and homosexuality in Catholic cartographies of power, but neither really tackles Catholicism's gender paradox in its entirety. How, we might ask, does the homoerotic charge Jordan identifies travel beyond the seminary walls to work among the laity? How is male homosexuality in the priesthood received and accommodated among the women who constitute the bulk of the church's faithful?

The Sensitive Priest

At some point during my research, I learned of the existence of a troubled young priest whom I never actually met but whose reputation preceded him. Younger lapsed Catholics told me many stories about him not only because he was a charming, outspoken figure but also because he was reported to be a hopeless alcoholic, as well as someone who was secretly active in the local gay scene.

Dona Jacintha, then in her seventies, was a devout, well-connected widow. An ex-mayor's wife from a landholding family, she lived in a big house that looked over the very town square where the troubled young priest had once been found drunk and unconscious following a public festivity. Dona Jacintha was a socially conservative woman, but she was also far from innocent. Fairly well-traveled and informed for her age, she was amply aware of the various new social and political movements happening across the country. Once she spoke to me in veiled feminist tones about the cruelty of her late husband: a "great man" in the town's official history, a former mayor, and powerful landowner. A man as great as he, she said cryptically, had done exactly as he pleased behind closed doors, and who could have possibly stopped him?

"My situation was terrible. Like that of [a] servant," she said. "Except that he never gave me any money. Would you believe that for all the money he had, I was forced to raise those children in absolute poverty?"

There was more to the story than poverty, I sensed, but Dona Jacintha said nothing more on the matter. Instead, she went on to tell me about the educational and career opportunities that she had missed out on as a woman.

"If I could have my time again," she said matter-of-factly, "I would choose to be born a man."

Such musings did not obviate her otherwise strong commitment to the rules and mores of a patriarchal society that was ultimately part of her make-up. For better or worse, the institutions that had oppressed her in her youth were also the source of her financial wealth in widowhood—and her social prestige as the surviving widow of a renowned patriarch.

One day, as we were taking afternoon tea together, I asked her what she thought of the troubled young priest who had not long been "moved on" from her local parish. Her face twitched at the mention of his name, but when she opened her mouth, all she had was praise: what an *homem sensível* (sensitive man) he had been, what intelligent homilies he had given, how *cuidadoso* (caring) he was. And then she said, as though reading my vague disappointment, "Not everyone got on with him, but most of us—us women I mean—really liked him."

I was familiar with such aphoristic turns of phrase. Devout older women were particularly likely to speak this way. By playing on widely held stereotypes of homosexual men as sensitive and caring, the locally salient trope of the "sensitive priest" manages to suggest homosexuality without actually naming it. At the same time, sensitivity and its attendant connection with homosexuality acknowledge an ideal facet of priestly masculinity, one that afforded women like Dona Jacintha a valuable alternative possibility in their relationships with men.

The Need to Be Heard

Flávia, a lower-middle-class woman in her thirties, had, like Dona Jacintha, suffered difficult relationships with men. Flávia's father left her mother and disappeared forever when she was just a baby. When Flávia was in her early twenties, she had three children in quick succession; however, one was born with a life-limiting illness and another with a severe mental and physical disability. Like her own father, the father of those babies disappeared, never to be seen again, when the children were infants, around the time that the severity of their conditions was starting to reveal itself. By the time I met Flávia, she had survived a string of relationships with jealous men and was living with her children in the house of her maternal aunt.

Flávia herself was a devout Catholic, and while she rarely left the house because of her constant caring responsibilities, she allowed herself time for church activities.

One day, she coyly described the recently arrived parish priest Padre Marcos to me as her latest obsession. It was nothing more than *loucura* (madness) on her part, she said, laughing, but how could she help it? In her view, Padre Marcos was the best priest the town had ever known.

Flávia went on to describe how Padre Marcos embodied masculinities of *cuidado* (care) and *segurança* (security) through his ministry and especially, she said, through the sacrament of confession. Flávia was an avid confession-goer, describing herself as the sort of Catholic who would "run" to confess the minute she felt ashamed of an action. Although she confessed on a regular basis, she was careful to match the gravity and nature of her confession with the appropriate priest. Even though she trusted utterly in the ritual itself, never doubting any priest to keep her confession a total secret, not all priests, she admitted, transmitted what she called "security." It wasn't a matter of trust; it was the quality of a priest's ability to listen, she explained. Some priests were cold and lacked empathy—they could not be trusted to guide a person with sensitivity. With Padre Marcos, however, Flávia felt safe. In him she had found a man who would listen not only to her sins but also to her problems—a man whose support for her was not predicated on expectation of financial or sexual return.

Close friendships between women and priests may or may not include sexual attraction, but they invariably emerge from a libidinal topography that combines faith, duty, and sexual politics. A desirable man, Flávia once opined loudly enough so her boyfriend in the next room could hear us, "is a man like Padre Marcos." We were sitting at her kitchen table talking, and her boyfriend was lying on the sofa in the living room, engrossed in his phone.

I looked at Flávia nervously, wondering if it was time to excuse myself, but she grabbed my arm, winking, and went on in the same loud voice, "What I need is a man who listens, who cares about me and not just about what he can get from me!" She laughed out loud, flashing her eyes flirtatiously.

Flávia's life may have revolved around constant toil, tending to her disabled children, but her capacity for life-affirming laughter never failed to delight me.

As Padre Adilson confirmed, being a priest means becoming aware of people's material necessities; traveling the region, he identifies gaps in provision and helps, where possible, to fill those gaps through pastoral work and the redistribution of money and material resources. The priest, like the politician, therefore, spends a good part of his time tending to needs that can be met. A good priest, however, addresses both needs that can be met and desires (of a spiritual or psychological nature) that cannot—or at least not without God's intervention. Along this journey, the priest must witness and make sense of the way human needs and desires intertwine and discover appropriate responses.

The priests I interviewed were, for their part, deeply sensitized to the dynamics of female desire their presence could trigger and were willing to reflect upon it.[12] The word they used repeatedly to describe people was *carente* (needy, lacking); the *grande carência do povo* (great lack of the people) manifested as demand for all sorts of things, ranging from food and water to the comforting *palavra de Deus* (word of God). The role of the priest was, in various ways, to respond to that complex deficit, and one of the techniques for doing so was *ouvir* (to listen). Padre Marcos, for example, was unequivocal about the importance of listening for "valorizing the other" and "raising a person's dignity." Listening, he insisted, had potent effects:

> Our people are very *carente* when it comes to listening. In the seminary, before offering answers, we are first invited to listen. For example, we are taught to listen to people in preparation for the sacrament of confession, and for the advice we know it is our responsibility to give out. So the course of confession is often like this: The person speaks, speaks, speaks, and finally the padre says two words, and the person leaves saying, "It was excellent! It was so good!" Why do they say this? Simply because at home no one ever listens to them; neither are they listened to at work or among friends! . . .

The desire to encounter "sensitivity" in the other is, in part, the desire to be heard—to exist in the witness of the other.[13] While not every priest is liked by women or conceived of as a good listener or confessor, good priests are, on the whole, good listeners, and good listeners give of themselves in some way, addressing people's desire to be heard.

An important overlap exists between the desire to be heard by priests and the desire to be heard by politicians. Indeed, whenever I asked people what made for a good mayor, the ability to listen came up time and again. "A good mayor listens to the *povo*," "someone who hears me," "one who knows how to listen." Phrases like this recurred so often that I asked Padre Marcos what he made of them. He responded:

> The mayor, too, must listen, but his listening is for the collective, is it not? The priest attends to the inner person, he listens to the dimension that is most personal. Not that he does not deal in the collective also, but for us it is listening at the existential level, listening so that the person might find themselves in the other—or, in the specific case of Christianity, find themselves *as a Christian*.

In Padre Marcos's view, priestly listening is distinct from political listening as the former attends to the inner desires of the individual person, while the latter attends to the material needs of the collective. And yet, as Padre Adilson described it earlier, the listening priest is already in the realm of politics. The political attractiveness of the priest derives precisely from his capacity to "hear it when people complain about the schools, the health system, when there is no work."

On the other hand, and as the work of numerous scholars of Brazilian political culture attests, the line between public and private, personal and collective, and hence between needs of the body that can be met and the desires of the soul that cannot—or at least not by human agency—is frequently blurred by the demands of friendship and kinship. For many, the call for a politician who listens is as much a call for listening "at the existential level," to quote Padre Marcos; a yearning for the kind of validation of one's personhood that only certain types of social relationship can provide.[14]

When priests talk about the "great neediness of people," therefore, they mean neediness in a sense that combines the spiritual, the material, and the psychological. Lay peoples' commonly stated desire to be "listened to" is not only about having one's identity recognized or validated; it is also a matter of economic survival. The priest, as divine mediator and trained confessor, is uniquely positioned to consummate such complex needs and desires, but his possession of a human, gendered body throws a libidinal spark into the mix, and this has certain consequences.

The priest is ultimately a human listener, and this fact makes him susceptible, as it would any psychotherapist, to dynamics of transference. Although the priest is heralded as a transformer of others' desires, he becomes an object of desire himself—whether in terms of his own gendered body, the divine institution he represents, or for the alternative visions of sociality built into it.[15]

A Space of Possibility

The pleasure of being listened to was as available to men as it was to women, but it was women who went to confession more often and flocked down vestry corridors after priests in great numbers in search of hearings, blessings, and other such encounters. In contexts where cultures of machismo prevail, the power of priests to queer dominant sexual relations may be more accentuated. Priests are generally unthreatening to husbands, not only because their nominal celibacy confines them reproductively and in social terms, but particularly when they are tacitly assumed to be homosexual. Customarily jealous men who tightly control their women's access to public spaces may attach no particular significance to the time that a woman spends with a priest, making the church feel like a space of freedom.

Priests who befriend women, particularly women from lower socioeconomic backgrounds, and who support them to take on roles of lay leadership may perceive themselves—and in turn be perceived—as the gatekeepers of such freedom. This was the case with twenty-eight-year-old Emiliana, whom we met earlier. Emiliana had a history of anxiety and depression, but when a caring new priest took over her local parish and showed her some attention, her symptoms started to improve. She had been bored and lonely, but the new priest "valorized" her, she said; he encouraged her to start up a Bible study group. Emiliana showed me a red notebook filled with her handwriting: the *trabalho* (work) she had done, she told me, that had brought her such contentment.

To understand Emiliana's relationship with that red notebook requires some background information about her life story and her experience of men. Emiliana's late father had been an abusive alcoholic, so Emiliana had grown up with a strong disdain for men who drank. When she was a teenager, her elder sister was raped by a man from a family with strong ties to the local police force. Those ties meant the crime was never investigated. The rape produced a child that Emiliana helped to raise, but the trauma her sister suffered and her mother's resulting illness weighed her down so heavily that she started to suffer from mental health problems of her own and never completed school.

Emiliana grew up ambivalent about marriage and about men in general, but had been willing to take a chance on her husband because he belonged to an evangelical church and therefore, very importantly to Emiliana, did not drink. He also had a good job at a local furniture factory and earned enough to support them. So Emiliana began life as a housewife but continued to suffer from *nervos e depressão* (anxiety and depression). Reading and writing had never played much part in Emiliana's life until the new padre encouraged her to study the Bible and keep her own spiritual journal. Sitting at her kitchen table in the evenings to do this work had brought her a welcome sense of calm.

Emiliana became very religious, at one point attending church up to four times a week. This made her husband jealous—a situation perhaps exacerbated by the fact that the new priest gave off heterosexual vibes. One day, Emiliana's husband threw her journals into the backyard and threatened to burn them. When she tried to retrieve them, he accused her of being "the padre's whore."

For a long period afterward, Emiliana's husband continued complaining about her excessive visits to the church, but he never prevented her from attending church events, nor did he choose to employ any of the more violent tactics men can feel pressured to inflict on sexual adversaries in such contexts. After all, the object of his jealousy was institutionally celibate and, without direct and incontrovertible evidence to the contrary, could be exempted from the normal rules of machismo and retribution that existed between ordinary men.

"Our people are *carênte* for listeners," as Padre Marcos proclaimed. But one of the mayor-priests was quite specific about what this meant for him. During an interview, he suddenly shared with me the following:

> Look, to talk of *carência* is to talk about the female parishioner. I always joke that although I have never studied womankind, I understand women well. It comes from confession. Many women seek out priests for confession because they want God's forgiveness but in a symbolic sense. They seek out the padre because at a deeper level, they don't know who else to tell when they are being beaten by their husbands, when their husbands are unfaithful; they don't know who to tell when they pick up a venereal disease from their husband. Perhaps they have been unfaithful too, and they don't know how to say it, how to even start reflecting on it.

We see from this testimony how in rural Brazil, where society is largely conservative and machismo-entrenched, acts of male listening can be profoundly cathartic. Within the confessional, the priest is a figure who simultaneously signifies and destabilizes the ultimate patriarchy. By virtue of his institutional celibacy—and in some cases homosexuality—his listening may become a *queering* of the dominant heteronormative structure, generating conditions in which alternative subject positions may emerge for women, even if such positions never take full possession of themselves.

In all of this it should hopefully be evident that although women may desire priests, it is not necessarily desire in a sexual or genital sense that is in flow but desire for a world in which men don't seek to rape, control, or decapitate them. For some women, a priest may be the only man who can incubate a vision of such a world, even if, as a foot soldier for an institution whose patriarchal values precede him, he can never fully complete it.[16]

Desiring the Desire of the Priest

It would be possible to describe what I have presented here as just another sexual economy, one that intersects with religious and political agendas in particular ways. However, resorting to the language of "sexual economy" risks imprisoning the concept of patriarchy in codes of conduct and rationalities of exchange, obscuring the role played by impossibilities and inversions.

Returning to the question with which I began this chapter, concerning why it is women, above all, who "flock" about priests, I have tried to answer it using a concept of a desire that is erotic in a sense animated by gendered longings and inversions, but not necessarily (or only) sexual in nature. Taking the term "libido" in its original psychoanalytical sense, as a "psychic drive or energy" connected with "passion/love/desire" but not limited to sex, I have striven to show how the priest, as a fleshly being, may come to serve as a focal point for desires both individual and collective and thus how religion and politics are ultimately the products of an overarching libidinous cartography.[17]

Using desire as a concept, it becomes possible to comprehend both the fantasies that underpin clerical power as described by Jordan and the searching drive of the women who flock—the women who "desire the priest's desire"—not only via the all-powerful fulfillment of the sacraments but via the pleasure of being listened to. Drawing on the notion of lack as a structuring principle of human existence, I have sought to recognize the embeddedness and, in some ways, the irresolvable nature of individual desires that emerge at the intersection of machismo, official church pronouncements on gender, and silent homosexuality.

As local discourses about *carência* (lack) would indicate, women's desire for priests is essentially utopian in the sense that it can never be fulfilled. From the lay perspective, the priest is at once intimately available ("sensitive," a "good listener") and completely unattainable. As an institutionally celibate man, socially "set apart" (in the Durkheimian sense of that which is sacred), he is sexually sterile—unable to fully consummate or lay claim to the fruits of any heterosexual relationship. To speak of the priest as an agent of social desire is thus to speak of his potential to activate desire at the individual and collective level without ever satiating it.

What is the significance of desire, then, for understanding the "gender paradox" of Catholicism? In her book on transnationalism and the Catholic Church, the anthropologist Valentina Napolitano presents us with a complex portrait of the relationship between the Vatican and its Latin American flock. The territory Napolitano traverses is one in which religiosity entwines with power, bureaucracy, and affect. The terrain is familiar to any scholar with an interest in Roman Catholicism as an institutional phenomenon. It is a terrain of rules and bureaucracy, canons and encyclicals, but equally a terrain of faith and passion in which the fleshly and laboring bodies of female migrants take up vital place.

In order to comprehend the church in its full totality, as a system that continually reproduces itself through flows of desire and rigid bureaucracy, Napolitano offers us the metaphor of the "passionate machine." The metaphor owes much to Deleuze's machinic notion of desire, which moves beyond the notion of desire as lack toward a conception of it as a kind of will that drives production. The machine part of the "passionate machine," then, relates to this sense of desire as production, but it also, I would say, captures something quite particular about the Roman Catholic Church—its nature as a system.

The notion of the church as a system whose complex parts are interlinked, however far removed from one another those parts may be in social, theological, or geographical terms, is integral for any understanding of Catholicism. The systemic nature of Catholic power cannot be ignored, as any campaigner working against the tide of clerical sexual abuse cover-ups knows. In acknowledging how homophobia, homoeroticism, and feminine desire run parallel and in connection with one another, it becomes necessary to zoom in on their points of articulation. The priest's body is one such point of articulation; consciously or not, it becomes the link point for "parts" and forces otherwise separated.

At such, it would be reasonable to ask just what Milene, Dona Jacintha, Flávia, and Emiliana's desires and experiences in relation to the opposite sex (and to various priests) can tell us about the mayor-priest phenomenon. For me, these women's stories show us how the political arena emerges from a more general libidinal cartography that is shaded by lack and forged out of promise. For women left to navigate matrices of machismo, any practice that allows them to court but ultimately circumvent the predatory male gaze is welcome. Safe male validations—listening nods, blessings, the touch of an arm—feed and embellish a woman's faith, as well as her libido.

The work of the priest is, as Padre Marcos remarked, to "attend to the inner person," channeling the formation of the Christian subject. The gendered and gendering nature of such work is evident, however, in the speech of priests who recognize themselves as "experts in women": professionals who must learn, over the course of their careers, how to "attend to" and enjoy, without falling prey to, the eager attentions of religious *beatas* and church-going spinsters.

Indeed, and as Padre Adilson's testimony made clear, priests who understand themselves as agents of and for such needs and desires also understand, at some level, that libidinous energy can be channeled into politics. In all this, it is important to recognize that it is not just women who will desire priests for the reasons described earlier; it may be men and gender-nonconforming people, as well. Men, despite their anticlerical performances, desire priests in similar and different ways and implicitly understand the attraction priests hold for women. By inviting priests to run for mayor, men leverage women's desire for priests to their own benefit. In other words, the priest's passage from church minister to municipal office holder is libidinally driven, made possible thanks to human desire that transcends the categories of the "religious" and the "political."

4   Virile Celibacy

It was over a year since I had followed Padre Jorge up the rectory stairs, and I'd heard nothing more about whether he intended to run for mayor. Back in Scotland, life had returned to its hectic pace, when suddenly items announcing Padre Jorge's candidacy started appearing on regional blogs and websites. Not wishing to let such an ethnographic opportunity pass, I got in touch with my research assistant, Rosa, who tracked down Padre Jorge on my behalf, and with three weeks to go before the election, I found myself on a plane returning to Brazil, with Padre Jorge's permission to follow the last days of his electoral campaign with my notebook and film camera.

In the long months prior to that moment, Padre Jorge had suffered a roller coaster of assaults and pressures, first from future political rivals who tried to stop him from running for mayor with bribery and threats and secondly from the bishop, who, increasingly suspicious of Padre Jorge's intentions, had tried everything in his power to prevent such an eventuality.

Unlike previous bishops, this one had little tolerance for mayor-priests and was keen to make an example of Padre Jorge in a bid to stem the tide of *padres na política* once and for all. He called all the priests and mayor-priests of the region to his headquarters to lecture them on the various avenues the church offered them for legitimate projects of social and political action. If working for social change is part of your priestly calling, he argued, do not submerge yourself in the polluting world of politics; use the church's own pastoral organizations. Next, as the political factions of the interior were busily organizing themselves for the start of the political season, the bishop arranged to celebrate Sunday Mass in the parish where Padre Jorge was preparing to run for mayor. At the pulpit before a church packed with potential voters, he launched into an angry critique of *padres na política*, declaring that any person who invited a priest to run for mayor, aided him in his campaign, or voted for him in an election was disobeying the will of God.

Finally, and perhaps because he sensed he was fighting a losing battle, the bishop sent forth a message to all priests of the diocese decreeing that any priest choosing to candidate himself in a political election would be immediately expelled from ministry without prospect of return. From this official warning, a rumor sprang up that the bishop intended to petition the Vatican for the laicization of any future deserters.

Laicization (the official process of returning a priest to a lay state) represented the most severe form of punishment the bishop could mete out, and while the possibility generated much conversation among the mayor-priests, none seemed unduly worried by it. For one thing, both the mayor-priests and, they assured me, the *povo* of the region rejected the theological veracity of laicization, even if canon law decreed it to be possible. For another, it was a long and bureaucratic process that the bishop was unlikely, in practice, to have time for.

All the same, Padre Jorge was deeply hurt by the bishop's treatment of him, as though he were a criminal rather than simply a man embarking on a legitimate new chapter of his life. He was still upset about the phone call he had received as soon as the news of his candidacy had gone public—the bishop's icy tone of voice, being ordered to vacate the rectory with immediate effect. Padre Jorge had hoped for a more formalized and dignified transition into political life, one that would have allowed him to bid his congregation a proper farewell. Being forced out of the rectory under the cover of dark was a shaming experience, a punishment by the very institution he loved and had devoted so much of his life to.

With nowhere else to go, Padre Jorge returned to his mother's house in the neighboring city and remained there for a few weeks, until one of his political supporters and campaign benefactors rented a spacious three-bedroom house in Iati that could serve both as a place in which to temporarily live and as campaign headquarters. The Iati house was where I finally caught up with Padre Jorge again, more than a year after our last meeting upstairs in the Jupi rectory.

Padre Jorge's journey from the parish rectory to his mother's house, and from there to Iati, marked the end of an era and the start of another. And yet, the journey from sacred to secular that now stretched before him was, in some ways, already familiar, as the life he had known in the church had always been regulated by journeys between religious and secular identities as a priest/man.

Being a priest, he had grown accustomed to the need for such passages, and while some had occurred only in his head, others had taken more spatial forms, involving cars, buses, and highway stops in repeated crossings of the scrub-dotted landscape. Where some such journeys had religious purposes, others, by contrast, had constituted secret departures from priestly vocation: temporary escapes from the intensity of the sacred role. Nonetheless, and up until that point in time, all such passages had involved returning to the place and position of parish priest. The journey facing Padre Jorge now was a more momentous one and offered no certainties. Like a sacrificial offering, it would see him pass over a threshold from which (according to this particular bishop) there would be no return.

This chapter is about the journey of men from priests to politicians. It is about how boundaries are negotiated between the religious and the political through the movements of people who make passage between religious and political identities. The notion of passage is essential, for a boundary between the religious and the political does not exist in any material sense; it is set and specified in the act of passage. As Brian Massumi observes:

> Every boundary is present everywhere, potentially. . . . The crossing actualizes the boundary—rather than the boundary defining something inside by its inability to cross. There is no inside, and no outside. . . . Only a field of exteriority, a network of more or less regulated passages across thresholds. (Massumi 1993, 27)

A network of "more or less regulated passages across thresholds" is one way of conceptualizing how humans in general engage with the sacred, but it is particularly apt for understanding the figure of the diocesan priest who, as the last two chapters have shown, serves the church by working on the religious/secular frontline, crossing between those domains at a more intense pace than the laity and, in so doing, reasserting religion's boundaries.[1] The trope of the passage is employed here in a dual sense: firstly, to get at the priesthood as an institution formed of myriad interlocking passages—material, psychological, and metaphysical—between worlds, statuses, and domains; and secondly, to point to an intensely personal transitional process that every priest adapting to life as a lay person must undergo once he leaves ministry.

One of the key aspects of the passage this chapter deals with is its social and gendered construction. For what is peculiar about priests in this context is how they perform vital separations between the domains of the sacred/religious and political/secular through their sexual relationship with women. In the former case, it is women's denial and exclusion that constructs the domain; in the latter, it is their controlled inclusion. Within this patriarchal system, women function as waymarkers along a continuous passage between the church and government that, as Massumi states, "actualizes the boundary" between them.

Vital Men: Virility and Political Culture in Northeast Brazil

Padre Jorge was generally deemed to be attractive. Tall and pleasant-looking, he had the middle-aged body of a once-towering athlete and the easy gait of someone who was used to being looked up to. Back in his youth he had been a professional footballer and local heartthrob.

"Ah, how delicious!" (*que delícia!*) whispered Rosa mischievously in my ear as we watched Padre Jorge emerging in the distance from a changing room in his goalkeeping gear.

The friendly football match we were gathered to watch was a staged event during Padre Jorge's campaign; the prospect of Padre Jorge returning to the football pitch had quickly drawn interest among his gathering supporters. Rosa's whispered comment was in keeping with the flashes of laughter that often emanated from the women who surrounded Padre Jorge, many of whom were there to watch the match.

Padre Jorge, for his part, did nothing very obvious to encourage such attentions and didn't seem bothered by them, but there were moments during those final weeks when the female attention directed at him left him looking a little unnerved, like the time a woman in a tight latex halter top took over the microphone during a rally to read out a long praise poem she'd composed to honor him. Or the time a young woman sporting a seductive sheet of shiny black hair walked up to him as he was leaving a restaurant with his political entourage and, putting her arms around his neck, said loud enough for those close by to hear, "You've left the church now, Padre Jorge. There's no going back—I won't let you!"

Padre Jorge's appeal among women was fairly evident, but that appeal was not just sexual; it was libidinous in a far broader sense. For many people, Padre Jorge was more than just the town's political savior; he was one of its founding heroes.

Padre Jorge had "saved" Iati once before, some fifteen years prior, when he had arrived to take over the municipality's newly founded parish. Up until that point, Iati had fallen under the administration of the parish of Águas Belas, which meant locals had to travel a great distance to receive the sacraments. However, from the local point of view, having one's own parish was more than just a simple practicality; it was a matter of pride and identity. A region with its own name needed its own financial, political, and religious center, which was why the people of Iati had fought—as communities of the interior have always done—for the right both to their own municipal body and to their own parish.

When Iati's long-awaited church was finally built, Padre Jorge was the first priest posted to it. Padre Daniel, in his recounting of this story, described Padre Jorge's relationship with the people of the municipality as being "like that of a first love one never forgets."

This purported nostalgia of "first love" may perhaps have explained the proliferation of love hearts during Padre Jorge's electoral campaign. During those weeks, I noted endless iterations of the heart shape: "Vote Padre Jorge" on heart-shaped stickers, hearts on campaign banners, heart-framed slogans graffitied onto walls. In Padre Jorge's garage, a team of adolescent girls gathered to produce wearable campaign accessories: writing "Padre Jorge" onto stacks of cardboard heart shapes, which they decorated with glitter and fashioned into earrings and hairbands.

In Padre Jorge's otherwise spartan bedroom, a heart-shaped cushion with "I love you" written on it sat on his dresser next to a "Hug me" teddy bear, a Bible, and a hairbrush. Under the window was a coffee table featuring an impromptu jumble of religious statuettes, rosaries, and other *lembrancinhas* (keepsakes) that Padre Jorge had received: plastic roses, figurines of angels, and an intriguing assortment of letters in torn-open envelopes addressed "To Padre Jorge . . ." and decorated with love hearts.

The hearts that inundated Padre Jorge's campaign might, at first glance, index the same libidinous cartography we explored in Chapter Three, in which female desire for the parish priest as confidante/confessor is driven by the wider context of machismo. But the desire that drives the electoral context does not have quite the same telos as that engendered by the silent homosexuality of the church and that finds expression in Catholic practices of listening and confession. Rather than dwelling in the sexual ambiguity of a celibate priesthood that symbolizes the glory of unity and an ephemeral "inoperativity" (Chapter Two), the desire that drives local elections feeds on the cut and thrust of social exchange and churns productively through material.

One of the abiding aspects of politics within the interior of Northeast Brazil is its implicit status as a masculine pursuit. Long before politics became professionalized under the modern liberal state, it was coterminous with the informal dealings that occurred in male-dominated social spaces such as bars, pool rooms, streets, and markets. Politics was, and to a certain degree remains, synonymous with that masculine sphere Da Matta famously described as "the street" (Da Matta 1987), a sphere in which alliances are formed and contested and the "poetics" of Brazilian manhood is played out.

This is not to say that women are not important players in political systems. On the contrary, women have always been active in patron-client networks as vote-proffering female heads of households, moral (and therefore politically influential) pillars of their communities, and, more recently, as legislative councilors, mayors, and even presidents in their own right. A detailed exploration of women's active roles in the political sphere is beyond the scope of this chapter; however, here it will suffice to note that party politics is still considered a macho pursuit.[2]

In small-town contexts, in particular, a prominent male politician takes on the mantle of a *paizão* (big father) who, like the classical Melanesian "big man," personifies a form of leadership based on principles of heteronormative virility and competitive exchange. The *paizão*, similar to a "big man," rises to prominence through a combination of informal persuasion and skillful conduct of wealth exchange, but his family plays an important role. While his wife and children index his capacity to protect and provide for those in his charge, rumors of extra lovers (or even a "second family" on the side) may serve, in accordance with the unspoken values of machismo, to emphasize his *força* (vitality) (see Gutmann 2007 [1996]).

As Aaron Ansell elaborates, in the political context, the term *força* is gendered as male and refers to a person's "combined physical and spiritual strength, their raw quantity of world-making agency" (Ansell forthcoming; see also Scheper-Hughes 1992, 188). The importance of this masculine kind of capital is continually present in talk about the capacity of prominent men to *botar chifres* ("cuckold") other men.

Gender, sexuality, and desire are therefore critical, if often tacit, components of local political worlds. In attempting to summarize the overall tone of the relationship between the politician and the voter, Padre Djalma, an ex-mayor-priest of Quipapá, described it as "like the relationship between lovers." Sitting in a highway *churrascaria*, where we were conducting an interview, he reminisced about his own experience of electoral campaigns and commented at length on the shadowy aspect to the voter-politician relationship. "It's like a game of seduction," he said. "Each party desires something from the other but cannot fully reveal themselves."

I noted that although married himself, Padre Djalma had chosen to use the term "lover" (*amante*) rather than "spouse" (*esposo*) to depict the political relationship, alluding to the erotic charge but also, perhaps, to some of the forbidden jouissance of the clientelist exchange (see Chapter One).

The hypersexualized nature of electoral campaigns in Northeast Brazil has been noted before in depictions of passionate voters seemingly unable to control their baser energies. As Ansell (2015) describes, the passion that takes hold of some voters at election time may be classed as an illness (*doença*) that causes people to behave irrationally and aggressively toward members of the opposite faction. Electoral sickness has different registers, however, ranging from the aggressive to the romantic.

Depending on the particular context, metaphors of seduction, battle, or game-playing may proliferate. Voters may taunt members of the opposition using sexual language and gesture, the intention being to "eat" (*comer*) the other side (Ansell 2015, 697). Women may adopt this active sexual register, particularly when taunting members of the opposite faction, but are also inclined to express their political commitment to male candidates in terms analogous to romantic longing. It is not unusual for male politicians to receive small sentimental gifts from female supporters nor to find themselves inundated with sexual offers.

If heteronormativity and reproductive virility carry weight in mayoral politics, this poses an obstacle for the political priest whose spiritual fatherhood, by contrast, is deeply bound up with the sexual ambiguity, silent homosexuality, and celibate sterility of the Catholic priesthood. In order to understand what is at stake for mayor-priests as they make passage into the world of politics, it is therefore necessary to keep several antimonies in view: virility and sterility; worldliness and other-worldliness; sexual promiscuity and celibacy.

In the rest of this chapter, I want to explore the responses of three priests to the challenges they faced while trying to balance the feminizing celibacy required of them by the church with the virility and *força* expected of them by the electorate. We shall see how this tension raised different issues for each of them as they sought to inhabit and negotiate what I term "virile celibacy": a style of celibate performance that is publicly and religiously vow-abiding while suggesting a vigorous heterosexual identity. The virile celibate is publicly chaste and privately sexually active: for all any member of the public knows, he may have secret lovers and have fathered several children.

Even for the most confidently (and demonstratively) heterosexual of priests, virile celibacy is not a given. It is an identity that requires expertise and a certain amount of collaborative willpower to cultivate. Virile celibacy opens doors into politics, but its ongoing negotiation can be fraught and difficult, as virility can just as easily be weaponized—used against priests to discredit their political pretentions.

The journey a priest undertakes, from parish to *prefeitura*, has several dimensions. At first glance, the journey is a literal one in the sense that becoming a mayor tends to involve a physical transition to a different location. There is also a certain duration to the journey in the temporal sense that it unfolds over a series of years, beginning the moment the priest is invited to run for election and ending the moment he demits from political office. But perhaps the most important dimension to the journey is the internal one, that which he undergoes as he transforms from one social status to another. That particular journey, unlike the other two, is marked by equivocation. While the chronological journey can only be one way (the priest sets out to win an election and complete a term in political office over a period of approximately five years), the transition of status he undergoes is far less linear.

That is, at any point along his passage from priest to politician, the priest may discover that he is perceived by others (or perceives himself) as more or less ontologically distinct from other men. The way he handles such equivocation can affect the course of his journey overall, for by the end of his term in political office he is likely to find himself facing one of two possibilities: either a return to ministry is still open to him, or he has forsaken that possibility forever.

Here it is important to recognize that priests do not travel alone on such momentous journeys; they are closely accompanied by friends, family, and adversaries. The course they chart is therefore influenced by a kind of collective energy. Critically, as we shall see, the mayor-priest's passage will be waymarked by social attitudes toward women and, in particular, by the intrigue provided by a single female associate. After all, to perform convincingly as a virile celibate, the priest needs more than the ambient attention of a devoted female flock; he needs what we might think of as a "shadow partner": a stable association with a particular woman with whom he *may or may not* be sexually involved.

In the ethnographic sections to follow, we shall explore the situations of three men at different points along that tensile journey from priest to politician. In each case, we shall see how private choices and public performances in connection with shadow partners have concrete effects on religious/political boundaries, in turn illustrating the conflicted nature of a church that enshrines celibate sterility but depends, for its continued reproduction, on the fecundity of the female body.

Seeking Office: Padre Jorge

Let us return, for a moment, to Padre Jorge, sitting in his rented Iati house with weeks to go before the municipal election. At that point in time, Padre Jorge's life was held together by women, but those women were either paid to cook and clean for him or they were his consanguineal kin.

Padre Jorge's sister and mother were particularly significant in this regard. Elisangela, his sister, tended to be present throughout the days at the campaign headquarters, exerting a calm, organizational presence and subtly overseeing Dona Vera's work as cook and housekeeper. Dona Clemilda, Padre Jorge's mother, was also an important female partner but more so in spiritual terms. She kept a distance from the day-to-day running of his affairs, only appearing at Padre Jorge's side for key ritual moments in the campaign process, like the "peace procession" instigated by Padre Jorge's campaign leaders in response to a gun incident between two men from opposing factions that had landed one of the men in the hospital.[3]

Dona Clemilda's role at the peace procession appeared to involve assuming the mantle of spiritual authority that her son had recently relinquished. Dressed head to toe in white, she issued blessings to all who greeted her and, once the procession started, led the collective praying of the rosary through a microphone. She was a statuesque woman with finely chiseled features—standing at the apex of the procession with her neck scarf billowing in the wind, she resembled a ship's figurehead. During the final moments of the procession, in a move that would have appealed to Iati's Pentecostal contingent of voters (of whom there were many in the crowd), she performed as a conduit of divine grace, praying for her kneeling son, her hands upon his head.

Padre Jorge may well have been romantically attached during this period of his life; however, despite following him quite closely over a two-week period in the lead up to the election, I gathered little evidence for it. Although some days he was nowhere to be found, and some nights he spent away from his house, the general assumption was that as a mayoral candidate in the final weeks of a campaign, he needed to keep long and unpredictable hours. As with any other priest, however, his to-ings and fro-ings still appeared to me enigmatically guarded. "The padre is traveling," would come the familiar line, or, "He must have stayed the night at his mother's house." Not wishing to appear indecorous, I accepted these explanations and pried no further.

A week before the vote, things turned bad for Padre Jorge. A wave of blue flags in support of the incumbent mayor suddenly appeared, rippling across the rooftops of the municipality. It looked as though Tenório's blue might overpower Padre Jorge's red, and this had the campaign committee worried.

Paulo, Padre Jorge's erstwhile campaign manager, suspected that the mayor's party was rampantly and illegally buying up blocks of votes and launched a mission to capture evidence. He allowed Rosa and me to accompany him on a couple of tense drives into the countryside in the dead of night, trailing expensive vehicles known to belong to people of the incumbent faction, in the hopes we would catch them distributing cash and favors to the rural citizens.

"For the love of God, what possible business does a brand-new pick-up like that one have in this stinking hell of a place, at this hour of night?"

he fumed as we bumped and careened down dusty, potholed tracks in the pitch-dark.

Every so often Paulo would pause the car and turn the steering wheel, allowing the headlights to illuminate a large pile of bricks in the middle of a field or stacked at the entrance to an isolated homestead. A stream of obscenities would follow: ". . . sons of whores, delivering bricks after 11 o'clock at night. Who does that?"

We never gathered any hard evidence, however, as the pick-ups we trailed would speed off and lose us or send other cars into our path to block our movement.

"The people of Iati are honest—that is our problem," said Padre Jorge dolefully. "If they promise to vote in exchange for money, they'll honor that promise."

A meeting had been called at the campaign headquarters to discuss what could be done about Padre Jorge's shrinking lead in the race to election. The vast majority of the region's voters were poor, and with barely a week to go before the vote, Alexandre Tenório's financial might was making a strong impression, flooding the town with blue stickers.

During the meeting, various strategic counter-responses were discussed, but the possibilities were limited. Given that Padre Jorge's campaign had no money, it was decided that the best plan of action was to continue promoting themselves as they had already been doing: as the faction that "stands for ethics."

Following that meeting, Padre Jorge upped the ante of his door-to-door work in the town's peripheries. Walking from house to house, he performed his ethics in a distinctively priestly way: initiating conversation with a "God bless you," extending a warm hand, sometimes placing it on a child's head or an adult's arm, inquiring about health, offering platitudes and more blessings before finally launching into a practiced spiel:

> Thanks be to God I am here today because I'm running for mayor, as you know. And with God's help, I intend to turn this municipality around, but I have one request to make of you, madam: if *he* [Tenório] offers you money, please don't take it. For that is the money which

should be going to the hospital, the schools, our roads, our community. By the grace of God, I know that you understand this, madam.

With only three days to go before the vote, the mood in Padre Jorge's camp had returned to fighting optimism. Small red flags started returning, springing like flowers out of windowsills and rooftops, and suddenly it was once more conceivable that the incumbent faction could lose the election.

"Tenório's time is over. That man has weeks left to live!" These words were uttered by Pimenta, an affable day laborer who seemed to divide his time between Padre Jorge's campaign headquarters, where food and company were always abundant, and foraging the nearby scrubland for the wild chilies to which he owed his nickname.

Members of the entourage were gathered in Padre Jorge's living room between outings, engaged in what had become a favorite pastime: listening to Pimenta's eccentric but astute predictions.

"When Tenorio loses the election and realizes the level of debt he's in, he'll kill himself," he said assuredly. "It's as simple as that." But for all his political acumen, Pimenta failed to predict what happened next.

They came during the night—a team from the opposite faction delivering copies of a DVD to dozens, possibly hundreds of homesteads across the town. The DVD, pushed hastily under doors and thrown onto porches, came in a paper sleeve bearing the title "Padre Jorge: Saint or Dragon?," under which was an image of two dragons spattered in bullet holes, as if shot down in action. The reference, not lost on anyone who received it, was to Padre Jorge's popular campaign mascot, the image of St Jorge. The film on the DVD opened with dramatic music laid over spinning screenshots of dragons and photos of Padre Jorge, fading to a woman's voice delivering the following warning:

> People of Iati, pay attention! Is Padre Jorge really what he seems? He may liken himself to his namesake, Saint Jorge the dragonslayer, but could it be *he* that is the dragon? Watch the following testimony and decide for yourself.

It then cut to the talking head of an attractive blonde woman in her early thirties, identifying herself as an ex-lover of Padre Jorge. Speaking to the camera, she described how their relationship began through telephone calls and developed via secret car trips to the nearby city. But the thrust of her exposé wasn't the fact of their relationship so much as Padre Jorge's mistreatment of her during that time: his promise to leave the church and marry her never materialized; he constantly borrowed money from her that he never paid back; and, finally, he betrayed her with another woman.

As day broke over Iati, supporters started turning up at Padre Jorge's campaign headquarters clutching copies of the DVD. Padre Jorge addressed those visitors as they turned up, dismissing the DVD as "one big lie" and waxing about the evident desperation of his political adversary ("only someone who knows he's lost the election would do such a thing"). Between hand clasps and blessings, he defended himself against the woman purporting to be his ex-lover, claiming he'd never laid eyes on her before and describing her as a prostitute (*uma garota de programa*), someone lacking morals (*sem moralidade*) whom his political adversary must have paid to deliver a script.

Meanwhile, Paulo, Padre Jorge's campaign manager, took the DVDs from those arriving and tossed them into a corner of his bedroom, ready for later disposal. He allowed Rosa and me in to film the pile, which was impressive, not only in terms of its size but also in terms of the physical energy that supporters had put into disfiguring the tough plastic discs, whether by snapping them in half, burning them with lighters, or scratching them with knives.

Paulo picked up one that had been miraculously warped, as though someone had tried to scrunch it in the palm of their hand like a piece of paper. "Look at that," he said. "They're bringing the DVDs here already destroyed. Proof, you see, of their anger."

Paulo's talk of anger niggled at me. Who were those angry people, and with whom, precisely, were they angry? With Padre Jorge? Tenório? Or with themselves for having been taken in by Padre Jorge's fake celibacy? Padre Jorge's female supporters did not seem particularly angry to me. They smiled knowingly, sometimes nervously, at the mention of the DVD, but did not seem too bothered by it. If anything, the DVD had injected a shot of unexpected jouissance into what was, at that point, a very fast-moving election campaign, providing them with something new to gossip about.

Among Padre Jorge's male supporters, the DVD was regarded as nothing more than entertainment—or proof of Tenório's debased character. The accusation it contained seemed to be of no relevance at all, except that it reinforced—perhaps even proved—the idea of Padre Jorge's virility.

"Who knows if the video is true?!" a local shopkeeper said with a flash of enjoyment in his eyes, when I asked him about it. "If I had to guess, I'd say Padre Jorge isn't going to last long as a bachelor outside the church!"

Not having been present in Padre Jorge's house at dawn when the first supporters had started arriving with their DVDs, I sought an account from Padre Jorge's housekeeper, Dona Vera. That account added an important clarificatory detail, one that Dona Vera had been most insistent about: the women who had arrived first at Padre Jorge's house were the "suffering elderly women" (*as idosas sofredoras*). None of those elderly women were from wealthy households; they had arrived on foot, visibly upset, some crying. One *idosa* had needed checking by a local nurse on arrival because the incident had caused her to collapse in what turned out to be an "attack" of high blood pressure. According to Dona Vera, Padre Jorge had spent the dawn hours in tears himself, holding court with those crying women, praying and reasoning with them.

Perhaps it was a coincidence that Padre Jorge's first and most emotional confrontation that day was with elderly women, but it is worth noting that poor elderly women, past childbearing age, would have had the most to lose if it turned out that Padre Jorge was sexually obligated to a younger woman. Structurally marginalized by their class, age and gender, the *idosas* perhaps depended more than other voters on the notion that Padre Jorge cared for them in a way that only a celibate priest whose heart belonged equally to all could do.

We can see in the *idosas*' angst that even if virility is part of the political sphere, a priest running for mayor must defend his celibate image, at least until he has firmly established himself in office. Failure to do so would be a threat to his greatest asset: his connection to that utopian celibate imaginary that claims to transcend the destructive effects of time and kinship, friendship and factionalism. It would therefore be surprising if the political adversary of a priest did not, as a matter of course, attack his celibate status, even understanding the capacity for such attacks to backfire.

Assuming Office: Padre Daniel

The tightrope of virile celibacy is one that, as I described at the start of this chapter, charts a transformation not only in terms of the priest's situation but in his very character. At any point along that journey, the priest becomes more or less vulnerable to revelations of a sexual sort. While Padre Jorge was, at the time I knew him, battling for office and therefore striving to maintain strict control over his celibate persona, the same was not true of Padre Daniel, who, by the time I met him, had married and left ministry for good.

Padre Daniel was a charismatic and intelligent man; able to speak knowledgeably and passionately on all kinds of topics, he was widely respected and was often asked to perform his support for political allies by giving speeches at their campaign rallies.

On a one-to-one basis, he was thoughtful and self-reflective. Speaking to me about the relative distribution of homosexual and heterosexual priests in the church, he mused over the fact that he and his heterosexual colleagues had always constituted a minority. "But I'll tell you one thing," he said, "without that minority, there would be no mayor-priests."

Padre Daniel was convinced that the mayor-priest phenomenon was rooted in heterosexuality and catalyzed into being by a common predicament among sexually active heterosexual priests: the reproductive drive. When contraception failed, he explained, or the woman decided it was time to have children, the priest had to decide whether to leave the church or risk a scandal. "For all that he might love her," said Padre Daniel, "the risk of a swollen belly is too much. The one sign he cannot hide from as it confirms to the public, you know, his double life (*vida dupla*)."

Padre Daniel was careful to clarify that pregnancy—or the mounting fear of it—did not jolt all sexually active heterosexual priests into leaving the church. "The world is full of fatherless children," he said, "many of them caused by priests."

He was alluding to the fact that priests who have children but wish to remain in the church are readily enabled to do so by much the same mechanisms of doubleness that allow them to enter long-term sexual relationships in the first place. But Padre Daniel was critical of such trends. He did not agree with the way some of his heterosexual colleagues had treated their long-term girlfriends: availing themselves of amorous play while evading all the obligations of a more formal partnership. In the end, he said, a man has a moral obligation to give a woman "the thing all women dream of."

"What would that be?" I had to ask, vaguely aware, as I did so, that as a woman I was meant to know what it was I supposedly most wanted.

"Marriage, of course," he replied, looking at me with bemused incredulity. "A woman's dream is to be respectable, is it not? Right or wrong, it is the man, through marriage, who gives her that respectability."

The story of Padre Daniel's relationship with his own shadow-partner-turned-wife, Darcyone, depicted the complex, contradictory forces that made up the collective imaginary of the virile celibate in the political sphere. The two had met when Padre Daniel was a recently ordained priest and Darcyone a novice nun. Their romance sparked during a religious retreat and remained a secret for many months, consisting mainly of stolen phone calls and longer trysts whenever circumstances allowed. As their commitment to one another deepened, however, they tentatively revealed their relationship to close and trusted friends and began to discuss the prospect of leaving their respective religious vocations.

Darcyone was the first to leave, but Padre Daniel clung on for longer. For all that he wished to live openly with Darcyone, he could not bring himself to leave the church until he had found an alternative source of income. In that period, a local man intending to run for mayor in the town's coming election asked Padre Daniel if he wanted to join his ticket as vice-mayor. As a popular priest whose relationship with Darcyone was still a well-contained secret, Padre Daniel could easily have seized that moment to go for the top office himself, but, knowing that a career in politics would not offer him a secure living in the long term, he decided against it. A stint as vice-mayor, he decided, would provide an ideal exit from the priesthood, for it offered a respectable reason for abandoning his vocation, a salary upon exit, and time to retrain as a lawyer.

It was clear that even as a ministering priest, Padre Daniel had struggled heavily with the injunction to keep his sexual status secret because, as he told me, maintenance of ambiguity in that area would be taken as a sign of homosexuality.

> The women of the parish would ask, "Padre, how do you want the flowers arranged? Padre, what color scheme shall we use when decorating the church?" And I would reply, "How on earth would I know, ladies? I'm not *that* kind of priest!"

However, while many suspected and some knew for sure that Padre Daniel was leaving the church for a woman, he was careful to keep his relationship secret until he had negotiated the terms of his departure from the church *and* won the election. Darcyone was often at his side during that time, but by not declaring the true nature of their relationship, Padre Daniel succeeded in maintaining a strong association with the church, even as he transitioned away from it.

Padre Daniel's special status, the status that elevated him above other men during his electoral campaign, was grounded in the public's understanding that he was not leaving his ministry altogether, just taking a temporary sabbatical from it. And it would have been important to protect that image for both political and religious reasons. Padre Daniel understood the implicit terms of the deal he had struck. He understood the transition he was undergoing to be a volatile one, structured by desire and subject to the complex expectations of the voting public. All the same, a conflicting ethics of care toward Darcyone ended up derailing the process.

It happened at the Mass of Thanksgiving (*Missa de posse da prefeitura*) that small-town mayors traditionally sponsor in the month they take up office. The event is an important one in the political calendar of any small town, as it brings together all the politically influential men and women of the municipality. Padre Daniel, who was freshly appointed to his new political role and still in possession of the bishop's favor, decided to use his moment of speech-giving to make his relationship public.

The decision to do this had been forced on him, he told me, by ongoing rumors that were casting Darcyone as the selfish party who had destroyed a good man's sacred calling. Padre Daniel and Darcyone had long accepted that they were the subject of gossip, but by the *Misa da posse*, the rumors against Darcyone had become so intense that they were having a serious impact on her.

"The *povo* were kinder to me than to her," Padre Daniel acknowledged. "With me it was all light stuff: 'Ah, the padre likes women'; 'The padre can't resist a beauty.' There was no mention of the fact that *I* had ended *her* vocation."

When Padre Daniel stood to address the crowded congregation, no one suspected what was coming.

"And one last thing, my good people," he said, wrapping up his speech. "During the election campaign there was a lot of talk that the priest was dating. Well, from now on, it's true—Padre has a girlfriend!" With that, he called Darcyone to join him at the front and introduced her.

As Padre Daniel left the microphone, the church, packed to its rafters with dignitaries and townsfolk spilling out into the square, applauded the couple. Yet, despite the celebratory atmosphere that prevailed in the immediate wake of Padre Daniel's revelation, all was not well. Traces of scandal and feelings of resentment lingered for key segments of the community, and a week following the *Misa de posse*, Padre Daniel received a letter from the bishop retracting his promise of a potential return to the church once his political term was up and pressing him to apply for canonical dispensation from the clerical state so he could marry in a Catholic ceremony.

The couple did go on to marry, but not in the church. Their decision to avoid a Catholic wedding was a deliberate act of resistance against the institution they had both given so much of their lives to but that they perceived had coldly rejected them.

Padre Daniel explained how priests who leave the church for women are routinely pressured into religious marriage by bishops because they know that, in the eyes of the *povo*, there is no such thing as laicization. Only a sacrament of marriage can fully override a sacrament of ordination, divesting the priest in question of his sacred status and religious power. Marriage, therefore, is the church's way of cutting its remaining association with—and hence, duty of care toward—any priest no longer under its full control.

Padre Daniel's stint as vice-mayor went smoothly. He retrained as a lawyer and, as soon as his political term was up, the couple left the small town to start a new life in the city. But Padre Daniel's abrupt rupture from his priest identity continued to weigh heavily on him. His sudden loss of status, coupled with the continuing coldness of certain members of his family toward Darcyone, left him emotionally depleted. Padre Daniel could not relinquish the sense that he was being punished not for the sin of involving himself in politics, but for the sin of devoting his life to the love of a single woman.

It could be argued that the lasting negative effects of Padre Daniel's revelation stemmed not from the content of the revelation but from its timing. Coming at the *Misa de posse*, a point when the flows of desire that had been oxygenating his political campaign were still too intimately entwined with his image as a priest, it had threatened the patriarchal fantasy of all-male celibacy that the church depended on. Padre Daniel's passage into politics had caused the church, through association, to temporarily immerse itself in a fecund but potentially polluting secular power. Such temporary immersions are not necessarily anathema. Members of the ecclesial hierarchy are well aware, for example, that Catholic priests who forge positive and successful careers in politics can make (and historically have made) excellent emissaries for the religious institution, particularly when they return to ministry. However, this is only possible if their celibate identities remain intact. Padre Daniel's too-quick public declaration of love for a woman disrupted that possibility.

Leaving Office: Padre Aldo

While some priests, like Padre Daniel, are clear at the start of their political careers that they intend to leave ministry for good, others remain undecided. Such was the case with Padre Aldo, who, at the time of our first meeting, was halfway through his second term as mayor-priest of São Bento and still deciding whether to return to ministry. Padre Aldo had remained unmarried and had enjoyed a remarkable seven years as a politician in which he had struggled, as any mayor would, against the machinations of certain political adversaries, but despite this fact had consistently succeeded at winning new allies, strengthening ties between the diocese and the municipality, and avoiding scandal.

"The bishop likes me—what can I say?" he nonchalantly replied when I asked him why he could return to the church if he chose to, while Padre Jorge was banned.

At the time of that conversation, Padre Aldo was still uncertain where his future lay. He had been invited to continue his political career as a state deputy and was tempted by the possibility, but the risks, he acknowledged, were great. He seemed to carry an inkling that politics, like gambling, was something one should "quit while ahead"—or rather, while the bishop was still open to the prospect of his returning to ministry.

Two years later, Padre Aldo prepared to return to the church, handing his municipality over to his faction's successor, the daughter of his longtime vice-mayor, the richest man in all the region.[4] If, for some, that election presented yet another case of vote-buying and nepotism, further proving that the air of moral decency Padre Aldo had brought to the administration was nothing more than a superfice, for Padre Aldo another electoral win for his side afforded an honorable exit. And it is in light of this fact, of his return to the priesthood as a *successful* ex-mayor, that certain aspects of Padre Aldo's personality and his masterful negotiation of virile celibacy stand out, starting with the first time I ever met him.

I had been invited, along with some men from Padre Aldo's political entourage, to lunch at his house. As we sat in the reception area of his cool, tile-floored house, Padre Aldo emerged looking smart but casual in jeans, a crisp white shirt, and pointy leather loafers of the sort Brazilian men of money and influence always seemed to favor. With him was one of his political aides, a slim and well-manicured woman in tight jeans and sunglasses. Taking a seat in the corner of the room, she ignored us for the large part in order to make endless phone calls. I wondered how she was able to screen out Padre Aldo's booming voice, which was naturally loud and dominated the entire room.

On that day, he claimed to be stressed. "It's this job of mine, my dear friends," he said. "It's not that it comes with problems—the job *is* the problem!"

We chuckled sociably at the irony.

"What I need is an acupuncturist!" he continued. "No, a masseur—that's the one, isn't it?" he corrected himself mischievously.

While we laughed along politely, the attractive aide flatly ignored Padre Aldo's joke in a manner that could have signaled mild annoyance or, perhaps, some deeper intimacy between them. Padre Aldo continued laughing, completely unperturbed by her blatant failure to appear amused by him.

He poured out glasses of beer with great delicacy then handed them around to his gathered guests. "Ah!" he lamented as he did so, "we're in Lent, which means I'm not drinking; what a bore! But the rest of you, drink up—please be at home!"

The conversation meandered around to the subject of a man Padre Aldo wished to hire for some work but could not because he was the alleged lover of his friend's ex-wife. "If only I knew who was the first to put the horns on who!" he cackled. "If my friend's wife cheated on him first, obviously I can't hire the guy, but if my friend was the cheat, I suppose it looks less bad. . . ."

There was more amused laughter.

"Oh, the poor, poor Northeasterner," he continued, slyly observing me, the foreigner, to gauge whether I understood the predicament. "It's the stuff of machismo for sure, but, for the Northeastern man, the worst thing in the world that can happen to him is to be cuckolded!"[5]

Before long, lunch was over, and Padre Aldo was urging his guests to take their time over coffee despite the fact he had to rush off on urgent business. "Let's go!" he called to his aide, getting up from his chair.

She lifted her handbag onto her shoulder, slipped down her sunglasses, and stood tall in high heels next to Padre Aldo. As they walked out the door, I noticed Padre Aldo's hand on the small of her back, propelling her gently toward his car.

Padre Aldo was wont to describe himself half-jokingly as a "poor Northeasterner" (*pobre nordestino*) and "unfortunate soul" (*um infeliz*) who, like his fellow unfortunate Northeasterners, was mired in backward machismo. One had to feel sorry for the "poor Northeasterner," he joked repeatedly, "he knows his life is a drama but is powerless to change it."

Padre Aldo's use of the term "poor" was freighted with literal and figurative meanings. The "poor Northeasterner" was, in his usage, more than the economically poorer compatriot of the rich southern Brazilian; he was "poor" in ways one was meant to both regret and admire: educationally "backward" (*atrasado*) and politically "addicted" (*viciado*), but, and for all that, loved by God.

I often wondered if Padre Aldo directed these observations at me to defray any moral judgments I may have held against the region as a cosmopolitan outsider. But I also sensed Padre Aldo to be something of an outsider himself. Coming from a peasant agricultural background but having lived, traveled, and studied in other parts of Brazil and South America, he was able to inhabit other perspectives.[6] By habitually identifying himself as a "poor Northeasterner," he seemed at once to distance himself from, and emphasize his connection to, the very culture he sought to critique.

In fact, Padre Aldo's successful career owed much to the artful way he straddled different worlds: he belonged but understood positions of non-belonging; he performed the priest when expected to do so and embraced the profane whenever it was necessary. His talent for using speech and humor in ways that spoke, always, to the maximum number of differently arrayed interests was undoubtedly part of his success, both as a priest and as a politician.

Learning of the DVD that had been sent to derail Padre Jorge's election campaign, he roared with laughter and went on to recount the attack on his own celibacy during his first-ever electoral campaign.

"The first thing the opposition do is give you several children," he told me. In his case, cars mounted with loudspeakers had been sent to cruise the streets of the municipality, broadcasting that he was the father of no fewer than seven illegitimate children. "It's their go-to strategy," he said, laughing.

> In my case it was so predictable. My mother rang me in tears, wailing, "Son, is it true?" I said, "Mother, much as I would love for this rumor to be true—how wonderful it would be to give you some grandchildren—sadly it is not. . . ."

We cannot know for sure from Padre Aldo's telling whether his mother would, indeed, have been happy to learn that the rumors were true.[7] But what may be noted is that Padre Aldo's response to his mother on the matter was the same as his response to his prospective voters.

"My dear people," he announced in retaliation from his own speaker-bearing car, "much as I would love for this rumor to be true, sadly it is not!"

Padre Aldo's defense remained faithful to the spirit of virile celibacy: by simultaneously emphasizing the intrinsic value of both forms of fatherhood (spiritual and biological), he was able to appeal to the widest array of social and moral sensibilities. Going on to win his election, he came first in every single ballot box across the region's largest municipality.

As an attractive, single woman, Padre Aldo's aide was an interesting part of his political armory. Always well dressed and constantly at his side, cell phone in hand, she did more than hold his life together with her organizational acumen; she produced his virility.

The pair had known one another for many years, long before Padre Aldo had become mayor, and an air of old gossip hung about their association. For example, the fact that she, despite having drawn the interest of many eligible suitors over the years, was still unmarried and without children, was supposedly evidence that the pair were secretly a couple or, at the minimum, that she was in love with him. But speculations on the matter never ran very far, in part, I suspect, because Padre Aldo was politically unassailable, being at the time on excellent terms with the bishop, the regional media, and the richest men of the municipality. Rather, the air of old gossip was just enough, it seemed, to cement the aide in the public's imagination as his shadow partner—that is, as someone *he may or may not* have been sexually involved with, and who therefore affirmed his hetero masculinity.

Padre Aldo's case illustrates how the power of the shadow partner to disrupt the celibate fantasy depends heavily upon two things: firstly, upon the priests' political network (the quality of his connections to other powerful men); and secondly, upon on how far he is on his desacralizing journey—whether at the start, in the middle, or at the end.

An interesting case for comparison would be that of Padre Alexandre, who, like Padre Aldo, was halfway through his second term as mayor-priest at the time of my research. While Padre Aldo was keeping his options open about returning to religious ministry (the option he took in the end), Padre Alexandre was open about the fact that he had no intention of returning to the priesthood. All the same, he had remained a bachelor, and this may have been why items about his having made a female colleague pregnant started appearing on regional political websites. In one of these items, a disgruntled ex-functionary of Padre Alexander's is reported as saying that the mayor-priest had announced the news himself to a gathering of his political functionaries. The ex-functionary continues:

> The town is unhappy at the news. How could a priest do this? Is it not enough that he betrayed the church when he entered politics?

Yet what is striking is how little punch this revelation packs. In the comments thread below the item, neither Padre Alexander's supporters nor his detractors express any outrage at the rumored pregnancy. While Padre Alexandre's detractors use the discussion to vent about his administrative failures (closure of schools, insufficient funds for the hospital, etc.), making no mention of his sexual morality, his supporters simply dismiss the grounds for his outing at all, as seen in the following comments:

> I'm not from Ibimirim but I admire the city and more still the courage of the padre when he decided to act as a politician. And whether he got [a woman] pregnant or not is his problem. . . .

Wow what idiocy. If she got pregnant, it was because she wanted it. And, after all, he is no longer a priest; he can get anyone he wants pregnant! . . .

Can I just clarify: when a priest stops serving the altar and becomes a politician like Mr. Alexandre, the canonical law that governs the Church's rules makes it clear that he is suspended from ORDER. When the priest leaves the priesthood for five years, he returns by decree of the bishop to the lay state. So I would stop treating this citizen like Father Alexandre; he is simply Alexandre, a common citizen. . . . [8]

As comments pages like this one reveal, the virile celibacy priests depend on for political survival is not an autochthonous production of the male sex but is constituted through female presence. However, as the different reactions displayed by the public on the topics of Padre Aldo's aide, Padre Daniel's wife, Padre Jorge's alleged lover, and Padre Alexandre's alleged biological paternity indicate, the forces that work to contain the mayor-priest within or disassociate him from his sacred status are complex and temporally unstable.

Virile Celibacy: A Mode of Religious Politics

The logics of priestly and patronal fatherhood runs parallel to a certain degree in that both kinds of fatherhood suggest the capacity to provide for a greater-than-usual number of dependents. Both priests and mayors sit at the apex of a growing arc of people, but the worlds and temporalities they exert influence over differ. At a certain point, these parallel logics pull in opposite directions: in the mayor's case, toward a worldly framework in which production and reproduction are valued; in the priest's case, toward an otherworldly framework of sterility and "final inoperativity." The priest who does not partake in the heteronormative system remains at a critical remove from the inevitable divisions but also from the fecundity that patronage and local democracy are premised upon. In response to this, mayor-priests must negotiate the tense and twisting expectations of virile celibacy, an image that allows them to serve both value systems at once.

The priest's personal journey from the sacred to the secular, as we saw, is punctuated by key events: the run-up to the election, the election itself, the *Misa de posse*, the first year of office, and the end of office. This is a desacralizing journey—one that inevitably weakens his association with the church and his power to symbolize it. And yet, the degree to which this desacralization takes place depends upon a range of factors, including—and perhaps most importantly—his sexual relationship with women.

A priest's success as a politician depends not merely on himself and his own work ethic, but on the way collective knowledge about his relationships and sexuality is handled by his community. For a priest's political adversary, the goal is to force secret knowledge that might already be in circulation about him out into the open, transforming it into something transgressive. Public revelations of this kind (about a priest's lovers or children) do not necessarily discredit a priest entirely, but they may certainly disrupt the clerical fantasy that a priest's heart belongs equally to all.

Virile celibacy is therefore one instantiation of a "secular passage" that a priest may take in the context of his career. The secular passage, whether it be spatial, chronological, or psychological, constitutes a necessary movement backward and forward from the church's cloistered, authoritative center. Contrary to the utopian inoperativity symbolized by priestly celibacy, such movement (or elasticity) constitutes a mode of operativity, an engagement with the world that has purpose and telos. Secular passages in the form of a move into party politics or a sexual "double life" do not necessarily harm the church as an institution—indeed, they may be necessary to its survival over the *longue durée*.

In returning to Schmitt's notion of the church as a powerful "container of opposites" and to the concept of Catholicism as embodying a particular political form, I suggest that it is only through passage that boundaries between opposites such as church and state (or the sacred and the secular) are constituted and, herein, that the power generated within each domain is produced and controlled.

What is so striking about the passage in the mayor-priest context, however, is its sexed and gendered dimension. In the stories told here, we see how processes of revelation and concealment concerning individual women—"shadow spouses," as I have called them—influence the priest's trajectory, radically determining both his electability and his capacity to continue representing the church. As Padre Daniel's case illustrated quite clearly, this sort of politics comes at a high emotional cost for priests and especially for their female partners who, sandwiched between the patriarchal institutions of church and local government, are often the first to be socially vilified.

Paradoxically, it is the shadow partner's essential exclusion from the institution of the priesthood that makes her so central to it. For the church, this paradox seems particularly founded on the unruliness of the female womb and its capacity to "swell up" (as Padre Daniel put it) in betrayal of a collectively held fantasy about the priesthood as a sacred oasis of all-male power. If virile celibacy is just one mode of religious politics, then, it is certainly not one that liberates men or women from the cultural constraints of gender, sexuality, and earthly bodies but invariably returns them to it.

5   Votes of Faith
Force, Power, and Political Form

In their classic ethnographic description of the small-town municipal election as a cultural phenomenon, the anthropologists Moacir Palmeira and Beatriz Heredia paint a rich and quite lyrical portrait of the *época da política* ("political time") as a species of sacred: a time "set apart." Elections, they write:

> constitute as critical a period of the social calendar as those calendrical rituals associated with the Church. Just as the cycle of religious festivals that extends, annually, from the beginning of December until the Day of Kings in January comprise a "time of feasts," or the liturgies that extend from the Ash Wednesday to Easter Sunday comprise a "time of 'Lent,'" the coming of an election opens up a "time of politics." (Palmeira and Heredia 1995, 34, *translation my own*)

And true to form, it was during the "time of politics," with only two weeks to go before the election in which Padre Jorge was running, that Paulinho became prone to reveries.

"When Padre Jorge wins the election and I become manager of the hospital . . ." he said, packing fireworks into a plastic carrier for that evening's march, "I'll sort that place out once and for all: order new drugs for the stock cupboard, fire those sons-of-bitches who never do anything. . . ."

"Padre Jorge is a good man," he continued on his hands and knees as he staple-gunned red fabric onto the plywood backdrop of the stage for the following night's rally. "He'll take care of us. I have faith in him!"

Paulinho was one of Padre Jorge's keenest campaign volunteers. Watching as he decorated the stage, I found myself swept up in his energy, as convinced as he was that Padre Jorge was about to win the election and raze every social hierarchy to the ground, turning that dust-filled plain into a new Garden of Eden. Like Paulinho, I had become a participant in the extended liturgy of the electoral period and was committed to its transformative properties.

Padre Jorge had agreed to let me film the final weeks of his electoral campaign. During that filmmaking Paulinho's great dedication to Padre Jorge had captured my attention. Perhaps what captured me was the possible unfolding of a rags-to-riches story: poor man makes good, thanks to the benevolent actions of a single, charismatic priest. Or perhaps I was simply at a point in the electoral cycle where fantastical thinking had gained a certain currency. Whatever the case may have been, there remained moments when I wondered what was really going on in Paulinho's head. Did he actually believe Padre Jorge would reverse the world and its entrenched social inequalities just for his benefit? And what was going through Padre Jorge's head? Did he genuinely intend to make Paulinho—widely known throughout the town as a poor, gay, cross-dressing sex worker—manager of the local hospital?[1]

There were moments when Paulinho's faith seemed naïve, but he was not the only one consumed by naivete.

Rosa, my brilliant and frequently cynical companion, had much the same look about her during those weeks. Wide-eyed and brimming with energy, she was deeply excited about the possible outcome of the election in her home municipality some miles away from Iati. Her optimism was due, like Paulinho's, to the *fé* (faith) that coursed through her, the *fé* she had in Marco, her chosen mayoral candidate. I questioned her: what made Marco so different from candidates of the past?

"I feel it," was her response. Then, pausing to reflect further, she offered that he was younger and seemed "more dedicated" to helping people. Perhaps, she reasoned, because he was a lawyer by profession.

There was, of course, a clientelist dimension to Rosa's faith: Marco had promised continued support for the children's home that she managed. However, it was not this alone that was animating her; it was the excitement in the air, the thickness of the atmosphere. Rosa explained that during the *época da política*, a person's faith—which was routinely present and intrinsic to who they were—suddenly grew stronger. This was true for everyone caught up in politics. Paulinho concurred.

"How do you know your faith has grown stronger?" I asked them as we shuffled on foot through the backstreets of Iati, laden with staple guns and rolls of red fabric.

"You know because every morning you wake up thinking about your candidate, feeling goosebumps," said Paulinho. He went on, likening his faith to a kind of energy that gave him strength to keep working. With enough faith, he reasoned, a person can live for days without eating.

Faith is such a quotidian concept in Brazil that it tends to blend into the background. It gets invoked and proclaimed so often in everyday speech that it can come to seem—like the words "please" or "thank you"—somewhat formulaic—empty of real meaning. But faith merits closer attention. As Paulinho and Rosa's reflections intimate, it has a key role in the rituals of democracy.

This chapter investigates localized meanings of faith, exploring how it functions, via ritual forms and practices, to bridge the religious and political. It follows in two parts: the first explores the overlapping meanings of faith as a folk concept, a theological virtue, and an ontological category. Extending the metaphor of the secular passage, the second part closely traces my own journey through the *época da política*—an intense and emotionally punctuated space-time in the Brazilian calendar.

Throughout this narrative, faith is to be glimpsed running parallel to other intensely affective states that result from the sonic clamor and festive tension of the electoral period: passion, heat, sickness, hope, inclusion, and exclusion. In such a context faith is not unlike a form of religiosity that precedes the particularities of religious and political identities and contains the seeds of potential that, in the heightened space of "political time," can become both productive and dangerous. Returning to the ontology of faith at the end of the chapter, I focus in on its causative, energetic nature—its capacity to deliver "goosebumps" or to "move mountains" (Matthew 17:20)—and ask what such a species of energy implies for our understanding of religion's role in politics and vice versa. I argue that how we theorize faith and whether we view it as something that precedes or results from social practice has implications not only for how we grasp the localized phenomenon of mayor-priests but also for how we understand the nature of power.

The Ontology of Faith

While "belief" (*crença*) is often taken to be a central paradigm in modern Christianity and has particular salience in Brazil among Protestant evangelicals who are described in contradistinction to Catholics as "believers" (*crentes*), the idiom through which religiosity most expressed itself among people was not belief but faith.[2] *Fé* (faith) could be marshaled as an explicitly religious sentiment to convey an attitude of trust or acceptance in relation to a divine being. Similarly, it could be used to convey a psychological attitude or inner strength necessary for confronting any situation deemed to be hopeless or challenging, as was the case for Paulinho, whose faith that he was about to bag a coveted managerial post in the hospital contradicted a lifetime of evidence that suggested otherwise.

In the Christian tradition, the word "faith" overlaps semantically with the term "belief," but whereas belief may describe an intellectual acceptance of facts and is generally used to signal one's assent to the core tenets of a religion, faith tends to signify something deeper and more affective. Both belief and faith imply an element of "trust" and therefore point to the possibility of doubt, but with faith, the trust dimension is stronger (Lindquist and Coleman 2008; Pouillon 1982; Robbins 2007; Ruel 1997).

According to the *Catechism of the Catholic Church*, faith is the "pledge of the presence and action of the Holy Spirit in the faculties of the human being" that "adapt[s] man's faculty for participation in the divine nature" (*CCC*, §182–83). To have faith is, in this sense, to adopt an attitude of loyalty and commitment toward a person or institution in the absence of rational or supporting evidence. In Christian thought, it is the divine gift that allows us to perceive the world as if "through a glass darkly" (1 Corinthians 13:12). In the English language, the semantic overlap that exists between having faith and having *a* faith in the sense of following a particular religion reveals the polyvalency of the concept and, in particular, its ability to signal both an interior disposition and the act of belonging to a social institution.

Here it is important to recognize that although faith is strongly associated with Christianity and hence religious belonging, it is not the preserve of the pious. Even the most religiously committed of my interlocutors asserted that faith could be found among people who did not believe in God.

Canvassing some members of a local parish youth group by WhatsApp on this topic, faith was described to me as "nondenominational," "a kind of love," and as something "anyone, even a child with no Bible knowledge, can have."

To some degree it is this quotidian, widely shared nature of faith that makes it ripe for political exploitation. Religious rhetoric is fairly normative in political speech across Brazil; generic references to "God" and "faith" are common on campaign trails and signal a politician's baseline morality. Accordingly, a "vote of faith," taken in its broadest sense, is an *exercise of faith*—an act that condenses hope and moral purpose. It is this broad semantic capacity of faith to signify human vitality and moral longing that politicians appeal to when they draw attention to themselves as "good Christians" or claim that "God" is "with them" and "on their side."[3]

As men of God, it only expected that mayor-priests will, like all politicians, mine the rich semantic depths of faith on their campaign trails. This was certainly the case during Padre Ivo's 2001 run for office in Jupi, when "Vote of Faith" became his campaign slogan. But the use of such rhetoric requires skill; priests who engage it must do so in ways that neither exploit their spiritual power over the laity nor limit faith's claim to the Catholic Church alone. Not all such endeavors are successful, however, as I witnessed for myself when, during Padre Jorge's campaign, his adversary started defaming his and his late father's character.

Wounded by this turn of events, Padre Jorge chose to retaliate at his next campaign rally. On stage before a massive crowd of citizens, he brought up the rumors his adversary had been spreading about him and his father and described them as a sinful attack, not only on his personal honor but, more pointedly, on the sacred institution of fatherhood, priesthood, and the Catholic Church more generally. Railing vehemently into the microphone, he shouted:

> A political enemy such as this has the nerve to enter a church and get in line to receive communion and to consume the consecrated host and then to lie to God, and then to lie so much about the Church, the padre, about the people of God! Brothers and sisters, whoever displays a sticker of this man is sinning! Is sinning!

At the end of the speech, there were claps and some scripted cheers, but the crowd remained, by its own standards, quiet—perhaps somewhat discomfited.

The supporters of Padre Jorge I spoke to the following day had indeed been disconcerted by that speech. Some said that Padre Jorge should not have passed religious judgment on his adversary, but mostly people spoke of having had their *fé* manipulated. This was a complex matter, for it was not that they entirely disagreed with Padre Jorge's assessment of the situation: it was true, they said, that his adversary had overstepped the mark, just as it was true that their support for him was bound up with their respect for the Catholic Church. Their discomfort came from the fact that their faith—something personal and inalienable—had been so blatantly manipulated by Padre Jorge for the sake of his political career.

When I spoke to Rosa about this communal reaction, she reminded me that faith was, first and foremost, a wellspring of individual energy and therefore open to exploitation by others. The *época da política* was a special season for faith, she emphasized, and although it was wrong for anyone to take advantage of another's faith for one's own gain, during elections, it frequently happened.

Here it is worth warning against understanding this sort of faith as a "mere" bodily energy, entirely immanent and secular. As Omri Elisha, in his research on North American Christian evangelical faith-based organizations, has likewise argued, the most empowering attribute of faith is its association with divine agency. This conception of faith, he writes, implies that the faithful "are subjects of a moral force not entirely of themselves" (Elisha 2008, 62) and experience religiosity as an "embodied otherness" (Csordas 1997; Elisha 2008).

As among Elisha's evangelicals, faith here implies some sort of external or supernatural force—a "rush of energy" that is both exterior and interior to the self (Durkheim 2008 [1912], 213), not unlike the feeling that Brazilian evangelicals in the suburbs of Rio speak of as grace. In Laurie Denyer Willis's depiction, grace is a "whoosh" that makes people feel "removed from feelings of abandonment and restriction" and produces a sensation of "being lifted from all that has so cruelly, cunningly captured them" (Denyer Willis 2023, 11).

In Catholicism, faith is classified as a "theological virtue" precisely because it has God for its object.[4] For Catholic theologian Leonardo Boff, faith's all-encompassing nature points necessarily to its divine origin:

> Faith is not an "act" alongside others so much as an "attitude" that encompasses all acts, all the person, all sentiment, all intelligence, desires, and life options. It is an experience of original encounter with the living God. This encounter changes life and the manner in which

all things are viewed. Through an attitude of faith we see that all is connected and re-connected to God, as that Father/Mother that created everything, accompanied everything and attracts everything so that all may live in happy communion with one another and with Him already in this world and fully in eternity. (Boff, *Fé e Política: Suas implicações*)

The attitudes and dispositions that faith as an "original encounter" with the divine provokes in people is, however, varied. Whereas for Elisha's Protestant evangelical subjects the embodied otherness of faith is experienced as a provocation to complete humility and submission to God's will, for my interlocutors, faith was present as an "embodied otherness" that required some orientating work, some effort to gain control over. Even if faith pointed an individual toward God's will, its common manifestation as a form of bodily energy (goosebumps, a compunction to get up in the morning) could lead in any number of directions. Faith, in this sense, is a species of energy before it becomes a commitment to a particular set of moral values or an allegiance to a specific religious identity.

Speaking to Rubens, a regional leader of the *Fé e Política* (Faith and Politics) social movement, I was told that *fé* was unalienable. "Without it we would not leave our beds!" he said. In a follow-up, he forwarded me the words of a song by the famous Brazilian singer-songwriter Gilberto Gil that describes faith in broadly animist terms not as the property of humans alone, but as an essence inhering in everything:

ANDAR COM FÉ (GILBERTO GIL)	WALKING WITH FAITH BY GILBERTO GIL
Andá com fé eu vou	Walking with faith I go
Que a fé não costuma faiá . . . (4x)	Because faith does not fail
Que a fé tá na mulher	That faith is in the woman
A fé tá na cobra coral, ô, ô!	Faith is in the coral cobra, oh, oh!
Num pedaço de pão . . .	In a piece of bread . . .
A fé tá na maré	Faith is in the sea
Na lâmina de um punhal, ô, ô!	On the blade of a dagger, oh, oh!
Na luz, na escuridão . . .	In light, in darkness . . .
Andá com fé eu vou	Walking with faith I go
Que a fé não costuma faiá . . . (4X)	Because faith does not fail
A fé tá na manhã	Faith is in the morning

A fé tá no anoitecer,ô,ô!	Faith is in dusk
No calor do verão . . .	In the heat of the summer . . .
A fé tá viva e sã	Faith is alive and healthy
A fé também tá prá morrer,ô,ô!	Faith is there to die, oh, oh!
Triste na solidão . . .	Sad in loneliness . . .
Andá com fé eu vou	Walking with faith I go
Que a fé não costuma faiá . . . (4X)	Because faith doesn't fail
Certo ou errado até	Right or wrong
A fé vai onde quer que eu vá, ô, ô!	Faith goes where I want to go, oh, oh!
A pé ou de avião . . .	By foot or by plane . . .
Mesmo a quem não tem fé	Even when I've no faith
A fé costuma acompanhar, ô, ô!	Faith accompanies me, oh, oh!
Pelo sim, pelo não . . .	For yes, for no . . .
Andá com fé eu vou	Walking with faith I go
Que a fé não costuma faiá . . . (4X)	Because faith doesn't fail.

In this depiction, faith exceeds the bounds of the human, constituting a kind of life force present in all worldly phenomena.[5] In this form it is something that everyone has access to—a resource that might be cultivated (or exploited) in order to gain psychological or supernatural control over a situation. The remit of religious, political, and civil organizations, Rubens clarified, was not to own or exploit faith, but to give it moral direction shaping it for the good of society.

"Things Are Catching Fire"

The days passed in a riot of activity. Following the *política*, Rosa and I and my film camera were permitted into people's cars and houses, up on stages, and onto the back of campaign trucks.

A group of men had coalesced around Padre Jorge. Sporting baseball caps, leather hats, and red T-shirts, they arrived early in the morning and settled all over his furniture. They waited on motorbikes parked outside and moved together after him whenever he left the house. This group, which grew and shrank according to the time of day, was made up mainly of youngish and middle-aged men, agricultural workers from lower-income homesteads. Some were prospective councilors on Padre Jorge's side or lending their casual service as supporters and political advisors; others were favor-hunters.

Rosa and I followed some of those men; we walked behind them filming them, we trained the camera on them as they talked, we watched those closest to Padre Jorge intently to see which way they would turn next. We jumped in the car and careened after them on political errands. We were invited to follow them, I should add. We were liked by some, tolerated by others. But the same men who were happy to be followed by us also wanted their privacy.

At one point, Padre Jorge discovered how to switch off our radio mic during filming to keep us from overhearing some of his conversations. This made white noise pour suddenly through our headphones, causing us to wince and giggle. Acts of secrecy continued off camera. Members of Padre Jorge's entourage would lower their voices and turn their backs on us, huddling tightly or moving away. They'd go into rooms for campaign meetings and shut the door, cutting us out of the action. It seemed at moments that we had entered a game where everyone was strategizing quite openly and where secrecy could be elaborately performed. Being shut out of rooms was simply one of any number of legitimate moves during the *época da política*; nothing to take personally.

If some spaces become smaller and more curtailed during the *época da política*, other spaces open up. In a study of Buritis, Minas Gerais, Christine Chaves elaborates on the important role of *festas* (festivities) in Brazilian political life, embedded in the local saying "politics is done through festivity" (*a política se faz com a festa*) (Chaves 2003).

Iati was no exception to this rule. During the final two weeks leading up to the election, the town was awash with noise and dominated entirely by two colors: red (the color of Padre Jorge's faction) and blue (the color of his adversaries). Blue and red spilled from the rooftops of houses, people clad in red and blue went about their daily business, and campaign jingles emanated from loudspeaker-bearing cars day and night. From a distance, the town seemed to be in the grip of an off-season carnival.

"The carnival of the interior!" said Rosa at one point, laughing as she perused the blue and red cat masks and sparkly antennae-style hairbands for sale in a local shop.[6] There was an inherently playful dynamic to the constant stream of public events going on: *comícios* (rallies), *carreatas e passeatas* (motorcades and marches), and *banquetes e grandes churrascos* (large-scale feasts, outdoor parties). All the same, the factionalist logic that guided those election-time *festas* differed significantly from the logic of Brazil's famous carnival, which is well recognized among social scientists as a temporary inversion that, far from upending the extant social order, ultimately revalidates it. Handelman explains the mechanics of carnivalesque inversion in the following way:

> Inversion keeps to the mold of the phenomenon, the foundation for inversion, that actually is inverted. Therefore, inversion maintains the relevance of its foundation and is a discourse about its validity . . . the aspects of order that are inverted remain the mold for the inversion. (Handelman 1998, 52)

Other theories of carnival speak of catharsis: carnival is like an enormous letting off of steam, which, to remain with the hydraulic metaphor, suggests that heat has been building up in ways that can endanger the stability of the social order (Babcock 1978; Bakhtin 1984; Da Matta 1991a). However, the playfulness of an election *festa* is not so much a "letting off steam" as a means of generating heat. In fact, in the run-up to an election, one often hears the phrase "things are catching fire." At this time, political gossip and stories of compromise and betrayal become the mainstay of casual interactions between friends and family. When running into people from neighboring municipalities, it is normal to ask, "How is the politics around your way?" and normal to reply, "Catching fire," without any need for further explanation.

Driving across the region, one passes through towns transformed by colors associated with the competing political parties. A cluster of houses sporting yellow banners here, a bandage of blue flags whipping in the wind there. Red and blue, or yellow and blue, or red and yellow dominate the landscape. The phrase "things are catching fire" is offered both as a metaphorical description of a period of time in which tensions are expected to reach fever pitch and as a moment of stepping back from the action—an ironic allusion to the incendiary, but also and perhaps more importantly, the *transformative* potential of it all. In short, unlike carnivals, elections and their ritual forms do not, in and of themselves, aim to reinstate the status quo.

During this period, Rosa and I were spending all our time among Padre Jorge's supporters, and this had me concerned. Although I was primarily interested in Padre Jorge, I wanted to see things from both sides. The problem was how to gain access to the blues.

At one point, Rosa and I started befriending a married couple who supported the incumbent mayor, but as soon as they connected us with Padre Jorge, they avoided our calls. A rumor spread that we had been paid to film Padre Jorge and make him look important, and from that moment onward, we were welcomed or shunned wherever we went. Palmeira and Heredia were right, I reflected:

> ... if the fronts of the houses and the streets with their decorated cars, as well as the constant music, gives such localities a festive air, the factional segregation of public, convivial spaces points to an intensification of the conflict that spreads fire-like through the community. It's no accident that *política* is associated with division. ... (Palmeira and Heredia 1995, 34)

One night, as a blue rally was preparing to start, we entered the town square and started filming wide shots of the gathering crowd. The political speeches had not yet started, but music was already blasting, and excitement permeated the air.

Before long we were recognized. A stage technician in a blue shirt strode up to Rosa, hands on hips, and a tense conversation ensued. As "members" of the political opposition, we were asked to leave.

Rosa argued politely for our right to remain there, part of the crowd. She then tried to placate the man with the promise that we would pack up and leave as soon as the speeches began, but his tone remained cold and hostile. As the crowd around us thickened and onlooking hecklers started throwing political insults, we were forced to move quickly out of the line of fire, our faces flushing with embarrassment, our camera bags half open, equipment in our arms.

Reaching a side alley where we no longer presented such an obvious spectacle, we paused to compose ourselves. Rosa started closing the bags and packing up, but I, concerned that there was not enough footage of the blues, tried to switch the camera on again. Rosa glared at me wildly: "Enough!" she growled.

Back at home, we sat in the darkness of the small backyard, batting off mosquitoes and drinking rum. Rosa did not speak. She was visibly shaken by what had happened. Rarely did her social charm fail her, but that had been an impossible situation—a total blockage of the convivial artery.

I, too, felt shaken and disconcerted. My arms ached from holding the camera all day, and my hair felt heavy, weighed down with dust and sweat from the constant journeying. Looking across at Rosa silhouetted in the doorway, I felt trapped by the electoral dynamics we were caught up in and concerned for our friendship.

As if to prove a point, at that moment, a loudspeaker-bearing car belonging to the blues passed by. The jingle being sung concerned the arrogance of Padre Jorge going about with his film crew: "Ah, how that pride will turn to shame when he is filmed being knocked out of the race. . . ."

"Sons of bitches," Rosa said.

After that incident, we gave up any pretense of neutrality and allowed ourselves to be entirely consumed by Padre Jorge's campaign. It was just as well, because from that moment on, everything sped up.

We stayed up late discussing his chances of winning and stuck close to Paulinho and Selma, whose energy for campaign work seemed to draw from a bottomless well that they attributed, in their own words, to the "animation of the season" and the force of their own faith.

"I don't want to think about him not winning!" shouted Selma above the chatter of people in her kitchen. "When people say he won't win, I get palpitations; I go weak!"

Selma was in her thirties but had the manner of a teenage girl in the throes of a crush.

"What if you put him in power but he's no good?" I asked her.

Selma looked at me blankly for a moment then narrowed her eyes at the unwelcome possibility. "If he's no good?" she reflected. "Well, just as we put him there, we'll simply remove him!"

The pace was exhausting; nights bled into days, and the days blurred together. Driving around after Padre Jorge, weaving through crowds, opportunities for filming were everywhere. At some point my stamina weakened, and I started opting out. What did it matter if I missed another rally or round of door-to-door visits? I asked myself.

On those afternoons, Rosa and I retreated to the little house I had rented and took refuge in ordinary activities: hand-washing clothes, sweeping the yard, watching DVDs. By dusk, I was often so tired I would collapse on my bed, sometimes missing dinner, falling asleep without even getting changed.

Rosa maintained a different rhythm. She needed the TV on to fall asleep. She moved her mattress onto the living-room floor so she could lie in front of the television, drifting off to its erratic murmur.

One night, I was woken up shortly after midnight by the most deafening noise. Encircled by a million horns at full blast, I lay there, heart pounding, wondering if the world was coming to an end. After some moments, I realized what it was: a midnight *carreata* (motorcade) going past our house.

I remained frozen in the dark, expecting it to pass like the peal of a fire engine traveling down a street. But the horns didn't diminish. They screamed on for some seven minutes or more without pause. The noise had a physicality to it that penetrated every fiber of my body and kept me pinned to the bed.

Unable to get up, my mind raced in all directions. I thought about my rental car parked in the street; I thought about my children thousands of miles away. What would they make of such a noise? Would they find it terrifying or delightful? Finally, I managed to turn myself over and, heart still racing, recalled Palmeira and Heredia's description of the political period:

> Preparation [for the election] becomes more intense, assumes a dramatic and festive character in the hours leading up to a rally, in the form of *passeatas* and *carreatas*. . . . If, before, the act of campaigning had been individualized through visits and invites by politicians, now it is transformed into a collective action. . . . The noisy bus parade, trucks, coaches, motorbikes, and other vehicles, sounding horns and trumpets, shouts, slogans. . . . (Palmeira and Heredia 1995, 42)

Just a ritual show of sonic dominance, I reassured myself. Not the beginning of the apocalypse.

The Rearrangement of Temporal Horizons

Paulinho and Selma's passion seem at first glance confluent with the philosopher Jacques Rancière's (2010) proposition that democracy must be thought of not as an individual quest for happiness, nor as a form of governing the social body, but as a contingent, constant force, an "anarchic element" that disrupts the oligarchy that persists. A vote cast is always fresh and prospective, even if only for a fleeting moment. As an "anarchic element," it retains a structural openness to future possibility—unfurling outward like the petals of a flower, it blooms in the subjunctive moment.

Yet Rancière's suggestion that democracy is a force remains a rather abstract one: it cannot tell us where such force originates, how it takes root in the senses, or how it comes to be manipulated and eventually configured into one constellation of power relations or another. For an answer, we must look to practice itself and to the idea that elections have important expressive dimensions in their own right.

The notion that politics is like theatre (see Geertz 1981) and that elections have liminal and other ritual qualities about them is well recognized in anthropology (Banerjee 2011; Herzog 1987; Spencer 2007). If people only voted because they really believed that their favored candidate would make all the difference, surely we would see far less participation in electoral politics. Yet in countries such as India and Brazil, where voter apathy is hardly a problem, it would seem that the clue to participation lies elsewhere, including in the pleasure of the process itself. As Banerjee observes, elections serve as "aesthetic and ritual moments of heightened awareness" where glimpses can be had of an alternative, more egalitarian order "otherwise hidden in the inequities of everyday life" (Banerjee 2011, 95).

The same could be said of the Brazilian election. No one thinking rationally on the basis of previous evidence believes that any mayor can really bring about that promised utopia. But the *época da política* is both a rational and a fantastical time. Like cupping a die in one's hands and shaking it, the anticipation generated is its own reward, the *época* itself an "art of organizing hope" (Dinerstein 2015).

Anthropologists of Christianity have shown how action becomes most powerfully charged in contexts where subjunctive dynamics hold sway: in moments of rupture (Robbins 2007), when expectations get foreshortened (Guyer 2007; Haynes 2020), or when time becomes virtual (Bialecki 2017). The same holds for secular utopian projects, where different temporalities interpenetrate one another to shape a subject's capacities and expectations. The Catholic-Marxist–influenced Landless People's Movement in

Brazil (MST), for example, rechoreographs linear time via its celebrated concept of *mística*, a kind of mysticism that keeps the utopian revolutionism of the organization alive by condensing "the experience of nowness" with "that which will follow and that which has already passed" (Flynn 2021, 169; see also Chaves 2000). Such suspensions of the linear are key to the enactment of utopia. As the philosopher Slavoj Žižek points out:

> In a proper revolutionary breakthrough, the Utopian future is neither simply fully realized in the present nor simply evoked as a distant promise which justifies present violence—it is rather as if, in a unique suspension of time—in the short-circuit between the present and the future, we are—as if by Grace—for a brief time allowed to act as if the utopian future is (not yet fully here, but) already at hand, just there to be grabbed. (Žižek 2005, 267, cited in Flynn 2021, 160)

Faith, likewise, has a hand in utopia insofar as it leads to a "short-circuit between the present and the future." Viewed as such, faith could be seen as a phenomenon that derives from the ritual aspects of political practice or from socially constructed temporalities that refuse linearity. After all, and as Rosa and Paulinho earlier insisted, faith becomes "stronger" during the *época da política*. However, faith is not merely the side effect of social practice; to see faith as wholly derivative would be to put the proverbial cart before the horse: in short, to misrecognize its a priori nature.

Passion, Sickness, and Fire

Halfway through that two-week period, the *época da política* started wearing people down. I had to drive Rosa back to her hometown and took the opportunity to drop in on Dora. I found her floating about in her backyard, her veined hands wringing thick ropes of wet laundry and hanging it on the line. Our best conversations over the years had always happened as she got her chores done, I testing out thoughts, seeking her opinion, she listening while working and sometimes pausing to pronounce on what I had said.

On this day, she seemed more tired than usual, so I took over the wringing and she went to make us coffee. She hadn't felt well since the start of the *época da política*: cars mounted with loudspeakers had been cruising constantly through the neighborhood, interrupting her every thought.

Worse still, a young man had recently been shot in association with the *política*, causing tension in the town to escalate. "Maya," she said, "during this crazy period, everything is politics, and politics messes with everyone."

The naked factionalism that takes hold during this extended moment is infectious; it works on people, as we saw in Chapter One, like an addiction (*um vício*), a drug. Allowed to run riot, it causes conviviality to wither, old tensions to spiral, and, sometimes, even death. When Paulinho had to rescue his friend, a young man known by the nickname of Veneno ("Poison"), from a barroom fight, he blamed the incident on Veneno's *paixão* (passion) that had "caught fire" as a result of the tension and madness of the *política*.

In the *Catechism of the Catholic Church*, faith and passion are closely related. Both emanate from within the person and constitute one of the ways in which "the Holy Spirit himself accomplishes his work by mobilizing the whole being" (*CCC*, §1769). However, the term "passion" "belongs to the Christian patrimony" (*CCC*, §1763); passions are emotions whose source is the "heart" (*CCC*, §1764). Neither good nor evil in themselves, passions are "natural components of the human psyche; they form the passageway and ensure the connection between the life of the senses and the life of the mind" (*CCC*, §1764).

In everyday Brazilian discourse, both faith and passion can have positive effects, moving the individual toward God. But faith and passion are not identical. Faith describes a positive energy, a primordial sense of purpose, whereas passion describes emotional states, good or bad, that may just as readily drain the individual of positive energy or even "catch fire," leading to "crimes of passion" and other misdemeanors.

The metaphor of fire used in the political context would seem to play on the similarity of faith and passion, resonating ambiguously with the Christian imagery of Pentecost in which tongues of fire come to rest upon Jesus's disciples, firing them up and filling them with holy charism.[7] But if the fire of the Holy Spirit ignites the senses in unambiguously positive ways, the fire of the *época da política* can be terribly destructive, as Veneno found out when, engulfed by its proverbial flames, he ended up with cuts to his face.

Writing about the 2012 municipal election in Passarinho, the town where he worked, Aaron Ansell describes how propaganda images and campaign stickers bearing the names and images of candidates came under critique. Many rural Brazilians, he reported, had stopped displaying them, especially in public places like shops and businesses because of the "sickness" they threatened: the mere sight of such images was enough to elicit a "visceral reaction" and a "revulsion at the virtual sound-scape ('noise') that it activated" (Ansell 2015, 688). At that time, photo-stickers were receiving widespread condemnation in leftist-liberal circles as an instrument of patronage, domination, and surveillance; but Ansell argues that voters were not rejecting them because they suddenly recognized them in quite the same way, but because they linked them with *doentes* (sick voters) whose mad, feverish passion for a candidate "drained" their bodies of *força* and damaged neighborly relations (689).

We should pause to consider the potential of this kind of power that, while open to cultivation and manipulation by other people and external conditions, is also said to have a bodily component and to be indwelling. It is significant here that both faith and electoral sickness seem invariably to draw on old folk taxonomies of inner vitalism described as forms of bodily energy that can be contained, concentrated, or drained away. Faith, herein, relates to power, but not in the commonly understood Foucauldian sense that construes power as a purely intersubjective thing, the product of relational exchanges. Rather, faith has something of a substance-like quality to it; as a form of power, it dwells in the body; its causative potential thickens up given the appropriate material circumstances and technologies.

The Election Result

Early on the morning of the election itself, a smartly dressed young man came to Padre Jorge's house, but it was his highly polished leather loafers that really marked him out as a member of the air-conditioned elite. Viewed among so many plastic flip-flops and dust-covered boots, they winked with arrogance, or at least that is how I perceived them.

Perhaps it was the first sign that I was becoming sick, because the man who owned the arrogant shoes was, in fact, perfectly likeable. A recently graduated lawyer, he had been sent from the state capital of Recife on behalf of the MDB party to advise Padre Jorge's faction on how to avoid unintentionally contravening new federal legislations that had been put in place to counter political corruption.[8]

"For example," said the lawyer to the large group of Padre Jorge's campaigners who now stood in a circle around him,

> today you go home for lunch. You do not eat here, in the house of the padre today. Padre Jorge cannot provide lunch to any one of you or it looks like vote exchange. Moreover, you cannot manifest as a group and seek to influence voting behavior next to the polling station. Manifest as a group: that means walking down to the polling station with all your friends and colleagues. Do not form yourselves into anything resembling a procession on your way to vote today. Do not use horns, drive a sound-car, sing as a group, make lots of noise. Walking in pairs *quietly* is OK, maybe two, maximum three people can go together, provided they are coming from the same household. But no more than that, or the opposition can report us for illegal behavior. What else can you *not* do? You cannot give out *santinhos* [voting cards] with images of your or your friend's face on it, on the streets near to the polling station. You do not exchange anything with anyone in that vicinity.

Soon the questions started: "Hey, *senhor*, what can we wear?"

"Dress normally, but no T-shirts with candidates, no obvious signs of manifestation. Better to keep things neutral."

"I have a question, oh, *senhor*!"

"Yes, friend, speak!"

"Is it better to avoid wearing red?"

"Yes, better to err on the side of caution. No red afro wigs, no symbols painted on your face. . . ."

"Excuse me, *senhor*, what about make-up, nail varnish? Say a woman goes to vote with red nails, red lipstick. Does that count as manifestation? Could one sue for that?"

"*Senhor*, you said there will be no lunch here today. But I already had coffee this morning. Does that count? What about a small piece of bread?"

The questioners were serious—they were anxious to control their "passion," their "heat." The polling booths were open, slowly deciding their fates. The lawyer, even though he seemed slightly bemused by the kinds of details he was being asked to clarify, kept patiently to his script. *Use your common sense*, was his standard response: *today of all days do not take risks. Anything loud, anything ostentatious, any obvious signs of manifestation are best avoided.* The mood in the room was serious but buoyant. Although the legal stipulations being issued had emanated in the first instance from a spirit of democratic idealism, they were being sold to voters via the logic of factionalism: be correct in your comportment and your opponent won't be able to have you disqualified.

The ballots closed at 5 P.M., and as the sun went down, the town turned quiet and expectant. Rosa and I had planned to stick close to Padre Jorge for the final vote count. Padre Jorge and his closest aides had been invited to await the election results in the house of Padre Jorge's prospective vice-mayor, a local businessman with political pretensions whose fancy house sat in a large compound, hidden from view behind a high concrete wall. Although I had driven past that very same compound many times in the preceding weeks, until then I had been ignorant of who lived inside it.

That evening, Rosa and I took care over our appearance, blow-drying our hair and putting on make-up. Rosa, entering into the factional spirit, painted her nails red and put on a bright red blouse. I had a red dress in my suitcase that Rosa urged me to wear, but at the last minute, I chose to wear black. If earlier I'd been irritated by the lawyer's shoes, now, it seemed, I was irritated by the color red. Wherever I looked, I saw bodies clad in red: orange reds, pinky reds, flames of red, threatening to engulf me.

"So, you're going dressed as a widow?" asked Rosa sarcastically.

Looking back, I realize exhaustion was starting to engulf me, but at that point it was manifesting mainly as a growing sense of irritation. It wasn't just the color red that was irritating me; as soon as we entered the prospective vice-mayor's I grew annoyed by its size and its owner's sense of status. The walls of the compound felt prison-like, and my suspicion of the local elite—a small group of men and women who had suddenly turned out in force for the final act of Padre Jorge's campaign story—started to intensify.

The men gathered on that wide veranda were similar in appearance: light-skinned, well-dressed, and chunky metal watch–wearing. They sat around clutching mobile phones and drinking whiskey. I recognized very few people at the vote-count party; Paulinho, Selma, Pimenta, and Veneno were absent, as were all the other campaigners who had worked so hard alongside Padre Jorge those past two weeks. Padre Jorge's faithful driver was one of the few men present I had met before.

"Maya, my child, have a whiskey!" he called, advancing toward me across the veranda, his large red face clashing somewhat with the redness of his T-shirt. He held out a glass, but I declined it.

"Whiskey not to your liking? There's rum if you prefer."

"I'm working," I replied.

He frowned. "Come now, tonight of all nights? You have to have a drink!"

"No thank you," I said curtly. Seeing the look of hurt on his face, I felt momentarily satisfied, as though I'd achieved something.

"OK," he continued, "now you might need to work, but later on you'll toast with us!"

He smiled, his eyes creasing kindly, and suddenly I felt guilt-ridden. What on earth was wrong with me?

It was a tense gathering. As the votes were counted, some women present started crying, praying, and clutching at one another's hands in nervous anticipation. The men, when they weren't glued to their phones, exchanged loud, self-conscious wisecracks, poured themselves whiskeys, and rummaged noisily through the ice bucket.

As the numbers trickled in, the results seemed, for the most part, to be neck and neck, and Padre Jorge's face, as usual, gave nothing away. But the young man who sat with a ledger kept totting up the numbers and looked deadly serious.

The tension reached a peak just as some firecrackers were going off, and the fateful phone call came in. A second later, everyone was shouting with joy. Padre Jorge had won the contest, though not by the widest of margins. The car mounted with loudspeakers parked in the compound was turned on, and the group started dancing wildly around it. From that moment on, I felt more than ever like an outsider peering in: present but unable to fully participate in the revelry.

As I looked at Padre Jorge speaking conspiratorially into the ear of his new vice-mayor, my cynical reason started to reassert itself. *This is the truth of municipal politics*, I thought, *Padre Jorge is on the inside now; he has left the* povo *behind. By tomorrow, all the old hierarchies will have simply reestablished themselves.*

Perhaps those miserable thoughts were written on my face, for no one tried to speak to me or offered me another drink. Music blasting, they danced around hugging each other, waving flags and sporting massive grins. The longer I filmed them, the more distant and disconnected I felt.

Rosa came over to me. "Let's get out of here," she said.

Once outside the compound, we made our way toward the central square where night had fallen and the party of the *povo* was in full swing.

Loud music, singing, and revelry, fantastical costumes, inebriated dancing. I came alive again: people kept jumping in front of my camera, speaking about the win, and the wild happiness of those elated masses was far more contagious than the elite gathering back on the veranda.

For a while, I filmed the craziness in the streets, but eventually the melancholic sense of disconnection came back. Young men charged past me with babies' dummies and empty suitcases, symbols of mockery directed at the losing side, who, according to tradition, would be crying like babies and packing their bags in preparation to leave town. With Rosa's help, I packed up the camera, and we negotiated our way back through the manic, jumping crowd to a little bar. From there, we said goodnight to Paulinho and his friends and returned home to bed.

Faith as a Species of Power

Dwelling with the memory of that exhaustion and disconnection, it seems necessary to bring it into conversation with the doubts I'd had about the intense electoral optimism that had surrounded me in the run-up to election day. In those initial encounters, I'd wondered if Paulinho and Rosa's election fever betrayed some naïveté, but today I see that the naïve one was me. At that point, I had not fully reckoned with the power of an *época da política* and had no idea what it meant for *fé*. I was raised and schooled in a very different system: a Western, secular society where voter apathy was a perennial problem and cynical reason reigned. Cynical reason—the term coined by German philosopher Peter Sloterdijk in the 1980s—describes a pervasive modern mindset emptied of political hope. The modern cynic is a borderline melancholic who does not believe in radical change. It is, writes Sloterdijk,

> that modernized, unhappy consciousness, on which enlightenment has laboured both successfully and in vain. It has learned its lessons in enlightenment but it has not, and probably was not able to, put them into practice. Well-off and miserable at the same time, this consciousness no longer feels affected by any critique of ideology: its falseness is already reflexively buffered. (Sloterdijk 1987, 5)

Knowing what I do today about Paulinho's failure to escape from poverty in the years that followed, I have found myself revisiting his intense *fé* during Padre Jorge's election and wondering what made it flow. My ruminations have returned me to notions of force and to the *época da política* itself as a unique period of time wherein the world splits in half and neutral ground disappears entirely. With the disappearance of neutral ground, political cynicism and apathy become harder to justify, a condition in which *fé* intensifies. The results can be powerful, overwhelming, exhilarating, sickening—as I found out in my own way.

From its inception until its end, the *época da política* constitutes an extended moment that, broken down, we could view as a set of practices, rituals, gatherings, and events that are separated from the ordinary flow of life. Within this extended moment, religiosity blooms, and dispositions need not mirror or represent patterns found in the ordinary flow of time. The extended moment is a thing irrespective of the broader social and political context, a nonderivative phenomenon. It is, as the anthropologist Don Handelman says of ritual play more generally, "inherently itself; perhaps even more so than any order erected by humankind" (Handelman 1998, 63).

Viewed within this context, Paulinho's *fé* that he would one day run the hospital was not based on what he knew from his lifetime of social and economic marginalization; it stemmed from the magic of political practice in which linear time is scrambled and utopian futures are up for grabs. Paulinho and Rosa's *fé* therefore needs to be understood in the same terms that anthropologists have used to interrogate temporality—as a method of radical presentism that circumvents all knowledge of the past in order to open up the future to different forces, different kinds of agency.

Yet *fé* also needs to be understood in the same terms that anthropologists have used to make sense of concepts of "force" that are experienced as external to the self and constitute an "embodied form of otherness" (Csordas 1997).[9] For although people draw upon faith, invoke it whenever they need it, there are also moments when it quite literally possesses them, when in casting votes, engaging in rituals, or navigating relationships, they are taken over by the vital energy of collective coexistence.

As Rubens from the *Fé e Política* movement asserted in a WhatsApp exchange:

> *Fé* is felt in moments of wow! You know, when something happens, when you achieve something, in that sensation of "hey that wasn't me

alone! there was definitely something else there; some power, something greater."

It is in moments of "wow," where power seems "something greater" and bodily motivations seem most to transcend distinctions between politics and religion, that we need to train analytical attention, for it is here, in the "wow," that we are also in the presence of magic.[10] Not magic in the sense of stage-based illusionism but in the sense of the ancient Persian root word from which the word magic derives (*magh*—"to be able, have power").[11]

In his study of contemporary mass politics and mass media, the anthropologist William Mazzarella (2017) revisits the classical and enigmatically magical concept of mana, famously defined by Durkheim as "a certain rush of energy" (2008 [1912], 213). Plumbing the idea of "magical resonances," he redescribes the power of mass society in terms of potential *resonances* in the world, "between things, and between things and people" and shows how the world may be sustained or changed by tapping into and harnessing such resonances (Mazzarella 2020, 155).

Faith functions in similar ways in its proclivity to sustain or change the world. Simply put, it is a causative agent. The danger of conflating faith with a (more secular) sense of hope, or else viewing it as a "mere" emotional or psychological coping mechanism, is that we overlook its causative nature—its existence as an a priori species of power, a mysterious substance of energy. Rather, by appreciating faith in its energetic and therefore productive sense, it becomes easier to see how politics and religion come to be lived as (un)conscious continuations of one another.

The strange means by which faith's power intensifies has been the subject of this chapter, illuminating yet another intersection of the desirous relation between politics and religion. However, claims about the vital, a priori nature of faith are significant here. If we take them seriously, we must concede that there is nothing inherently "religious" about faith in such a context, just as there is nothing inherently "political" about the human capacity to dwell, as Žižek puts it, in "the short-circuit between the present and the future" (2005, 267). Such capacities point, rather, to the fact that religiosity is always already threaded through politics—if we define religiosity as a quality of attentiveness to thresholds of power and possibility. Faith, in this sense, is an embedded aspect of being human and may thicken up in any situation at all, without necessarily implying a particular relation to ideology.[12]

This is not to say that specific religious configurations (as in specific social and institutional traditions) are entirely independent from faith understood as a vital form, for as we have seen in this and preceding chapters, desire—of which faith is one manifestation—invariably grafts itself onto (or is co-opted and intensified by) cultural identities and religious institutions. For better or worse, mayor-priests have a hand in this sort of process, and this makes them particularly interesting figures for understanding Catholicism's role and contribution to broader structures of governance.

All the same, if faith is already present in everything and therefore inherent in every vote, we must understand the church as a political actor that feeds on the faith that is already there, rather than one that introduces it into political proceedings. In conclusion, if the Catholic Church (and, by extension, the figure of the mayor-priest) enjoys a particular kind of political influence in the rural interior of Northeast Brazil, it is not because it generates faith ex nihilo, but because it is ideally positioned to co-opt and repurpose a dynamic resource that is already immanent.

Victory Parade

The day after Padre Jorge's election was the day of my departure. By 8 A.M., the sun was scorching, and an air of festivity lingered on.

Rosa phoned around and discovered that Padre Jorge had left Iati at the crack of dawn to celebrate his election win with his family. He was unlikely to be back anytime soon, which meant I had missed my chance to bid him farewell. This made me sad, but Rosa insisted we go looking for Paulinho instead.

Paulinho, however, had also disappeared. We phoned him, texted him, trekked across town to clap outside the door of his house; we searched high and low, but Paulinho, it appeared, was nowhere to be found. We returned to our rented house to organize our departure. As we packed, swept, and tidied, I tried to focus on what lay before me. Tired as I still was, I could not afford to relax; I had to drive Rosa back to her hometown, drive from there to the airport in Recife, return the car at the rental depot, board a flight home, grade a pile of student essays, and somehow remain fully charged for my daughter's sixth birthday party, the day after my arrival home.

Rosa stopped sweeping and tried Paulinho's phone again. She was annoyed at his disappearance.

We packed the car, bid our farewells, and by late morning were heading out of Iati. On the way, we ran into a snake of revelers crossing the high street. It was the beginning of a gigantic victory parade. People were running along, singing and chanting, forming congas and breaking away. And there in the middle of it all was Paulinho, bobbing up and down, his face a picture of cheerful abandon. He didn't notice us.

"Paulinho!" Rosa called out of the car window, but he did not hear, and bobbed away. The procession surged onward, down the street.

Rosa followed Paulinho with her gaze. "Slag," she breathed under her breath. "Watch him gyrate."

And with those malicious words' of affection ringing in my ears, I turned onto the dual carriageway, and we sped away.

6 The Miraculous and the Mundane

In 2014, I returned to Northeast Brazil to visit Padre Jorge in office. The region was in the midst of a terrible drought. Traveling inland from the region's capital, I was stunned to see just how sparse and grey the landscape had become.

Rosa joined me for that visit, and as we drove north across the Borborema Plateau, she filled me in on what she knew of Padre Jorge's administration and the intense antipathies that had continued to shape political relations in the town. Rosa's impression was that Padre Jorge's administration was *fraca* (weak), as he was never present, being constantly in the city of Caruarú, where he was rumored to have a second home. His closest allies were becoming disaffected. Water problems continued besetting the population, and, worst of all, it had been reported that his new residence in Iati contained a swimming pool.

"That can't be true!" I exclaimed, unable to believe that mild-mannered Padre Jorge had the audacity for such a blatant luxury. Private swimming pools were rare in those arid climes, even among the region's elite.

"I don't know if it's true or not, but we're about to find out," Rosa replied. She had already prearranged our visit to Iati where, she assured me, Padre Jorge was waiting to put us up in his new swimming-pooled residence.

In the Convento São Félix de Cantalice in Recife, there is a small museum in memory to one of the region's most famous religious figures: Frei Damião, a Capuchin missionary who spent his life traveling through the backlands of Pernambuco, offering confession and celebrating the sacraments. Popularly venerated during his lifetime and even more so in death, he has been called the "Apostle of the Northeast" and is currently on route to beatification. In a little glass display case is a potted biography of the priest, which opens with the words, "Frei Damião spilled onto the dry lands of the Northeast Sertão his rivers of grace."

The liquid metaphor used to describe his sanctity is by no means incidental. The area Frei Damião traversed was part of those famously semi-arid heartlands of the state where access to water has long been a problem. Words such as "cracked," "parched," and "austere" are often used to describe the topography of the interior—a landscape that for vast tracts appears thorny, grey, and abandoned, broken up only by occasional brick houses and fields of spiny cacti. Jesuit archives record droughts in Northeast Brazil going back as far as 1559. Over the centuries, these cycles of drought have had calamitous effects: intensifying political conflicts, entrenching social inequalities, and decimating local populations through hunger and disease (Arons 2004; Hall 1981; Kenny 2002).[1]

Taken collectively, notes Arons, "the literature of drought seems like the result of a group of good Brazilian writers getting together and deciding to write the most depressing stories they can imagine" (2004, 26). For Levine, meanwhile, the Northeast's religious art "was always the bloodiest, portraying the suffering of Christ in stark detail, celebrating, as it were, saintly pain and humiliation" (Levine 1992, 217).[2] Today, a drought-themed genre of folk art retells the story through images of barren landscapes and *retirantes* (drought-fugitives) and grafts it onto the story of the Christian Passion—the heat of the interior being equivalent to that of Gethsemane, the struggle of drought victims equivalent to the parched suffering of Christ (Campos 2008). Examples of such art can be purchased in galleries and tourist shops throughout Brazil, speaking to a wider "natural-cultural" (Latour 1993) ecology in which water is not merely necessary to live, but deeply connected to Christian notions of life eternal.

Intersecting this ecology are questions of political economy and ongoing concerns about corruption in water management. As the oft-used term *indústria da seca* (drought industry) attests, controversy besets the way drought gets exploited by politicians to attract votes and government payouts while failing to invest properly in its future prevention.[3]

During a conversation with Padre Jorge in 2010, before he became mayor, thirst cropped up as a measure of spiritual devotion. We were talking about the beauty of the liturgy, and I asked what made the Mass, in his opinion, such a "beautiful" event. He answered:

> People say it is in the music or in the words, but if you ask me, the beauty lies in the people's thirst: their thirst for salvation, their thirst for God. The poor who suffer poverty, suffer injustice, they find in the Church a place . . . in life they are often rejected, badly attended to in the banks, in the hospitals. So in the Church, the Mass, they find themselves accepted, loved. . . .

In Padre Jorge's words, thirst offers another way to think about the interlocking nature of need and desire we have already encountered in the preceding chapters of this book. "Thirst" and, by extension, water bridge different temporal needs (and desires) for justice and satisfaction in the here and now and for love and abundance in the life hereafter.[4] This culturally laden idea of thirst, spanning different kinds of materiality and temporality, plays in particular ways upon the physical properties of water itself, producing what Webb Keane calls a semiotic "bundling" (Keane 2003).[5] As water in the form of liquid and vapor traverses both the visible and invisible, thirst has similar affordances—switching between the visible and invisible, the literal and metaphorical. The way leaders and politicians deal with the "bundled" nature of water (and, by implication, thirst) is of critical importance: electoral gains and losses, levels of popularity, the capacity to run a second term, all invariably intersect with this fluidic ecology.

Water (and thirst) therefore come to represent two interlocked but contrasting economies: a mundane economy of limited good that determines the material quality of life within it and a miraculous economy of unlimited abundance in which thirst is satiated through the grace of divine power. This chapter concerns these two contrasting models of economy—mundane and miraculous—to which water and its associated metaphors give expression and explores how they construct the social imaginary that accompanies the mayor-priest's office.

In the sections that follow, I trace Padre Jorge's own attempts to reconcile and balance these divergent models of economy during and after his election to office. Using his experience as a window onto the broader question of how religion and politics become co-present, I revisit the concept of desire through an exploration of the rumors, fantastical expectations, and critiques that surrounded him and show how the utopian faith that puts politicians in power quickly gives way to mundane and immediate questions about who gave what to whom and on what terms.

Such dynamics are true across the board, but for the mayor-priest there is one significant difference: the mayor-priest can never entirely escape the promise contained in his ontological difference from lay people, and for this reason he faces a unique challenge, one that casts light on the way that politico-religious fantasies are structured. My claim is that it is precisely as the mayor-priest assumes formal secular office, as he seeks most explicitly to balance and negotiate between two interlocked but opposed kinds of economy, that the dual and turbulent nature of his identity as a mayor-priest reveals itself and the personal costs embedded in the secular passage he has chosen become most evident.

Following Padre Jorge's story to its end, we catch a glimpse of what, in structural terms, the mayor-priest is destined to become: a sacrificial victim whose high-stakes passage into politics enables a fertile sort of communion and sharing of power between church and state while preserving the "separation" of those institutions.

The Miraculous and the Mundane

Perhaps not coincidentally, these diverse ways of thinking about water (as scarce or infinite) are mirrored in a broader set of Christian discourses about the nature of prosperity more generally. Christianity's incarnational logic has long allowed for models of economy that reject any notion of a limited good, though its expression of such ideas has varied across time.

One of the most widely discussed examples of Christian economics concerns the prosperity gospel, also referred to as the "health and wealth" gospel so prevalent among Pentecostal adherents (Hunt 2000).[6] The basic principle of the prosperity gospel is that God wants people to be rich, healthy, and successful. All that is required to access such prosperity is faith in God's power coupled with rituals of gift exchange involving "seed offerings" that, given in faith, are expected to yield dramatically increased harvests (Haynes 2013).

The prosperity gospel has been viewed both as a response to late capitalist market conditions (Comaroff and Comaroff 2000), a means of survival under the flexible labor conditions of the post-Fordist economy (Martin 1995), and a "Weberian training ground for neoliberal participation" (Haynes 2013, 87). It has also been analyzed as a complex form of gift economy in which acts of sacrifice are a central feature (Coleman 2011) and where the construction and maintenance of correct social relationships within church hierarchies are at least as important as the achievement of financial wealth (Haynes 2013). The prosperity gospel adherents' expectations about what constitutes divinely ordained prosperity may also vary in kind, from miraculous windfalls and great riches to small but steady advances up the economic ladder. Such expectations point to different Christian eschatologies, or theories about *when* to expect divine rewards, whether it be in the "expansive present" (Haynes 2020) or sometime in the distant or indeterminate future. In short, Christian time is supple and multivarious, and people can move between different models of time and economy depending on circumstance (Bialecki 2010, 2020; Coleman 2011; Daswani 2020).[7]

The model of economy I shall describe is not that of the prosperity gospel so popular among Pentecostal Christians throughout the country, nor is it merely one model of economy but two, or what would *appear* to be two: a mundane economy of limited material goods in which only some are able to prosper and a miraculous economy of sudden material abundance that is the product of God's mercy, where everyone benefits equally. In what follows, I use the term "abundance" rather than "prosperity" in order to differentiate between the largely capitalist cosmo-economics of contemporary prosperity gospel ideologies and the more socialist-utopian concept of collective wealth equally distributed that prevails in this particular context.[8]

The two economies I shall describe are co-extensive but divide in terms of their temporal and relational dynamics, as I shall explore. This division relates to a particularly melancholic take on the Fall in which Adam's sin causes a "doleful abyss" to open up between the "absolute perfection of God and the radical wickedness of man" (Sahlins 1996, 396).[9] Scholars have interpreted this originary myth as an event in time that crystalized a fundamental separation between creature and creator, leading to one of the central dynamics of Christian thought: the paradoxical understanding of God's simultaneous presence and absence from the world (Engelke 2007). This sense that there are "two" economies follows the notion that God, though eternally present in spirit, maintains a strategic distance from the mundane world, leaving humans to manage the material punishments for their original sin. Yet God, in infinite beneficence, sometimes intercedes, producing reminders or glimpses of an alternative world in which material goods are infinitely abundant and do not have to be haggled over. In the following two historical accounts, glimpses of this miraculous economy are conveyed through the idiom of water.

The Miraculous Economy

In a historical analysis of the career of Dr Feitosa, a much-celebrated mayor of Juazeiro do Norte, Maria Auxiliadora Lemenhe (2006) analyzes a series of "mystical events" associated with Feitosa's life that were repeated to her by numerous townsfolk.

Dr Feitosa held office between 1945 and 1965 and had strong personal and symbolic connections to his famous political antecedent, the popular saint and mayor-priest Padre Cícero. One of the stories that surrounds him concerns how he hit an underground "lake" as he excavated ground to build his house. Although this source of water would eventually serve only Feitosa's family, it is nevertheless recounted as a discovery that benefited the whole community. Feitosa, who understood the political meaning of such myths and connections to his late *antecedor*, Padre Cícero, would eventually become known as the *Anjo da Lagoa* (Angel of the Lake) (Lemenhe 2006, 257).[10]

In another story recounted to me by the late Frei Juvenal, a liberationist priest of the local Franciscan order, the people of a small farming community where he ministered in the late 1970s were "led by the gospel" to discover a communal source of water. This water needed to be transferred to a part of the community where people "had the greatest thirst" as a result of a micro-climate of persistent drought and a lack of roads, which obstructed their access to the region's water grid.

During one Ecclesial Base Community meeting, it was collectively divined that God "willed the water to cross the highway" so that it could be accessed by those whose needs were greatest. Subsequently, a political campaign was launched to get the water canalized, but endless difficulties were encountered along the way—each setback working to reinforce the isolated community's self-perception that they were politically forsaken. Although Frei Juvenal's faith remained strong despite the many setbacks, he nevertheless had to contend with what he described as several "doubting Thomases" of the community who refused to believe that the project would succeed.

After much effort, however, water finally reached the area. In celebration, Dom Hélder Câmara (the internationally venerated archbishop of Olinda) traveled to the community to hold an outdoor Mass in thanksgiving for the success of the canalization project. It was at this event that providence announced itself, as Frei Juvenal recalled:

> For at the moment he [Dom Hélder] was giving his sermon, with his thin white arms lifted to the sky, a little cloud appeared. And this cloud grew very suddenly, almost like a miracle, completely taking over the sky, and released a downpour of torrential rain so sudden and so strong there was no time to escape from it! Well, we rejoiced, danced in that rain! Certain that it was a sign from God.

In both these stories, prosperity (water) arrives in an unexpected and abundant fashion like a blessing from God, offering a glimpse, however brief, of boundless beneficence. In both these examples, moreover, prosperity is a collective issue. The underground lake, though on private land, is construed as a blessing for the whole municipality; the rain cloud that bursts pours down indiscriminately on the gathered community. In both cases, the narrative concerns justice for the rural *povo*, who, in the mystical Catholicism of Padre Cícero's era and the Socialist-liberationist Catholicism of Frei Juvenal's time, made up the "meek" who would "inherit the earth."

The miraculous economy, then, is characterized by three features. Firstly, it has a communal nature, recapitulating a logic of "perfect kinship" discussed in Chapter Two in which the poor achieve equality with the rest of society through God's unconditional beneficence. Secondly, it relates to goods that are tangible and shareable, like food and water, as opposed to more inalienable forms of wealth like health or beauty that cannot so easily be shared or redistributed. Thirdly, miraculous abundance is not simply (or only) the result of everyday acts of faith or discipline on the part of prosperity-minded individuals but a more unexpected phenomenon, one that seems to depend directly upon the physical and mediating proximity of one of God's favored emissaries. In both stories, the favored emissaries—Padre Cícero of Juazeiro and Dom Hélder Câmara—were priests but priests of an extraordinarily charismatic sort who, in their lifetimes, achieved a level of popularity and influence beyond the average.

How the average mayor-priest fits into such imaginaries is a complex question, for while he can no more depend on the discovery of unexpected water sources or poetic weather events for political success than any other politician, he is nevertheless recognized as a godly emissary with a pressing stake in the matter of how material resources get distributed and as an individual with special access to divine power—one that would, in theory, give him something of a head start over non-priest mayors when it comes to performing miracles.

For some sort of answer to this question, we must start with the as-yet-unelected mayor-priest and with the concept of the "cheap campaign."

The Cheap Campaign

One hot afternoon, I found myself hitching a lift to the city with Tonio (Dida's brother, whom we met in Chapter One, lamenting the vice-like nature of politics). On that journey, we talked about *política* at length. I asked him if he could imagine himself running for *prefeito*.

Tonio laughed and shook his head. "I doubt it, Maya, unless I suddenly win the lottery."

He cast me a knowing glance before turning his eyes back to the road, and I could tell he was trying not to be too explicit, but we both knew he was referring to vote-buying.

Tonio's glance reinforced the point that a person needs to be very wealthy indeed to run for the office of mayor. Coming from a family of smallholding *agricultores*, Tonio understood himself to be categorically poor in relation to the wealthier landed elites who cultivated the more prestigious offices of the executive. As a smallholder, his access to resources was unlikely to ever be great enough to allow him to progress much further up the political ladder. Only a small elite were ever generally wealthy enough to compete for the top municipal office, causing power to be concentrated among the same political families, generation after generation.

Reflecting on Tonio's financial limitations, my mind turned to our mutual friend, Padre Jorge, whose political future, at that time, still hung in the balance. As a priest, his salary was modest. He, too, came from a humble agricultural background. How, I wondered, could he afford to run for mayor and Tonio not?

"But a priest is something else entirely," replied Tonio. "He does a cheap campaign."

As we sped past grey-green pasture dotted with odd, lonely palms, I puzzled over the phrase "cheap campaign"—it was not the first time I'd heard it in connection with mayor-priests. As the erstwhile mayor of Jupi had said during an interview only the previous week, "The priest can enter an election without a single centável and take the seat from the richest man in the place."

I asked Tonio to elaborate, and he went on to tell me about the election campaign of Padre Ivo, who had served a single term as mayor of the municipality where Tonio was now head of the chamber of councilors. Tonio had been heavily involved in that campaign and remembered it well. What had been so remarkable about it, he related, was how "cheap" it had been, and he went on to recount how Padre Ivo's campaign committee had struggled on in the absence of substantial financial backing.

"Everything had to be gifted or borrowed. It was the hardest we'd ever worked as campaigners. No money for anything, not even gasoline—we did it entirely on foot!"

I asked Tonio whether there had been money for the "buying" of votes, and he explained how there had actually been no need, as everyone knew the padre had no money. "That's why it's a cheap campaign!"

I laughed.

Tonio smiled, keeping his eyes on the road. After a moment of silence, he said, "But it's not just that everybody knows the priest has no money with which to buy their votes; it's the fact he's a priest. Suddenly the *povo* recognize that voting isn't all about 'me' and what I can get for myself; it's also about the community."

The "cheap campaign" is a common motif when it comes to priestly candidacy, but it is also complicated by the mystery of what goes on behind the scenes between those with money and those without. For not all priests enter the race in a state of financial deprivation. Some embark on political careers in partnership with wealthy individuals who agree to bankroll a campaign in exchange for a slice of power at the other end: the role of vice-mayor, for example, or an assurance that the priest will support them as political successor when the next election comes around.

For others, however, the option of partnering up with a wealthy backer remains unavailable or defeats the purpose of their political excursion, as priests tend to be invited to run in elections precisely because their capacity for a "cheap campaign" allows them to defeat the wealthiest of adversaries. In poor municipalities where life is precarious and political aspirants with capital to spare are few and far between, priests are often the only people truly capable of diverting power away from the local big man.

Such was the case with Padre Ivo and Padre Jorge, both of whom had found themselves pitted against families whose lengthy possession of the municipal machinery had augmented their wealth and sedimented their power. In such cases, as Tonio emphasized, priests are not merely alternative figures through which one performs individual, vote-buying exchanges; they come to stand for the "common good."

Priest campaigns are strongly recollected and narrated as stories of collectivism, democratic idealism, equality, and sacrifice. As Dona Silene, an agricultural worker in her fifties who had campaigned alongside Tonio on Padre Ivo's campaign, recounted for me:

> There was no money—it was like squeezing a stone! So we walked for miles on foot; it was a great sacrifice. Ah, it was so good—everyone working together like that; good people, good work! Well, that's how we won.

Dona Silene's nostalgic recollection painted an alternative picture of local politics to the one of poverty, transactionalism, and political addiction that was all too familiar. Like Tonio's, it conveyed a sense of self-sacrifice and democratic energy; a willingness to work as a collective and in solidarity for the greater good. But the question of how a "cheap campaign" based on austerity and sacrifice also comes to evoke the kind of material abundance normally associated with the miraculous economy remains. To address it, it is necessary to look more closely at the peculiar reversal of the normal terms of electoral reciprocity that happens when a priest is invited to run.

Store-Cupboard Dreams

Padre Jorge's electoral campaign headquarters was full and bustling. Red-clad men filled the front room; red-clad women congregated at the back of the house, bantering and carrying out domestic chores.

On entering the house, I was grabbed by Edilma, a breezy woman in her fifties whose bright red lipstick matched her red-framed spectacles.

Edilma's constant, energetic presence in Padre Jorge's house was something of a mystery to me, as she neither lived nor voted in the municipality; neither did she appear to be an employee of Padre Jorge's campaign. Dona Vera and Dona Maria were the sure-footed women who managed the space between the kitchen table and the backyard.

That morning, Edilma had a wild look in her eye. "You have to see this!" she said and marched me through the house toward a cupboard door off the back porch. "You have to see this!" she said again gruffly, opening the door and nudging me in.

As my eyes acclimatized to the darkness, I realized I was in a small windowless room filled to the rafters with food-packed shelves.

"This is where we keep it. Just see how much there is!" she exclaimed.

I scanned the shelves: sacks of rice and beans, tins of powdered milk, boxes of margarine, baskets of onions, and liters of oil. Several kilos of dried meat hung from the ceiling. On the floor were bunches of bananas piled one atop the other, as well as baskets of pineapples, oranges, and other kinds of fruit. I had to concede it was pretty impressive, like a compact but plentiful grocer's shop.

"These are the donations!" Edilma exhaled. "All donations! The padre hasn't wanted for anything. He wants for nothing! These gifts just keep coming."

I was genuinely impressed, and this seemed to satisfy Edilma. But my interaction with the store cupboard was far from over.

The next day, Edilma asked me if I had managed to "film" inside the cupboard yet. And on several further occasions, the overflowing store cupboard was alluded to by women talking excitedly about the campaign. In all such conversations, the tone was both acclamatory and proclamatory.[11] The general abundance of food was a sign, they said, that God, Jesus, and all the saints were working in collaboration through Padre Jorge. In the collecting, storing, and sharing of it all, only *o bem* (goodness) and *alegria* (happiness) could come to pass.

One elderly woman's gift to Padre Jorge was to arrive at his house early every morning in order to make a large vat of sweet black coffee that she would then pour carefully into a collection of thermos flasks for the rest of the day's consumption. The woman's gift of early morning labor habitually included a loud, lilting stream of words:

O, Padre Jorge, child of Jesus! God bless him and protect him! There is nothing to fear. With God on side there is only happiness. Everything a person needs is granted, my child. We love you, Padre Jorge! We'll get there in the name of Jesus! And in the name of Padre Damião, Our Lady, and Padre Cícero who are all looking after us. . . .

With the smell of roast coffee thick in the air, the continual bustle as food was prepared, and the sound of prayerful proclamations, an atmosphere of spiritual and material abundance materialized in which everyone was able to partake and enjoy the fruits of their aggregate donations.[12]

Gifts to mayor-priest candidates are often transitory and perishable, manifesting as goods, services, and materials necessary for day-to-day living but that get used up quickly: food, soap, toothpaste, petrol, detergent, stationery, an electricity bill, a phone bill, a canister of cooking gas, a month's rent, a loaned car, a few days' work as a general errand runner, cook, cleaner, driver, etc. But what is most gifted to the priest is food.

The food donations to Padre Jorge were constantly redistributed via the priest's *casa aberta* (open house), in which anyone who entered was urged to eat.

The morality of the *casa aberta* and of extended food sharing in political process has been richly documented in the context of Brazil, and it is not unusual for mayoral candidates of all descriptions to incorporate food sharing and hospitality into their campaign outgoings. But in the case of Padre Jorge, food sharing and hospitality were, in some ways, the absolute engine of his campaign.

When Padre Jorge was at home, there were essentially three places in the house he would be: either sleeping in his small single bedroom, sitting at the kitchen table, or standing in the passage between the reception room and the kitchen, greeting visitors and ushering them toward the kitchen table. Padre Jorge's constant ushering of people to eat would have been tiring had it not been so habitual. Whenever someone entered the campaign house and greeted him, he greeted them back instantly with a "God bless you" followed by a smile and a "Go eat, go eat!"

This encouragement to eat was not merely an enactment of his priestly status as everyone's father; it was a method of redistributing the resources that he was already, like a mayor in action, in receipt of. Each mealtime could hold up to ten people squashed around the table, while others stood around the edges of the kitchen looking on. When one set of visitors finished their food and departed, another set would take their place. So it was, through this constant stream of visitors and gift bearers, that a pervasive sense of plenitude was created, stoking hopes for a fairer administration to come. One in which, as the elderly coffee woman proclaimed, "everything a person needs is granted."

At the same time, however, a ledger was being kept by Padre Jorge's small team of aides in which all the gifts coming in were noted. Not long before the day of the vote, I was present as Padre Jorge was pulled into a side room by his team for an impromptu meeting. Later that day, I cornered Tiago, a young, business-like aide who had been in the room, and asked him what the meeting had been about.

"The meeting was to keep track of accounts," he told me. "We were just reminding the padre that there comes a time when you have to be careful what you are accepting and from whom, because it becomes impossible to pay it all back."

In the view of Padre Jorge's team of aides, the proliferation of gifts was less evidence that they were suddenly all part of a more socially democratic society and more a sign that the *povo* were maneuvering themselves into a position of power over the priest through ambiguous gifts that would soon be reframed as loans to be paid back. And yet it was not entirely clear whether Padre Jorge perceived the situation in quite the same way or if he was aware of the fact that the terms of his habituated role as a receiver of gifts (small tokens of thanks, religious gratitude, etc.) had the capacity to shift.

As a priest, he was quite accustomed to being the object of so much prestation, but whereas the gifts he received from parishioners on behalf of God—offered either in return for blessings achieved or in expectation of future reward—did not leave him materially indebted to anyone, the gifts he was receiving as a mayor-priest candidate carried quite a different spirit (cf. Mauss 2002 [1950]).

The Mundane Economy

If exceptional divine emissaries like Padre Cícero or Dom Hélder Câmara produce glimpses of shared and equal abundance, the ordinary politician is forced to negotiate a zero-sum economy in which one person's gain is another's loss. This is what Padre Jorge's aides seemed to be most concerned with.

Skillful management of the mundane economy is an infinitely laborious task, synonymous with the complexity of municipal politics, not to mention the failures of *politicagem*. Unlike the miraculous economy, prosperity in the mundane economy is never unconditional, for it remains grounded in micro transactions of a more equal nature between patrons, clients, friends, and family. A good politician manages a zero-sum economy through the skillful manipulation of different sorts of human relationships, thus diverting and redistributing whatever limited goods are already in the world. While he does not perform sudden miracles of abundance, he can still manage resources in such a way that they benefit the maximum number of people.

But communal projects of this sort require a longer time frame to realize. As one ex-minister for agriculture lamented to me on the topic of regional water shortage, "The tragedy is that there *is* water in the region. Water is only scarce because we allow it to be."

This comment was followed by a sophisticated summary of the machinations that made drought a political rather than a natural problem. But then, in a remarkable moment of frankness, he confessed his own complicity in the system.

> What the voters were asking for more than anything was water, so we had the choice either to invest the money in a larger reservoir project that would take some years to build but would service the whole municipality, or to buy ten tanks that would help around seventeen families but guarantee us votes at the next election. We opted for the tanks, of course. This is just normal politics.

When I asked how he felt taking that decision, he said it had left him with a sense of regret. Then he thought for a moment before offering up another common line among local politicians: "But the problem is not just the politician; it is the *povo* who just don't know what is good for them."

The administration's decision to channel water to seventeen families rather than to irrigate the entire region may have been made, on some level, in bad faith, but it also points to the widespread sense of frustration and entrapment described in Chapter One.

It might therefore be said that while both the mundane and the miraculous economy deal in the same goods and are ultimately the products of the same divine, incarnational ontology, they are separate insofar as they recapitulate an originary sense of separation between two imagined orders: one in which God is sensed to be immanently present and another in which God remains (strategically) detached from worldly affairs.

This distinction between the mundane and miraculous does not map neatly onto neighboring dichotomies such as the religious/secular or the immanent/transcendent; nor does it necessarily point to different ontological theories about the nature of the world. Rather, it describes different relationships to wealth in a singular overarching cosmology constituted by diverse but intersecting temporalities. In both economies, material abundance is the result of connectedness to others, whether those others be gods, saints, friends, or patrons. But whereas in the mundane economy wealth is tactically identified and intentionally worked for, in the miraculous, it has the aura of something bestowed, often indiscriminately, in response to some collective need or action.

The ledger being kept by Padre Jorge's aides was an iteration of the continuing power of the mundane economy, partially hidden by the effervescence of the *época da política*, as we saw in Chapter Five, but ever-present all the same. For despite the promise of the miraculous store cupboard bestowing limitless generosity to all, this promise could never break free of the gravitational pull of campaign debts and interpersonal obligations.

In the following section, I chart Padre Jorge's abrupt landing in this world of the mundane economy by following him through a day in his life as mayor.

A Day in the Life of a Mayor-Priest

It was true that Padre Jorge's new Iati residence was slightly grander than the one he had rented for his electoral campaign. After a long drive, Rosa and I pulled up at a large, yellow-colored house and parked inside its cool tiled garage. I was excited to be back and flattered that Padre Jorge had invited us to stay with him.

Padre Jorge wasn't home when we arrived, but we were welcomed in by a housekeeper and shown to our bedroom. Accustomed to roughing it when traveling together, the hospitality that awaited us was deeply appreciated. There were fresh towels folded on the twin beds and individual soaps on top of the towels. There was a fan to keep us cool and bottles of mineral water by our bedsides.

After exiting our bedroom to explore the house, we walked into a large, open-plan room decorated in shades of cream, with accents of red. This space was filled with plush leather seats, polished glass tables, and large, baroque-edged canvases of religious scenes. The color scheme was neatly considered: the red of the cushions matching the red of the fake flowers in a vase; the brown of the doors matching the brown ceramic of a set of ornamental bowls.

Leaving Rosa in the kitchen helping herself to coffee, I slipped through the back door in search of the rumored swimming pool, but all I found was a sandy yard dotted with chickens and criss-crossed by washing lines. The absence of a pool was barely surprising, but my urgency to discover if the rumor could have been true indicated something of the importance of that fluidic economy. The rumored pool had pointed suggestively in so many directions: to the continuing problem of water in the region, to Padre Jorge's uncertain level of popularity, and to the character of his detractors—those who had probably started the rumor in the first place.

I wondered what sort of a home it was to Padre Jorge. There was something strange about the set-up. It wasn't homely so much as hotel-like. The atmosphere in the house was calmer than it had been during the electoral campaign, but there was a continual flow of people either waiting for Padre Jorge on the leather couches or helping themselves to coffee or water in the kitchen. Rosa and I had even been given a key to our room to protect our belongings from the nameless citizens wandering in and out. Turning the key over in my hand, my feelings of specialness at having been invited to stay in what I believed to be Padre Jorge's home started to dissipate.

An hour after our arrival, Padre Jorge was still nowhere to be found. His housekeeper told us he had been expected back some hours ago but was still "traveling." Calls were made to cell phones. The padre was reportedly "still in the city," then "on the highway." Messages were left on his voicemail. Finally, the padre was "on his way back to Iati," but no one knew when he was scheduled to arrive. Rosa and I whiled away the late afternoon on the front veranda, people-watching and playing on our phones. Eventually, Paulinho appeared on the entrance path, and, happy to see someone we knew, we ran down the steps to greet him.

"*Meninas!*" he cried, arms raised in welcome. "They told me you were here!"

We laughed and embraced.

"But just so you understand straight up: I've come here for your sake, not to see that *safado prefeito* [rascal of a mayor]." Paulinho was sporting a T-shirt randomly stamped with the English words "Sexy" and "Style." His recently bleached hair, longer since I'd last seen him, puffed out softly like a cloud behind him.

"I've got so much to tell you," he said, "but not here in this good-for-nothing's place. Let's walk into town."

Rosa and I were glad to leave the mayoral residence for a while. We walked down to the central square with Paulinho, conversing all the way.

Paulinho told us that he was fed up with Padre Jorge and his continued failure to deliver. Many people felt the same, he stressed. Using expletives, he went on to tell us how his promised job as manager of the hospital had never materialized, going, instead, to a young woman, the daughter of "*um rico*" (a rich person). Paulinho continued relating how the young woman, in all her inexperience, had made such a mess of the job that it had been passed on to someone else, this time a woman who wasn't even local to the area. This second woman had been better qualified for the position than the first, Paulinho conceded, but the overall morality of appointing someone from another municipality was, in his opinion, worse.

Rosa agreed with this, arguing that if the right sort of experience and expertise could not be found locally, the mayor's duty was to train and capacitate locals for positions, not give their jobs to outsiders.

Paulinho took us to visit the little bar he had opened in the central square's underpass, in a room no more than three square meters in size. The underpass was home to a couple of other desultory recreational amenities: a snack bar with a pool table and a lottery stall. It was too early for custom, but Paulinho opened for our benefit, switching on the boom box and multicolored laser lights.

Grinning in bewilderment, we shouted our praise for Paulinho's latest entrepreneurial turn over the deafening sound. Paulinho smiled wryly and wiped down his bar with a defiant sort of pride before bringing us glasses of whiskey cut with coconut water that, unsurprisingly, contained far more whiskey than coconut water. By the time Rosa and I left to return to Padre Jorge's house, darkness had fallen, and we were drunk.

I arose the next morning to finally encounter Padre Jorge dressed in dark blue jeans, a black blazer, and a red shirt. He was already at the breakfast table surrounded by citizens and aides. Padre Jorge smiled and welcomed me, asking me if I was ready for the day's work. I replied that I was and thanked him in advance for allowing me to shadow him for the day.

In the cream-and-red reception area were various men—older ones in traditional, leather *vaquiero* hats, younger ones in baseball caps. They hung around leaning against walls or perching awkwardly on the plush soft furnishings.

Upon leaving the breakfast table, Padre Jorge moved into the reception area and took a seat at a large, glass-topped dining table. His breakfast entourage followed, and before long, other members of the administration arrived. Pen in hand, Padre Jorge listened in turn to their updates on various developments and signed the numerous papers pushed under his nose.

Suddenly it was time to leave the house for the municipal building, where Padre Jorge was scheduled to attend *povo* in his office. Several cars made to leave the residence, and I was ushered into one with Padre Jorge, Padre Jorge's driver, and a well-dressed man called Carlos, who introduced himself to me as a journalist there to collect material for his "independent" regional news portal (an online WordPress blog), which he matter-of-factly related was funded by various mayors across the region.[13]

Arriving at the *prefeitura*'s office, Carlos and I followed Padre Jorge into the building in procession with other members of Padre Jorge's entourage. To my surprise, Paulinho was already there in a floaty tie-dye shirt. His resentment for Padre Jorge wasn't in evidence as he smiled and hugged us, then stalked ahead to open the door to the mayoral office.

As we entered the office, others swarmed behind us, but Paulinho batted them off and set himself up as gatekeeper to the room, coming in and out as he pleased, while making others wait their turn. The office was of medium size, though somewhat cramped by the highly polished L-shaped desk standing in its center. Behind it was a stuffed leather office chair and three giant flags, for Brazil, the state of Pernambuco state, and the municipality, that drooped down grandly, like stage curtains. On the desk before him was an ancient-looking laptop, a remote control for the air conditioning, and a pen holder. On the corner of the desk, in a more ornamental arrangement, was a wooden crucifix, a brightly painted statue of a winged St. George brandishing a sword, a large blue book embossed in gold with the words "Municipal Budget," and an open Bible.

On the other side of the desk and all around the room were chairs, which had quickly filled up with local citizens and municipal workers, plus me and Carlos. The office felt like an affably chaotic prosthesis of the public sphere, a space that belonged to everybody and nobody. Padre Jorge, sitting at the center of it all, appeared overwhelmed as people talked to him and over him. And then a small, angular *senhora* (older woman) arrived with a convoluted problem to do with her pension. She had not been receiving it for some reason to do with missing papers, a false identity, or perhaps—it was not clear from her gravelly voice—a stolen identity.

The *senhora*'s problem was discussed loudly between Carlos and the municipal workers with greater legal and administrative experience than Padre Jorge. Carlos then advised Padre Jorge publicly, in front of the woman herself, how he should respond. The *senhora*'s problem, it was conceded, was real enough, but it was not of the sort that a mayor could resolve.

It was clear from her clothes and demeanor that she was poor; her dress was old, and her thick, unadorned hands betrayed a life of manual labor and hardship. Padre Jorge offered the *senhora* a seat, but she refused to sit down, preferring to tower over Padre Jorge, who sat hunched and weary behind his desk. The others and I watched in fascination as she raised her voice at Padre Jorge and started banging a fist against her hand in response to his beleaguered insistence that this was not something he could resolve for her.

"You may say that," she yelled, "but as far as I'm concerned, the only one who rules around here is you! You, sir, are the lord, the justice, the father and everything. . . ."

Padre Jorge interrupted her drily: "Yes, *senhora*: who metes out the justice around here is me, the padre, but let's not forget the part played by God in His infinite wisdom!"

"And the prison service!" called Carlos ironically from the back of the room.

Smiles of amusement broke out among the watchers, but the *senhora* did not seem to care—if, indeed, she noticed.

Leaning further over Padre Jorge's desk, she jabbed her finger on his desk in emphasis: "To me you are everything! Everything! I don't listen to anyone else in this room. I say *you* will resolve this for me!"

Never learning her real name, I dashed her down in my notes as the "Everything Woman."

Then it was time to leave the municipal building in order to visit a school in a rural neighborhood that had just been renovated under Padre Jorge's administration, and I struggled to keep up in the ensuing rush of the entourage to exit the building and grab a place in Padre Jorge's chauffeur-driven car.

As the driver started the engine, Padre Jorge turned around from the front passenger seat and commented, "Maya, observe how important it is for one to keep moving throughout the day, or you never get away from people."

Driving away from the town, we passed fields of scrub and rural hamlets, eventually pulling up at a freshly painted school whose gates were locked shut. Someone arrived from somewhere with a key to open the gate, and in no time at all, children flocked to greet us. Padre Jorge placed a hand in blessing on the head of every child who came up to him. Turning this way and that, he seemed in his element, embracing his subjects and giving out blessings.

Attempting to capture some of those scenes on my phone, I found myself continually edged aside by Carlos at work with his expensive digital camera.

After leaving the school, we visited a local rubbish processing site, and, on the way, Padre Jorge started talking about the importance of overcoming the factious and divisive logic built into local politics. The sheer force of the enmity among the region's leaders was overwhelming, he said, and the will to maintain divisions and distinctions between factions was greater than any will to work for the greater good. He went on to explain how the rubbish processing site we were about to see was undergoing major restructuring and improvement and how he was particularly proud of the fact that this was a project he was continuing to invest in, despite the fact it had been started by the previous mayor.

> Here in this region, many mayors refuse to touch the projects started by their adversaries. Even if a source of state funding exists just for its completion, they let it stand unfinished so their adversary cannot take the credit for it.

We walked around the gigantic cavity trying to ignore the impolite stench, followed at some distance by a straggle of male aides. Evidently uninterested in the rubbish question, the aides were using the moment to check their phones.

"But I don't think in this small-minded way," continued Padre Jorge, shielding his eyes to take in the horizon.

> For me, this is a project that is going to benefit the whole community. Some people worried about the politics of it. They told me, you know, to just leave it. But you can't just walk away from something this big just because your adversary was the one who initiated it.

Next on the agenda was a visit to an abandoned manioc mill, full of antiquated machinery. I was not entirely sure why we were there, but Carlos kept taking photos of Padre Jorge peering into empty vats and standing next to gigantic rusting implements.

While this was happening, a little girl approached Padre Jorge. "Mama wants to see you," she said.

"Tell her I'll be along shortly," Padre Jorge replied. But by the time we returned to the car, that promise was all but forgotten.

As the driver was turning the key in the engine, there was a tap at the window. There stood the little girl. "You promised to come and see Mama," she said.

Padre Jorge looked wearily down at her and replied, "OK, the car will wait—tell your mama to come here."

The girl ran off (the house was only a few yards behind us) and returned again, breathless. "No, Mama won't come to you. She says *you* have to come to her."

Padre Jorge tensed up with what could have been embarrassment and stiffly opened the passenger door. "OK, let me just deal with these people before we go," he muttered under his breath, getting out of the car.

The remaining entourage appeared uninterested and settled down in their car seats, phones in hand, to wait, while I slid out of the car to follow Padre Jorge.

Approaching the small brick house, I saw two women on plastic chairs in the front porch. One was removing nail varnish from her fingers; the other was sorting beans. Neither stood up to greet Padre Jorge; indeed, barely did they glance up.

"Where is my job?" asked the woman doing her nails in a clipped voice.

Padre Jorge reassured the woman that he was doing everything he could to help her. He knew her situation was difficult, he said, but she needed to show patience. A back and forth continued to that effect, followed, finally, by a cold farewell as we returned to the car.

As we drove away, Padre Jorge clearly felt he owed me some sort of explanation for the scene I had just witnessed. The woman, he explained, was a single mother to six children whose husband had recently died, leaving her without any income. Padre Jorge had promised her work as a health-post cleaner, but at the present time there were no spare jobs. "This is the reality around here," he sighed. "It's nothing but need and more need."

We returned to Padre Jorge's house for lunch.

Walking into the kitchen, I was surprised to find a mélange of neatly dressed municipal functionaries and members of Padre Jorge's extended family queuing up to take a seat at the kitchen table, where lunch was laid out. The kitchen had transformed itself into a lunch canteen with people arriving, eating, and leaving in quick succession.

After lunch, I spoke to Elisangela, Padre Jorge's sister and the person in overall charge of his house. In epilogue to the "cheap campaign," she told me that the food bills were *pesado* (heavy); every week she shopped to provide daily breakfasts and lunches for fifteen to twenty people. When the padre was around, she commented, those numbers could double.

"You'll Be a Pope!"

After lunch, I was invited by Padre Jorge and one of his erstwhile secretaries into his home office to watch as he attended the *povo*. First in the queue was an officious-looking white-haired man in a well-ironed shirt, with a walking stick. Settling into a laid-back, wide-legged posture, he launched into a conversational preamble, laced with hints about his social standing. Evidently, he was wealthy, a local landowner: both his sons were studying abroad, and his daughter was married to the son of So and

So (Padre Jorge nodded in respectful recognition of the name). He then digressed into a spiel about his hatred for the *Movimento Sem Terra* (Landless People's Movement).

"I don't know what the world is coming to," he chaffed loudly. "My land is constantly being trespassed. Only last week I had to shoot a man."

Padre Jorge steadied his gaze, struggling to contain a look of shock.

"That's right," continued the man. "Got my gun and scared him off!"

Having asserted his social status, not to mention his masculine virility, he went on to deride the family of the outgoing mayor, praising Padre Jorge into the bargain. He claimed to have faith in Padre Jorge's administration, adding that he was looking forward to helping him "make Iati great again." Eventually he got around to business: he was there with a proposal he claimed would "solve the water problem in the area once and for all." The proposal involved Padre Jorge forming a partnership with a neighboring municipality to buy a portion of his land and using it to construct a reservoir.

"You and I both know it, Padre," he said, leaning forward conspiratorially. "Water is the biggest problem around here. But just imagine: if you are the one who solves that problem, you'll be more than a padre—you'll be a pope!"

Padre Jorge squirmed slightly in his seat, his expression betraying incredulity and embarrassment. In my notes I underlined the words "you'll be a pope!" I was intrigued by the old man's audacity—his unabashed attempt to turn the region's socio-spiritual "thirst" to his own economic advantage.

After several more petitioners had passed through, Padre Jorge halted the flow of people coming into his office so I could squeeze in a one-to-one interview with him. Outside, the horizon was an orangey pool of pink. The day had whipped by, and the sun was starting to sink.

As I moved from the corner of his office where I had been attempting to remain out of the way into the chair directly opposite Padre Jorge's desk, I noticed him taking out a hanky and wiping his brow with exhaustion. Finally, with recorder on and the door behind us firmly closed, he put the hanky away and began talking.

"It's an endless stream of demand. An endless business," he said. "The water conflict in this region causes constant suffering, as you've seen today."

From his body language, I sensed that he perceived our conversation as a welcome interlude—an opportunity to offload some of the clamor in his head. Following is a condensed edit of what he said:

> The situation is bad. Everyone wants employment, but I have already exceeded my legal quota for municipally funded workers. This municipality is extremely poor. . . . There is no agriculture, there is little left of the milk industry that many used to live from. In this sort of situation, the municipal government becomes, in people's minds, the solution to everything. But it cannot be like this. We are super restricted. There is the law, after all, and it governs what we can and can't spend on. . . . It hurts to not be able to help people more, but what hurts more, in a way, is how people who are meant to be on my side want constantly to exploit the situation. Politics here in the Northeast is like this. They warned me it would be bad. It is as bad as they said it would be. In fact, it is worse.
>
> You asked about the house, right? How it is always full of people. Open houses are part of my nature. I grew up in a big house, with a big family, where the doors were always open. This was also my experience of living in a parish. My parish house was also an open one, with people arriving, staying, and eating. The only difference between this house and the parish is that at the parish things were calmer. How so? Well, if someone arrived at the parish with a problem, we would converse and resolve it. Resolution would be reached there in that conversation, with a blessing, with some advice. The difference is that people come to the mayor's house to resolve problems of a different nature. Financial problems, family economics, problems of work. We can't resolve the problems of everyone who arrives. Some, yes. But not all. . . .
>
> I like an open house. Yes, it's expensive, yes, it is tiring. Sometimes you just want a moment alone. But it is impossible because people are constantly here to speak to me, from early morning until late at night. Maintaining this lifestyle is draining. It's a sacrifice, a sacerdotal gift of yourself. Sometimes you have to withdraw, to reform yourself, rejuvenate yourself . . . to pray. Once a week, or every fifteen days, you have to shut the doors. But a politician needs to be available. If, before, the expectation was that I be an angel, now it is that I be Superman.
>
> You want to know what is the difference between shutting your door as a priest and shutting it as a politician? In the church, I receive people if I please. As a politician, I am obliged to receive. It is as if they paid me to be there; the mayor is their property!

Another difference would be that the word of a padre is absolute; the mayor's can be questioned. As a priest, on a saint's day, I can suggest a route for the procession and everyone instantly agrees with it. As a politician, as you know, there are also processions. But at least ten people will argue with any route I suggest. Whatever you do, it will displease someone. When I fill the pot-holes, they ask why I did not use the money to repaint the school; when I repaint the school, they ask why I did not use the money to stock the new health-post. . . .

How do the people address me? Most address me as padre, but some use prefeito or padre-prefeito. Personally, I prefer padre. When they address me as prefeito, it always means they want something! You've seen for yourself today how forceful people can be. They'll practically grab you by the collar to make their demands!

At this point, Padre Jorge grabbed comically at his own shirt collar, recalling the "Everything Woman" from earlier, and together we laughed.

In a serious voice, he went on to describe his sadness at not yet having managed to garner the extra resources so hoped for.[14] His deputies at state level had "betrayed" him: the resources they had promised in return for his loyalty had never materialized. Worse still was his sense that people within his closest circle were moving secretly against him, like chess players plotting six moves ahead. If the situation carried on, he said, he was likely to lose the next election.

At that point in the conversation, Padre Jorge's driver opened the door to his office and reminded him that he still had to attend a man who had been waiting to see him since morning.

Feeling guilty for having taken up so much of Padre Jorge's time, I stood up to leave and thanked him for the opportunity to observe him at work and for all his generosity. As is often the way after an intense day of fieldwork, I was exhausted, and after returning to my room to lie down for what I believed would only be a brief moment, I fell fast asleep. By the time I awoke it was dark, and the house was quiet. Rosa was smoking on the veranda, and Padre Jorge was nowhere to be found.

Through the walls of the house, I heard latecomers at the door being turned away with the usual lines: "The padre is traveling," "The mayor has left home for the weekend," and "No, we can't say when he will be back." Knowing that my trip to Brazil was at an end, I despaired at the realization that, once again, I had missed my chance to bid Padre Jorge a proper farewell. And yet, deep down, I knew that the house Rosa and I were staying in was not his home at all, and having spent a day in his company, I was starting to understand why.

Chasing Abundance

As rumors about swimming pools and promises of becoming a pope suggest, mayor-priests do not enter the field of politics via a singular and shared definition of economy. The path they chart is the product of two somewhat competing understandings of the way resources circulate: one miraculous, the other mundane.

On the parched plateau, water bridges both economies in being at once a limited resource that requires careful management and a substance that can surface from the ground or pour down from the heavens with suddenness and in great abundance. As the ethnography discussed here suggests, narratives that circulate in relation to water are about more than water: they are about the distribution of wealth writ large. The differing models of economy that water exemplifies may map onto quite different politico-economic kinds of ideologies about the way resources can or should be distributed, but as models of economy, they exist in an interlocked conversation with one another.

In the febrile time-space of the *época da política*, anything seems possible. The miraculous economy hovers like a rain cloud, and drops of it can be felt in the peculiar reversal of the normal exchanges that occur during the cheap campaign. In the subjunctive temporality that takes over the mayor-priest's headquarters, plenitude rains down in the form of goodwill and prestations, filling up storerooms and overflowing kitchen tables.

That sense of abundance is helped along by the proclamatory song of the women helpers who, for a short time only, are transformed from "the ones who flock" (Chapter Three) into the "ones who gift." And yet, the mayor-priest candidate, at such a juncture, treads a delicate path: with every passing day, he moves further away from the charisma of the institution that once protected him. Unlike the intensely desired deluge of rain or the secret underground lake, the store cupboard he commands is an unstable symbol of harmony in abundance, and as election day draws closer, it reverts, once again, into transactionalism and debt. Knowing this, he must carve out a new identity for himself somewhere between the miraculous and mundane: either by proving himself to be one of God's extraordinary emissaries (like Padre Cícero) through the enactment of miracles or by establishing himself as an averagely competent civil servant.

Once the election has passed, the priest finds himself at the center of a zero-sum economy, managing a finite set of resources. As Padre Jorge reflected during his final interview with me, when he was a parish priest, the spiritual resources he managed were limitless: "Resolution would be reached there in that conversation, with a blessing, with some advice." As a mayor, however, he could no longer simply offer blessings and a listening ear to people; nor could he only receive petitioners when it suited him. As a mayor, he was indebted to the *povo* and, despite the prestige of that title, no longer commanded the absolute authority and respect that he had enjoyed as a priest.

Here it is possible to glimpse how in taking up municipal office, the priest enters an intense new landscape strewn with strange and fantastical expectations: that he differ from all other politicians on the one hand; that he conform to mundane rules on the other. As a mayor, he lives under a certain pressure to be a "superman" (to use Padre Jorge's own words), a weight of expectation not dissimilar to that which he lived as a priest, but as a politician, the terms are more exacting. To succeed as a politician in this context, he must reposition himself within the matrix of machismo (Chapter Four) and learn to redistribute wealth through whatever means possible, *rebolando* (turning tricks) like any other politician.

Shadowing Padre Jorge that day, I sensed he had become all but an ordinary man. And yet I knew this not to be true, for he was still a padre. The public significance of this fact may have been slowly waning in the scuffle and fray of the political day-to-day, but it would always hold profound meaning for Padre Jorge, just as it would for the many who voted for him.

After all, a priest is still—for all that he may turn out to be an ordinary person full of lacks and failures—ontologically different and, in that sense, a great potentiator of desire. Utopian imaginaries have been imprinted upon his physical body; divine promise has been "indelibly sealed" into who and what he is. As revealed in the example of the "Everything Woman" who called dramatically on Padre Jorge's priestly status in a bid to extract an instant (perhaps miraculous) resolution to her political problem, once a priest, always a priest.

Conclusion

Even in places where secularism is an old and established ideal, it is unsurprising to discover that the distinction between politics and religion remains blurred in practice. What cannot be known in advance, however, is what particular configuration any given religiopolitical intertwining will take: what articulations it will give rise to and how those articulations will be challenged or received.

In Brazil, for a while now, religious identities have been aligning themselves ever more tightly and ever more consciously with political ones, a situation most visible in the well-documented association of Protestant evangelical Christianity with right-wing party politics (see Almeida 2020). While Catholicism is equally embroiled in national political life, its association with particular political viewpoints is perhaps less clear-cut, for whereas the mainstream of the Brazilian church is still commonly associated with moderate leftism and liberal progressivism, many Catholics at the charismatic end of the spectrum are outspoken supporters of right-wing political positions.

As I completed this book, Brazilian voters re-elected Luiz Inácio Lula da Silva as president, defeating the far-right incumbent Jair Bolsonaro and giving the leftist former leader another turn in power after a tumultuous nineteen months in prison on a bribery conviction. This electoral run-off—set against a backdrop of worsening poverty, rising authoritarianism, and destruction of the Amazonian rainforest—was classed as one of the most divisive in Brazil's history to date and held the front pages of newspapers around the world.[1]

Even in the volatile environment that has characterized Brazilian politics for decades, the levels of animosity and barely concealed violence in this election were unprecedented. One of the things much noted in the secular Brazilian press was the dramatic increase in religious leaders making their political intentions public,[2] coming under pressure from their congregants to do so,[3] or receiving threats from right-wing voters for their left-wing leanings.[4] While both evangelical pastors and Catholic priests entered these political discourses, it is interesting to note that their participation was received in the press quite differently. In neither case was this merging of the religious and political seen as particularly positive, but whereas in the case of evangelical pastors it was presented as unsurprising and even expected, in the case of Catholic priests it attracted surprise and a deep sense of unease.

The astonishment of the Brazilian mainstream media at the numbers of Catholic priests either declaring their partisan feelings in public or receiving threats from right-wing parishioners for being supporters of Lula is, in its own way, surprising, for, as this book has shown, Catholicism's deep and enduring intertwinement with Brazilian politics goes back centuries. Perhaps we would do well to take the media's surprise as itself an "ethnographic fact" (Strathern 1992), one that reveals just how unmarked a category Catholicism is in Brazil's social imagination of itself. For despite the huge demographic shifts in Brazilian society and the rapid increase toward evangelical Christianity and away from the Catholic Church, the figure of the Catholic priest remains ironically pivotal to the construction of Brazilian secularism.

This book has sought to understand Catholicism's role in the construction of secularism, not at the level of national politics and presidential elections but rather through an ethnographic study of the mayor-priest, who as we have seen is not an ideological figure in the "left" versus "right" sense but more an elected civil servant—a figure whose administrative skills matter but whose ideological allegiances are of relatively little importance. As I hope to have shown, this does not make him any less political, nor any less connected to organs of power on the national scale. At its broadest measure, the mayor-priest has offered a window onto the functioning of certain trans-local institutions, showing how Brazilian democracy, the Catholic Church, and normative institutions of gender and sexuality interlace in ways that mutually reinforce one another.

Beneath those broad intersections, however, lies another story: of emergent religiosity and queer religious identity. That story—shaped by laments about corruption and disunity on the one hand and energetic proclamations of faith on the other—threw light on alternative forms of politics and utopian visions of wealth distribution, illuminating how silence, lack, and desire combine in ways that pre-figure the very categories of "religion" and "politics." In that story, the mayor-priest emerged as both an institutional and transgressive figure and the vote of faith as both an ideational and material thing. Following native conceptions, this book has reckoned with the *forceful* nature of faith, exploring its role as a species of power.

If we can take home a simple message from this, it is not that secularism in Brazil is "weak" or underdeveloped in comparison with other parts of the world but that religion and politics are, everywhere, deeply articulated and that understanding the secular is really none other than understanding the rhythms, methods, and modes of those articulations: when connections are made and unmade, who makes and unmakes them, and how such categories get reconfigured.

For the philosopher Giorgio Agamben, it is economy, not sovereignty, that is key to understanding the enigmatic link between theology (or "religion") and politics. By "economy," Agamben does not have simply the management of wealth in mind but any cohesive system that is constituted by separable spheres or parts. Examples range from the Greek *oikos* (household) to the Christian conception of the Trinity, in which there is a sovereign (God) but one that is nevertheless split into three parts: the Father, Son, and Holy Spirit. Agamben's key point is that in Christian traditions, sovereignty is necessarily dissimulable ("articulated" like a juggernaut truck), for if it were not, God's will would simply be the same as humanity's, or, looked at differently, humans would have no free will of their own to speak of (Agamben 2011).

In light of this, it is important to recognize how separation and flexibility mark the relation between theology and politics and hence how a distinction persists between the notion of a kingdom (a sphere of divine being) and the notion of a government or "self-government" (a sphere of action, free will, or second-level cause and effect). Agamben (2011, xx) views this conceptual distinction as analogous to a "splitting between being and praxis" and suggests that it is this principle of "splitting" that lies at the heart of the word "economy." An economy, therefore, is a vicarious structure in which all the parts depend on one another, such that "the mystery of being and of the deity coincides entirely with its 'economical' mystery. There is no substance of power, but only an economy, only a government" (139).

(Dis)connecting Passages

Agamben's reflections on being and praxis constituting a primordial "economic" relationship between transcendence and immanence (or being and praxis) afford an interesting vision of the mayor-priest as an economy rather than as a sovereign. By embodying separations at different scales—between heaven and earth, church and world, religious and secular—the mayor-priest is one who participates in a system that separates divine being from human action. This fundamental separation works by holding God near but deferring the question of divine efficacy and direct intervention. In light of this, the mayor-priest who fails to govern through spectacular miracles can still serve the social imaginary as a symbol of hope through his role in the divine, interlocking economy.

Such articulation emerges through motion. As Simon Coleman (2021) has shown in his work on pilgrimage, "articulation" exemplifies the pilgrim's "ongoing labour of making, remaking, and denying [of] connections—temporal, spatial, ideological" (251). Working outward from the notion of a purposeful journey through time and space, Coleman shows the purchase of thinking with (and through) pilgrimage as a process of separation and (re)connection that applies across a range of more ordinary contexts and practices, illuminating the entangled reality of the "religious" and the "secular" (cf. Menezes and Bártolo 2019).

In this book, I have used not pilgrimage but an adjacent notion—that of passage—to suggest how spheres become differentiated from one another.[5] Working through some of the dynamics that beset the life of a mayor-priest, I have been prompted to think about priests as passengers whose agency is free but whose journeys are obstacle-laden. This has drawn attention to the way boundaries, refusals, and gravitational pulls suddenly make themselves apparent through motion itself, whether that motion be figurative or literal.

In the Introduction, I discussed how the priest is sacramentally tethered (through ordination) to a sacred and authoritative center, and therefore how his movements through the secular sphere (i.e., beyond the protected all-male sphere of the priesthood) are always centripetal in relation to it. In the movements that take place—to, from, and around that center—the boundaries demarcating the religious from the secular become signified. Such "secular passages," as I have glossed them, are a particular feature of the lives of parish priests. The celibate parish priest does not live the same sort of life as his flock (like a Protestant pastor), but neither is he entirely removed from it (like a cloistered religious). It is through constant passage and shifts of intensity—literal and metaphorical—in and out of secular and profane settings and between rituals, Masses, blessings, and prayers that "the church" becomes marked as a sacred center, a sphere "set apart."

This book has not sought to retell an established narrative that posits a gradual, post-Reformation invention of boundaries between church and state (Taylor 2007). It points to a Catholic boundary-work that pre-dates the Reformation, one coterminous with gender distinctions and rules of sexual abstinence. As the long history of Brazilian mayor-priests attests, the church has always depended on "secular passages" created by the inherent motility of its non-cloistered diocesan priests as they journey (or transgress) back and forth between sacred and mundane domains.

Such journeys do not dissolve the borders between the secular and the religious so much as reinforce them and are exemplified through practices around gender and sex. Viewed from such an angle, mayor-priests are not merely an instance of a secular politics co-opting religious energies but also of a reverse dynamic. Mayor-priests show us how the Catholic institution has long articulated itself in contra-distinction to spheres beyond itself and how negotiations with the power of those spheres can have a religiously vitalizing purpose. Such vitalization would not be possible if all were merely a seamless extension of the sacred.

The Church and the Challenge of Brazilian Democracy

Through such passages, the mayor-priest emerges as both challenger and champion of Brazilian democracy. By symbolically relating to everyone (as "father"), he is mobilized against the failed promises of Brazilian democracy and, in particular, its promise to serve the poor by representing the majority. Here, Catholicism comes to function as a symbol of equality and universalism via kinship in all its life-giving dimensions. The fact that priest-politicians tend to proliferate more at municipal levels than at the state or federal levels of government is an interesting reflection of this. In rural areas with smaller populations, the mayor-priest's influence derives from the intensity of his relationality—his emotional contiguity with the lives of his parishioners. Such relationality may scale up, but only to a certain point. It is perhaps not surprising that priests rarely if ever become mayors of large urban cities; not only are cities far more religiously and politically diverse in their make-up, but their populations are denser and their sacramental (and relational networks) somewhat more fragmented.

Where Chapter One revealed the cut and thrust of municipal politics as a particular sort of existential problem—an "addiction" or entrapment—Chapter Two described the utopian theology of the celibate priest as one possible answer to that problem. There I discussed the "final inoperativity" of celibacy as a pre-empting of an eternity in which people no longer have to work, conjoin, or divide themselves with others because there is none other to be in a relationship with but God. Such theology feeds Catholic imaginaries of a unifyingly "flat," spiritual form of kinship (i.e., one father, many equally loved children), which stands in opposition to a perennially segmenting and corrupt world of party politics.

And yet, the unifying properties of "flat" spiritual kinship are formally signaled not just through the priest's celibacy, but also through his maleness. The celibate priest is a patriarch who embodies certain fantasies about all-male power and whose status therefore rests on sexual and gender-based exclusions. This constitutes an argument running implicitly throughout this book: that to understand Catholicism as a political form, it is important to foreground the gendered grammars of exclusion that structure the priesthood as an institution.

Sex, Eros, the body, and "passion" are central to Catholic religiosity, and in developing this argument, I have paid close attention to how these elements emerge in the course of everyday practice (Mayblin 2022). Building on Valentina Napolitano's (2015) description of the church as a "passionate machine," a term that describes how Catholicism uses emotions and affects that exceed rational calculation to produce Catholic subjects, I have sought to illustrate some of the crucial ways that passion entwines with faith and desire.

Desire, too, has a history, what Alexandre Kojève (1980) named "the history of desired desires," and in the preceding chapters, I have traced some of this history across different scales of analysis—from the micro-politics of a confessional encounter or the gentle blessing of a pregnant belly to the notion of the church as a vast bureaucracy that functions a bit like a "machine" constituted by "passionately" articulated joints and openings.

CONCLUSION 183

In Chapter Three, I asked what form of desire moved women, in particular, to actively want priests as lovers and confessors, mentors and mayors. This question emerged from the observation—banal and controversial in equal parts—that most church-attending Catholics are women, and significant numbers of Catholic priests are held to be homosexual.

Following the desire of some Catholic women for priests, I have sought to depict it not only as a longing for the divine but also as a "flocking after," a pursuit of alternative experiences of male power in a society steeped in values of *machismo*. Women's visions of emancipation in such contexts nestle in their religious desire; it does not necessarily manifest explicitly as feminist or pro-LGBTQ+ discourse. But the indirect manner through which many lay Catholics in socially conservative societies positively accommodate and orient themselves toward homosexuality within the priesthood (without naming it) remains significant for its potential effects: like an under-the-radar force, it animates the church from the ground up, consequently reinforcing its global political influence.

The figure of the priest here is primarily as a potentiator of desire but a desire that, if worthy of the name, must not be fulfilled. His job is not to satisfy people's longing but to direct it toward the word of God and respect for the church. Even so, he (and those around him) who realize the potential of his power may recognize, also, that faith-like desire can be readily directed to achieve other goals. In the figure of the mayor-priest, we get a sense for how religiously oriented desire may be captured and mobilized to multiple ends.

In Chapter Four, I focused on the high-stakes passage that some priests choose to undertake through the profane and polluting sphere of party politics. As the priest ventures into that world, the list of things he is forbidden from doing becomes evident. These things range from celebrating Mass in the same community to which he is a politician and using church buildings for campaign work to proselytizing religiously at public or political rallies. In short, the ideational boundaries of Catholic secularity become visible through the process of passage.

While some such boundaries can be transgressed with relative impunity, other transgressions can have very real consequences—in particular, the abandonment of celibacy. This particular religious/secular boundary, I argue, does not prohibit sex per se but, rather, a priest's public acknowledgment of sexual commitment to a particular person. In the cases that were analyzed, it was a heteronormative model of commitment that most threatened the integrity of the priesthood's inner sanctum: one in which a woman's womb comes to constitute something of a leaky, swelling threat to the collective celibate fantasy—her body a gateway between the religious and the secular that a priest can venture through, but not always successfully return from.

To succeed in politics, therefore, mayor-priests cultivate identities as "virile celibates": heterosexual men who are publicly celibate but privately sexually active. Such an identity may seem to point, once more, to Catholicism's capacity to triumph through a complex of opposites: with virile celibacy, bishops, politicians, and even voters appear to have it both ways. But through the stories of particular priests and their lovers, it became possible to glimpse the pain and exclusion this system of doubleness generates.

If the church remains a significant political agent in the world, it is not simply down to the choreographed passages of its priests or to the unique forms of desire that it is able, through them, to graft on to political agendas in secular domains of power. It is powerful because it is uniquely situated to channel a faith that is already present in the world.

In Chapter Five, I explored how this faith is experienced, in some contexts more than others, as a form of longing, a form of energy, an inalienable source of personal power. Through the intensity of the electoral moment, the ritual "time of politics," I traced how faith waxes, wanes, and co-opts other passions, all in relation to others and in relation to broader social conditions but not, entirely, the product of those conditions. In doing so, I compared it with Deleuze's notion of desire as production, as a constant movement forward or manifestation of a religiosity that is prior to "religion" and "politics" as socially elaborated categories.

In Chapter Six, I explored two oppositional models of economy (miraculous and mundane) that beset the mayor-priest as he adapts to a life in secular office. Thinking through a climatic geography in which thirst and water are deeply significant, I examined Padre Jorge's experience as a mayor and his struggle to hold the religious and political in productive tension despite a chronic lack of resources. Through Padre's Jorge's negotiations with agitated citizens, all demanding more than ritual blessings and absolutions, I retrained attention on the political and charted Padre Jorge's battle against failure as the infinite gave way to the finite, equality to hierarchy, and relations of unconditionality to short-term transactionalism.

The Imponderable Church

If this book has focused on the lives and longings of ordinary people, me included, the Roman Catholic Church in its guise as a centralized institution held together by rules and infrastructures has admittedly been more implied—a presence in the background. This presence has nonetheless been a grounding condition for this study, and with these closing paragraphs, I turn to one of the central questions that the Catholic Church as a global institution that claims to be "one, holy, and apostolic" has always posed for me.

The question is a familiar one for scholars of "world religions": how can any phenomenon so textured by the specificities of a particular place and its politics also constitute something universal? Put differently, what is the church? And how should such an entity be analytically conceptualized?

Social scientists have long made it their business to dismantle concepts with the aim of demystifying them, reducing them to their constituent parts to better understand them. But the Catholic Church is not, perhaps, a concept that can ever be truly understood in social scientific terms, because it seems to call for an opposite process: a complication; a layering-on of meanings. As a divine institution, its infrastructural trappings (hierarchies, bureaucracies, buildings, resources) are layered with the hidden dimensions of transcendence. As the catechism itself proclaims:

> The Church is essentially both human and divine, visible but endowed with invisible realities, zealous in action and dedicated to contemplation, present in the world, but as a pilgrim, so constituted that in her the human is directed towards and subordinated to the divine, the visible to the invisible, action to contemplation, and this present world to that city yet to come, the object of our quest. (CCC, §771)

The impossibility of reducing the church is echoed in the cornucopia of images and metaphors used to describe it: flock and field, rock and spouse, humble and sublime. The church is

> both tabernacle of cedar and sanctuary of God; earthly dwelling and celestial palace; house of clay and royal hall; body of death and temple

of light; and at last both object of scorn to the proud and bride of Christ! (CCC, §771)

All the same, the meaning of "church" most frequently offered when one looks the concept up is still, quite simply, a group of people, the word "church" deriving from the Greek word *ekklesia*, which translates as a convocation or assembly. The people in question here are the whole body of the faithful, not merely those alive on earth, but those in heaven or purgatory who form part of the communion of saints: the church militant, church suffering, and church triumphant.

The current study hasn't attempted to resolve the vexed question of what Catholicism or the church is so much as to open a fold in that body of faithful. Extemporizing on the universality and inalienability of faith, I have approached the church in its most anthropological sense, as a communion of desire present as lament, energy, and eroticism.

Zooming in, that church was Milene, a lapsed Catholic schoolteacher observing the priesthood with detached skepticism; Dora, an ex-nun guided by deep spiritual principles; Vitor, a beleaguered councilor reflecting on the impossibility of politics; Paulinho, a marginalized voter filled with faith and energy. The church was also Flávia's desire for Padre Marcos, Padre Aldo's manicured "shadow partner," Padre Daniel's love for Darcyone, Padre Jorge's electoral victory.

Zooming out, the church becomes a network of provinces, a spotting of steeples, a clustering of bodies across a vast landscape. And priesthood, a tangle of passages both spatial and temporal. We might visualize that tangle as lines across a spinning blue planet, connecting continents, nations, and communities. Or as traces, only partly ponderable, of journeys, only partly visible.

Epilogue

Padre Jorge did not win a second term in office. He was abandoned—first by an increasingly disaffected electorate, then by members of his own administration, who, one by one in the run-up to the next election, defected to the opposition's side. When I next returned to Brazil, it was a few months after that humiliating defeat, and Padre Jorge had left Iati. I tried in vain to track him down but with no success. He seemed to have disconnected his phone, and nobody had any knowledge of his whereabouts.

Unable to make contact with him by any media or via anyone in his family, Rosa and I visited Iati to catch up with some of its citizens. Vitor (the beleaguered councilor in Chapter One) was still in his post and agreed to meet us at a roadside *churrascaria* (restaurant and grill) to talk. As he greeted us, wearing a crisp white polo shirt and sunglasses, I noted he had filled out a bit and seemed more relaxed. His newfound contentment was, he reported, down to the woman who had rescued him following his recent divorce, as well as to the fact that he was now permanently resident at his *sitio* (small-holding) where his cell phone had no coverage.

Over servings of salty grilled meat, he gave us his own take on why Padre Jorge did not make it to a second term. In his view, Padre Jorge was a decent man but had never been cut out for politics. Too much of his time had been spent engaging in spiritual practices that had failed to yield the necessary results. For example, there was the 500-mile pilgrimage he had made on foot to the shrine of Padre Cícero, in thanksgiving for having won the election—and in an effort to avert Iati's looming financial crisis. The entire trip had taken him away from Iati for the best part of a month and was all of a piece with his general tendency to resolve political problems through prayer. It seemed he genuinely believed that if he only prayed hard enough and frequently enough, miracles would happen: money would appear; the town would be saved.

But according to Vitor, Padre Jorge's refusal to take advice from his colleagues and advisors was equally to blame for his downfall. Even in the face of imminent defeat, when being offered strategies from his closest political aides, Padre Jorge's preferred action was to shut himself off in prayer or absent himself, leaving the administration in the hands of Elisangela, his sister. Elisangela's proxy leadership had made Padre Jorge unpopular, but perhaps the biggest problem he had generated for himself stemmed from his constant "travels." Throughout his term, he had spent too much time away from Iati—according to rumor, visiting his common-law wife and daughter.

Rosa and I glanced at one another in surprise. Yes, responded Vitor with a laconic smile, Padre Jorge's rumored "wife" and child had likely contributed to his political undoing.[1]

Having bid farewell to Vitor, Rosa and I popped in on Selma, who informed us that since our last visit to the region, Paulinho had married a slim young man, barely out of his teens, who "dressed like a rapper" and was notoriously *machista*. Apparently it was Elisangela, Padre Jorge's sister and effective vice-leader, who, during Padre Jorge's term as mayor, had paid for their wedding.

Following our visit to Selma, Rosa and I stopped by Paulinho's new house on the outskirts of town, where he lived with his husband, and clapped to get his attention. Paulinho, who was home alone, came out of his front door and, beaming at the sight of us, invited us in.

We sat at his kitchen table as he set about getting out glasses and bottles of soft drink and caught up on all the gossip. When conversation turned to the topic of his wedding, he proudly fetched a large, ornately decorated wedding album, sunk into its own satin-lined box, to show us. The cost of the wedding photographer and the baroque photo album had also been a gift from Elisangela.

Not long into that visit, however, Paulinho's husband returned and, looking displeased to find us in his kitchen, pulled Paulinho into the next room. A few heated moments later, Paulinho came back into the kitchen and explained, with much apology, that, given his husband's jealousy, he was no longer allowed to entertain friends. By then it was getting late anyway, and as Rosa and I still had a long drive ahead of us, we bid him an affectionate farewell and departed.

Regret enveloped me. I had wanted to spend longer with Paulinho and had hoped to see Padre Jorge one last time to hear his version of events and offer my condolences. While I knew Padre Jorge was under no obligation whatsoever to meet up with me, I nevertheless felt that between our first conversation in the rectory all those years ago, when he'd discussed his dilemma about whether or not to run for mayor, and our final conversation about his time in office four years later, a friendship of sorts had been established. But Padre Jorge could not be reached.

Paulinho thought he was now living with his woman and daughter in an upmarket neighborhood in the city of Caruarú, in a gated residence he could ill afford. Rosa guessed that he was unemployed and struggling to make ends meet. Some reported having seen him working as a vegetable trader. Others claimed his relatives had sent petitions to the bishop, asking for his reinstatement within the church.

With every thread of gossip and speculation, my curiosity grew stronger. But my efforts to get in touch with him continued to hit dead ends. Wondering if it were just I he was avoiding, I begged a reluctant Rosa to call him from her phone and leave a message. "Tell him I am on his side, that I only wish the very best for him," I instructed her desperately.

Rosa tried, Padre Daniel tried, many tried to make contact with Padre Jorge on my behalf, but others fared no better.

Making my way toward the coast, from where I would catch a plane back to Scotland, I stopped in Caruarú to spend the night with Padre Daniel and Darcyone. It was the very city in which Padre Jorge was rumored to now be living, but with a population of some 365,000 people, I knew my chances of bumping into him were minimal.

Sensing my melancholy, Padre Daniel reassured me that Padre Jorge was not avoiding only me; he was avoiding the whole world—hiding in "humiliation."

"But," I insisted, "Surely, given all our previous contact, he knows I'm not here to judge him?"

Padre Daniel regarded me with a flicker of frustration. Taking a breath, he tried once more to elaborate.

Padre Jorge had suffered one of the biggest humiliations a man can imagine, he said, for it was rare for any mayor to not make it to a second term, let alone a *priest*-mayor. An incumbent mayor has the machine in his hands and therefore the means to run a powerful re-election campaign. A second term is generally expected. Failing to get re-elected is a serious sign of failure. Added to that failure was Padre Jorge's estrangement from the priesthood and his inability to find a respectable new means of supporting himself. That was why, explained Padre Daniel, he had gone into hiding.

Padre Daniel was speculating based on his own experience, but speculate was all he could do at that moment—all either of us could do as we sat on his balcony looking out toward the horizon where, somewhere on those arid planes, ran the Rio Ipojuca. Exchanging our knowledge of small-town life, of the Catholic Church, of what it meant to be a priest in politics, we speculated late into the night, trying to intuit what Padre Jorge would do next and which new priests were about to candidate themselves.

Whatever the reality to come, one thing was clear: Padre Jorge's sojourn into politics had not ended well. His secular passage had left him burned, but he was not the only one to suffer. There had been others before him, and likely others would come after him—priests willing to sacrifice their livelihoods, reputations, and self-respect for a fleeting turn in secular office.

Acknowledgments

This book would never have seen the light of day without the immense generosity of so many people. To all the people of Pernambuco who contributed to this project, each in their own way, I am profoundly grateful. Four exceptional women have shaped and enabled all my work in Brazil: Auxiliadôra Cardoso da Silva, Maria Silene Rodrigues, Rita Cassia Oliveira Cadete, and Gilsyara Guaraná de Lima. Their friendship and support over the years has made the difference between my sinking and swimming.

I will forever be grateful to the priest politicians who found time to participate in my study; particularly to Padre Daniel Texeira da Paixão, Padre José Aldo Mariano da Silva, and Padre Jorge de Melo Elias whose warmth, hospitality, and honesty made this book possible. Rubens Pita, José Amauri Cadete, Fabiana Cadete, Katiana Oliveira, Margarida and Almir de Oliveira, and Rigoberta Cardoso da Silva have also provided friendship and logistical support at so many junctures.

The research for this project was first made possible with a British Academy award, with subsequent fieldtrips being supported by several small grants from the University of Edinburgh. Engagements with colleagues over the years have helped me form many of this book's arguments. In Brazil, I have benefitted immensely from the hospitality and intellectual generosity shown to me by colleagues such as Ana Claudia Marques, Jorge Villela, Marcio Goldman, Renata de Menezes, Christine Chaves, Aparecida Vilaça, Claudia Barcellos Rezende, and the late Clara Mafra.

Outside Brazil, conversations with Josep Almudever Chanza, Andreas Bandak, Tom Boylston, Janet Carsten, Katherine Clough, John Collins, Magnus Course, Alexander Edmonds, Naomi Haynes, Casey High, Diego Maria Malara, Rebecca Marsland, Kristin Norget, Adam Reed, Shari Sabeti, Jonathan Spencer, and Susannah Wilson have provided essential stimulation and encouragement. Special thanks goes to Jon Bialecki for making intimidating philosophy appear potentially relevant to the data I was working with in the early phase of this project, and to Aaron Ansell for all his clear-sighted input as I struggled to haul the manuscript over the finishing line.

I would also like to thank John Seitz and John Garza at Fordham for supporting this book's transition to print, Adriano Godoy and Leandro de Paulo for readings of specific chapters and help with Portuguese spelling and translations, and Eduardo Dullo and Valentina Napolitano for their careful feedback on the entire manuscript.

I hope it goes without saying that while this book has benefitted from so many shining intellects, I reserve sole rights to its mediocrities and failures.

Sadly, the writing of this book was marked by the death of my late-step mother, Andrea Levy. As a writer herself, I'm sure she would have been proud to see this project finally reach fruition. I am deeply indebted to Carmen Miranda and Bill Mayblin, for giving me the courage—mental and physical—to go forth in the first place. Without their support through every stage, from fieldwork to cover design, this book would still not be finished. I would also like to thank Margaret Course and Andrew Amos for holding the home fort over so many work trips.

To Magnus Course I owe both my gratitude and an apology—for the many unquantifiable costs of this project. His supportive interventions despite it all were nothing short of heroic, and will never be forgotten. Finally, I would like to thank Ezra Course and Willa Course, for valiantly leaving school, friends, and home, to join me in Brazil during the research phase. May the niche general knowledge of Brazilian mayor-priests they have subsequently (if reluctantly) acquired as a result, one day stand them in good stead!

Notes

Introduction

1. The parish priests I refer to were those who worked for the diocese. Unlike priests who belong to religious orders, diocesan priests are ordained for a particular diocese, and their main work is to serve in a parish. In the region where I worked, most ministerial work of the diocese was carried out by diocesan priests, though in some more inaccessible rural parts, it was shared by clergy belonging to the Capuchin and Salesian orders.

2. In common conception, the secular constitutes a series of neutral public spaces free from religion, set aside for the business of state. Such an understanding of the secular is relevant to this study insofar as it centers upon a religious figure (the priest) who, somewhat anomalously, enters such a public space. But my argument in this book builds upon a more complex understanding of the secular as a culturally grounded orientation toward "modernity"—one that does not so much deny religion as profoundly shape what we hold it to be (see Asad 2003 and Charles Taylor 2007). It also speaks to Ashley Lebner's discussion of secularity as distinct from secularism, as a lived condition in which religious differences between friends and family are negotiated even in the absence of any formal doctrines of secularism (Lebner 2021).

3. According to the historian Eul-Soo Pang, since the Republic, Brazilian priests have been politically active in four key ways, as:

> politicians (holding public offices); partisan bureaucrats (working for a political party or government); reform-mongers (ascetic-messianic thaumaturges and organisers of rural or urban trade unions) and pressure-group lobbyists (spokesmen for church-affiliated social and political groups). (Pang 1974, 342)

These "four types" of political action have been more or less favored by priests of different eras for complex intersecting reasons, including where in Brazil they came from (whether they were coastal or of the interior, northern or southern). From the time of the Republic onward, however, the kinds of political roles priests took up tended to map onto their positions in relation to ultramontanism. By this time, Brazilian priests' prolific (and often seditious) engagement in Brazilian political parties and social movements was increasingly perceived as a threat by certain contingents of the secular state and the church, and measures to curb levels of political activity among priests came into force (Santirocchi 2011).

From 1840 to 1962, the Brazilian church became definitively ultramontanist; the pro-Roman bishops who dominated the episcopate during this period worked tirelessly to "wrest priests from politics, the Enlightenment and Gallicanism, and the embrace of women" (Serbin 2006, 54). Nevertheless, priest participation in politics continued throughout this period in different ways. Those who moved among the cosmopolitan elites of the coast tended to be more progressive, nationalist, and in favor of a Brazilian Catholic Church in which celibacy would no longer be mandatory, whereas those in the interior tended to be more messianic, conservative, and pro-Rome (Serbin 2006).

4. For example, of the 80 deputies chosen in the first general election organized in Brazil, 23 of them were clerics. The Constituent Assembly of 1823, in turn, had 21 clerics, including bishops and priests, and in 1826, out of a total of 103 clerics, 23 were elected to compose the legislature of the Chamber of Deputies. Although the numbers of clerics participating in legislative and executive chambers did gradually decline after 1890 following the decree proclaiming the separation of church and state, they never disappeared entirely (Ciarallo 2011, 86).

5. See, for example, Jan Hoffman French's (2007) discussion of two priests from rural Sergipe whose political careers have oscillated between Catholic ministry, political work outside the state on Indigenous and Quilombo land movements, and periods as mayors and councilors in local municipalities.

6. Social pastorates, an outgrowth of the CNBB, were consolidated throughout Brazil throughout the 1970s and '80s alongside the Base Ecclesiastical Communities. According to the booklet published by the National Conference of Bishops of Brazil, the role of the social pastorate is to solicit answers to social questions in light of the Gospel:

> Today as yesterday, she [the church] is concerned with issues related to health, housing, work, education, in short, the real conditions of existence, the quality of life. . . . She expresses the compassion of Jesus and the love of the mother, translating them into a social action that promotes humanity towards the poorest sectors of society. (CNBB 2001, 18)

The dynamic between action of a charitable and political nature in the Brazilian church's pastoral organizations is discussed by Claudia Neves da Silva (2006), who finds that actors involved in pastorates at all levels are moved by a dual commitment to charitable helping and the political promotion of civil rights. For Andrea Muehlebach (2013, 455), the Catholic discourse of love that infuses welfare organizations in the Italian context constitutes a Catholicization of neoliberalism, generating an ethic that "couples the market to moral sentiment, and economic rationality to the emotional urgencies of caritas." For China Scherz (2013), the ethico-temporal framework employed by a charitable organization of Ugandan nuns that places emphasis on the present eschews the commitment to "fix things" and "end poverty" and is therefore at odds with more secular forms of political advocacy and development work.

7. The precise semiotic ideology underlying this woman's statement remains unknown. Did she accept the Catholic doctrine of the priest as ontologically different from other people—as *alter Christus*—or did she simply see him as a Bible expert? This question opens onto an old debate within the anthropology of Christianity about the extent to which Protestantism changes people's ideas about the agency of materiality (Keane 2007) and concomitant debates about the degree to which conversion to Protestant worldviews entails "rupture" from older cultural and conceptual frameworks where material objects, including bodies, can be divinely enchanted (Robbins 2007).

In Brazil, this debate has taken form in particular ways, with some arguing that the same (or similar) ontologies of divinity traverse what appear, on the surface, to be different kinds of religious faith (see Brandão 1986; Negrão et al. 2009), and those who find greater levels of discontinuity between Protestant and older cultural forms (Mafra 2002; Machado and Mariz 1997; Novaes 1985). Others have suggested that temporality and length of immersion have a determining effect on how likely subjects are to think differently from Catholics on questions of enchantment (Mariz and Campos 2011).

Brazil's religious landscape has been changing for some time. Census data from the last few decades show a continual reduction in the percentage of Catholics in Brazil in the population as a whole, though as Menezes (2005) notes, such statistics do not accurately convey the continuing cultural hegemony of Catholicism in Brazil nor the vitalism of its growing popularity in the form of media and charismatic movements and saints' cults (on media and charismatic Catholicism, see also de Abreu 2021). At the time of my research, Protestant denominations were still very much a minority, and their influence was still quite marginal in comparison with that of the Catholic Church. However, my point about shared attitudes toward priests in this region does not necessarily entail a shared concept of the priest as *ontologically* altered but a shared cultural experience of the priest as an institutionally significant figure. Priests, because of their lifestyles, are assumed to have heightened access to the sacred in the sense originated by Durkheim (2008 [1912]), which defines the sacred as an ambiguous power and as that which is "set apart." A shared conception of the sacrality of the priest derives from growing up in a culture where Catholicism is the dominant religion and priests enjoy roles as father figures, men of Bible knowledge, power, and authority.

8. Among those of a more secular disposition, Catholic priests were held to make better mayors than local evangelical pastors because of their higher levels of education, administrative experience, and skill at maintaining role distinctions. But on the inverse assumption that evangelical politicians are less adept at maintaining the correct sorts of separations between their religious/political and public/private roles, see discussions by Dullo and Quintanilha (2015) and Paula (2020).

9. In 1891, Padre Cícero was permanently excluded from sacerdotal ministry for "false miracles" and disobedience to the hierarchy. Despite this, his popularity among pilgrims remained undiminished, and his power only continued to grow. In 1973, the Brazilian Catholic Apostolic Church proclaimed Padre Cícero a saint, to the derision of the Roman Catholic Church. In 2015, the Vatican formally reconciled Padre Cícero to the fold, a decision that his devotees hope will open a pathway for official beatification and eventual canonization but has yet to materialize.

10. See Gamba, Cucolo, and Takahashi (2019).

11. Since the Constitution of 1988, municipalities have had the exclusive authority to organize transport, pre-school primary education, social welfare, and healthcare, as well as to develop and enact urban development plans and collect revenues from tax sources. Although federal and state laws are hierarchically superior to municipal laws, central government has no legal jurisdiction to interfere with municipal laws, provided they do not contradict them. In practice, this makes Brazil the most devolved country in Latin America and one of the most decentralized federations in the world.

12. The captaincies referred to a system of land tenure that concentrated huge swathes of land in the hands of a small elite, the legacy of which can still be seen in the vastly unequal distribution of land in the region today (Green and Skidmore 2021).

13. For an overview of Brazil's history of racial ordering and the construction of the myth of racial democracy, see Skidmore (1992). For the Northeastern context in particular, Rebhun (2004) analyzes how sexual and racial orderings coalesce as a form of stigma among lower-class women, while Hoffman French (2009) discusses land claim processes built around new forms of black and indigenous identity. On the continuing persistence of forms of racial ambiguity that reinforce long-standing narratives of racial democracy, see Sullivan's discussion (2017, 2) of how blackness may be "at once readily apparent and somehow seemingly non-apparent."

14. The Brazilian municipality derives from an old colonial system of governance. As in Portugal, each colonial village and city in Brazil had a council

(*câmara municipal*) whose members were prominent figures of colonial society (landowners, merchants, slave traders). Colonial city councils worked under the aegis of provincial governors and were responsible for regulating commerce, public infrastructure, professional artisans, and prisons. When Brazil became a republic in 1889, provinces were solidified into states, and municipalities were granted new levels of autonomy. Such autonomy, in practice, came under the auspices of *coronelismo*, an extra-legal system of loyalties in which regional chiefs (who sometimes also held roles as municipal mayors) were granted free reign over their territories in return for providing state deputies with the votes they needed for the legislature (Hanley and Lopes 2017).

Under the dictatorship of Getúlio Vargas (1930–40), government power became more concentrated at the federal level and municipal autonomy declined. With democratization in 1945, new rules delineating and bolstering the power of municipal governments were inserted into the constitution. Municipal bodies were granted new forms of revenue from state and federal government, and for the first time in Brazilian history, it was mandated that all municipal officials be elected. On paper, these were significant advances, but in practice, revenue transfers remained sporadic, if they occurred at all (Nunes and Serrano 2019).

There were no great advances for municipal bodies under the military period despite it being the period of the Brazilian economic "miracle," as all revenue was reinvested in heavy infrastructure or retained by the richest 3 percent of the population, who, in the 1960s, received around 20 percent of Brazil's total income. It was only with the return of democracy in 1985 and the new constitution of 1988 that municipalities gained legal status as federal entities, along with increased levels of political and fiscal autonomy (Nunes and Serrano 2019).

15. Data from "Títulos Públicos Sustentáveis," *Tesouro Nacional*, https://www.gov.br/tesouronacional/pt-br.

16. Recently, it is friendship rather than patronage that has become the more dominant concept grounding political relations in Northeast Brazil. The rise in what Ansell calls "amico-politics" (choosing to classify politicians as "friends" rather than "patrons") indicates movement away from older, more rigidly hierarchical forms of social relation across the Northeast connected to changes in patterns of land ownership and diversifications in labor arrangements. It also intersects with localized reinterpretations of liberal anti-corruption messages issued at a national level (Ansell n.d.).

17. See, for example, the work of Agnieszka Halemba (2015) on the authority of priests at a Marian shrine; Christine Lee (2019, 2021) on indigenous diocesan priests of the Andes, and Andrew Orta (2004) on Andean catechists and deacons. Both Lee and Orta tackle themes of cultural and religious mediation

in combination with questions of clerical identity. Other important studies have addressed Catholic religious living in spiritual communities (Irvine 2010, 2017; Lester 2005; Scherz 2018). Within the anthropology of Protestantism, the work of Blanes (2014) and Werbner (2011) stand as examples of research centered on individual religious leaders, exploring their roles and reception as church founders, prophets, and pastors. See also Reinhardt (2017, 2018) and Tomlinson (2020) for discussions of how theologians, pastors, and leaders are formed in seminary and other institutional contexts.

18. Catholic diocesan priests do not make easy research subjects. Not only are they frequently beholden to very taxing schedules, their livelihoods depend on a certain level of compliance and submission to secretive forms of ecclesiastic authority. Opening up to secular researchers is a risk many diocesan priests are not prepared to take. This does not make research among priests an impossible task, for as public figures they are obliged, on some level, to represent the church to the passing researcher. However, the front they present to researchers may be somewhat cautious, representative only of the church's most formal positions.

19. All except the sacrament of Holy Orders, which he can only deliver as a bishop.

20. The extent to which laity are even aware of the intricate theology that makes up the priesthood is an ethnographic question. It would be fair to assume that lay knowledge about the principles behind celibacy and the ontological transition that occurs via the "laying on of hands" varies substantially (see also note 8). But it is arguably true that most if not all Catholics around the world understand a priest as a man "set apart" from ordinary society by his living arrangements, dress, and ritual activities. The customary term of address for a priest, "father," plus common cultures of deference (or disparagement) toward priests in parish contexts, further mark them out as distinctly other. In practice, lay, embodied understandings of the priesthood work in tandem with, or even in lieu of, formal theological knowledge about it.

21. Formal references to the priest's "efficacy" in relation to his status as an *alter Christus* finds alternative expression in local discourses and beliefs about priests having supernatural powers, from stories of priests who heal, harm, and raise the dead (Badone 1990; Lawrence Taylor 1990) to those who fly (Hauschild 2010).

22. The "set apart" or sacred nature of the priest informs an originally Catholic notion of secular. Secular (or diocesan) priests live among the laity, carrying out their mission in the profane spaces of society to a greater degree than cloistered religious. For a more detailed discussion of the many conceptual distinctions (spiritual/temporal, religious/secular, visible/invisible, natural/supernatural, worldly/other-worldly) that have been historically

operative in Catholicism enabling the church as institution to function on multiple levels in society, see Casanova (1994, 11–40).

23. With the exception of married priests who joined the Roman Catholic Church from other Christian traditions. For example, a married Protestant minister (whether Lutheran, Episcopalian, Anglican, or otherwise) who converts to the Catholic Church can, with special permission from the Holy See, be admitted to the Catholic priesthood.

24. Elsewhere I have employed concepts of gymnasticity and elasticity to think through the church's capacity to contain within itself lapsedness, dissent, and heresy without the same proclivity to schism and breakage found in Protestant history (Mayblin 2014, 2017a, 2019a, 2019b). However, it is important to emphasize that the church's heavily materialized and authoritative center prevents such elasticity from stretching ad infinitum. Catholicism cannot properly be conceived of as endlessly elastic, nor can its reproduction be conceptualized in Deleuzian terms as "rhizomic," for it exists in perpetual tension with a decisionistic sovereign center.

25. Although Schmitt's thinking on this point was always rhetorical, never empirically founded, it is being increasingly taken up by anthropologists seeking to understand how Catholicism operates on the ground as a contemporary lived religion (Bandak 2017), a colonial institution (Mosse 2012), a politico-economic force (de Abreu 2021; Muehlebach 2009), and as a "theopolitical" form (McAllister and Napolitano 2020). Within this literature, some scholars have sought to engage the generative potential of Schmitt's concept while recognizing some of its conceptual vagueness. For example, David Mosse's work (2012, 106) on the propagation of Catholicism into Tamil Nadu life by seventeenth-century Jesuits shows how "the apparent universality, and authority of the church were (and still are) produced through struggle and contingent action," and how the emergence of a coherent realm of Catholic religion is possible only by "concealing these messy processes and constitutive exclusions." In Andreas Bandak's treatment of the apparent contradiction between the Syrian Catholic Church's material opulence and its moral teaching on simplicity, Schmitt's concept points at once to the complexity to be found "in practical life more widely," as well as to Catholicism's own capacity to hold oppositions in tension as a form of power (Schmitt 2017, 167).

I argue that while Schmitt's *complexio* provides a useful conceptual tool for thinking about Catholicism as a political form, it nevertheless has serious moral and intellectual limitations. For one thing, Schmitt's thesis in "Roman Catholicism and Political Form" was never empirically founded but relied on a somewhat fictional notion of a Medieval Catholicism long past. It was also deeply ideological, born of radical anti-Semitism, and driven by fascist intentions quite at odds with Christian principles more broadly. Because it was never intended as a theory of religion as such but as an exposition of Schmitt's political ideology, it risks having the same imperial effect on thought that it sets out to describe: in accommodating all possible incommensurables, it becomes impossible to think outside of it.

The limits of the *complexio* need to be acknowledged, for although Catholicism's elasticity has allowed it to grow and adapt in tandem with politico-economic systems, and although it has resisted schism more often than the Protestant church, the fact is that there are limits to such elasticity: Catholic schisms do occur, other ontologies do gain the ascendancy. As David Mosse (2012, 106) warns, "too often Catholicism (or Christianity) is attributed an independent coherence, power, and ideological encompassment. . . . But the unity and coherence of a Catholicism—its capacity to embrace rather than to be embraced by various cultural elements—are not to be presumed."

26. Elsewhere I have elaborated on this logic using the notion of the church as a "thinking self" (Mayblin 2019b).

27. Reinhardt (2015), following Jon Bialecki (2012), seeks mutual clarification between two approaches to immanence and transcendence in modernity: a received Christian one in which transcendence is above and beyond the immanent plane and the other, a more immanent vitalist approach favored by continental philosophers such as Deleuze that derive from a Nietzschean tradition that scorns Christianity. Reinhardt's elaboration of a contrapuntal analysis in relation to his ethnography of Ghanaian Pentecostals seeks to avoid the dangers of total theoretical blending, wherein anthropologists and their subjects are described as sharing the same ethical and intellectual project. "Contrapuntalism" provides a more honest depiction of the often-awkward traffic between life-forces and the categories they connect (religion, politics, economics) within the broader setting of what he calls a "Christian plane of immanence."

28. However, it also manifests in contexts that are not necessarily, or explicitly, religious. Like the famously hard to translate concept of *saudades* that denotes a bittersweet sense of longing, concepts of lack, desire, and melancholia have long played a role in Brazilian discourses about culture and national identity. From Paulo Prado's (1962 [1928]) "Essay on Brazilian Sadness," which casts Brazilians as the outcome of the miscegenation of three sad races, and the literary tragedies of modernist authors like João Guimarães Rosa and Euclides da Cunha, to Claude Lévi-Strauss's *Tristes Tropiques* (2012 [1955]), literary meditations on loss and humankind's endless quest to redeem itself from suffering have captured the imagination of generations of Brazilian anthropologists. Such melancholia has also been connected to Brazil's exceptionally brutal colonial history and to its grounding in one of the largest and longest-running transatlantic slave trades the world has known (Conrad 1986).

29. The mayor-priests never explicitly disclosed to me how they racially identified. All were light-skinned men who would have likely been viewed as *branco* (white) or *pardo* (mixed). It is worth noting that race in Brazil can be somewhat fluid. Priests, because of their many years of education in seminaries, exposure to foreign clergy, and elite forms of cultural capital, can shift class-racial categories, coming to seem whiter as they become more middle class (cf. Lee 2021).

1. Politics: Endless and Addictive

1. A classic example of this redemptive anthropological genre is Lisa Björkman's work on elections, patronage, and vote-buying in Mumbai, which leads her to conclude that:

> Ethnographic attention to cash transactions demonstrates that electoral democracy in Mumbai is the site of deeply political contestation through which Mumbaikars aspire to best position themselves—with the help of a trusted and able representative—to navigate the complexities and contradictions and possibilities inhering in the contemporary city. (Björkman 2014, 632)

2. This was during the run-up to the Petrobras scandal that broke in 2014, leading to the infamous Operation Car Wash that resulted in the impeachment of Dilma Rousseff in 2016. For a useful overview, see Turner (2018).

3. In Ansell's (n.d.) usage, "amico-politics" is the practice of folding patron-client relations and political forms of *assistencialismo* into the ideology of friendship. See also Introduction, n. 16.

4. But see also Jose Casanova (1994), who points out that by the mid-twentieth century, the Brazilian meaning of "the people" came to stand against the traditional elitism of Brazilian political society and its narrow representation of interests. In the new political discourse, "the people" were "civil society" and no longer conceived of as an extension of the state but as something autonomous from it. "In this respect," he writes, "both concepts, that of civil society and that of 'the people,' were not so much principles of mediation between states and society as principles of organization of society without mediations and without the state, principles of direct communitarian democracy with strong affinities with Christian anarchism" (131).

5. Dida's salary came out of a regional state funding stream, rather than directly out of the municipal budget. Functionaries whose salaries are funded at state level are more protected from the vagaries and *politicagem* of the local municipal economy.

6. See also Palmeira 1996; Villela and Marques 2006.

7. It is important to recognize that the decreasing size of families and the gradual undermining of older, more rigid forms of patriarchy have decreased the number of votes that the average household head has to bargain with.

8. As Palmeira (1996, 144, *translation my own*) also observes, "It is common for the most ideological candidates to complain that they are being forced to 'put their hand in their pockets,' that is, in order to be able to establish ties with voters they have to accept the 'logic' of donation and favour."

2. Celibacy as Theopolitics

1. But see Andrea Muehlebach (2013), on voluntarism in the Italian welfare economy, for a discussion of how the logic of agape can be adapted for different social and politico-economic ends. Muehlebach argues that Catholic imaginaries of loving paternalism shore up neoliberal forms of governance by serving as "as a crucial corollary to the marketization of welfare and as a key sentiment in the restructuring of care" (454). Such paternalism "tends to make the poor objects of love, not subjects of justice," the result of which "maintain[s] unequal relations between the giver and receiver" (463).

2. Discussion about hierarchy and difference within Brazilian society is, as one might expect, immune to easy summary. Here, I am drawing from my own observations as well from other anthropological accounts that highlight the impossibility of full trust and fidelity between couples (Dainese 2017; Shapiro 2016), constancy among friends (Lebner 2012, 2021), the existence of blood feuds (Villela 2004), and the role of factionalism in kinship and political lineages (Marques 2002, 2013; Goldman 2013; Palmeira 1996).

3. This classical justification for celibacy follows from Saint Paul's view that the unmarried state frees the ordained minister from the cares of personal family life so that he may devote himself entirely to the needs of the whole Christian community: "The unmarried man cares for the Lord's business; his aim is to please the Lord. But the married man cares for worldly things; his aim is to please his wife, and he has a divided mind" (1 Corinthians 7:32–33).

4. For a more detailed engagement with Agamben's concept, see Marmont and Primera (2020, 10), who describe inoperativity as:

> an attempt to rethink acting in terms that could neutralize the productive force routinely governing it—the necessary exhaustion and "passing into actuality" of potentiality, as he puts it (e.g., Agamben 1999, 180). Production, in this case, is to be taken in the broadest possible sense as the attainment of results, the achievement of an end, the successful completion of a process: a realization, so to speak, or, we may even say, a closure. In other words, what inoperativity indicates is a subversion of

the established relations between means and ends, the radicality of which has far-reaching implications for debates in politics, ethics, and aesthetics.

5. See Stoler (1995), who critiques Foucault's account of sexuality for the way it marginalizes the connection between European bourgeois order and the colonial management of race and sexuality.

6. According to Giraldi (2010), studies of the Brazilian Inquisition records reveal that the punishments meted out for sexual sins were less harsh than they were in Europe during the same period. However, it is also important to note that Brazil's understanding of itself as a nation with a distinctive sexual history is part of its founding mythology and one that is intimately connected to discourses about race (Hoornaert 1993; Parker 1991; Sacramento and Ribeiro 2013).

7. The start of the Second Empire in 1840 marked a long and intense period of Romanization for Brazilian Catholicism in which popular practices were curbed or reinterpreted in line with orthodox teaching and the clergy were brought under the more centralized authority of the Vatican through the establishment of standardized Tridentine seminaries (De Groot 1996; Serbin 2006, 54). Compare with Grant Kaplan (2014, 50), who argues that clerical celibacy functions as a "spiritual declaration of independence for the modern Christian citizen." Clerical celibacy, he writes, preserves Catholic identity "not by petitioning the state for rights but by mounting a theological counteroffensive against the pretensions of the modern nation-state" (50).

8. Igreja Católica Apostólica Brasileira a Igreja que ama Você, https://www.igrejabrasileira.com.br/; last accessed September 4, 2022.

9. See Silva (2008) and www.padrescasados.org. The MPC today has a branch called the Movimento das Familias dos Padres Casados and has since become a chapter in the International Confederation of Married Priests, which, according to its website, has a membership of some 150,000 priests who have been discharged from priestly ministry from around the world; http://www.padrescasados.org/archives/132/movimento-mundial-dos-padres-catolicos-casados/; last accessed September 3, 2022.

10. Proportionalist theologians reject deontological forms of reasoning based on the notion of intrinsic good and evil acts, arguing that nothing is good or bad in itself; the goodness of an act depends only on its foreseeable and calculable consequences (Kaczor 2010). The development of proportionalist theology allowed the conservative conclusions of the papal encyclical *Humanae Vitae* on the question of contraception to be soundly criticized (Curran 2008, 105).

11. For an overview of this decline, see Drogus (1995).

12. The priestly practice of maintaining a spatial and psychological distinction between the self in a celibate sacred role and the self as a sexual individual happened to be a strong feature of the mayor-priest cohort I worked with and needs to be recognized as one among a number of possible adaptations to the demands of clerical celibacy. In studies of priests who sexually abuse children, a relative psychological inability or unwillingness to create such distinctions are reported, with sexual acts often occurring inside sacred church spaces (Keenan 2011; Orsi 2017, 2019).

13. Elsewhere I have discussed celibacy as a "stable instability" at the heart of the church (Mayblin 2019b).

14. For a detailed discussion of the way exemplarity functions in relation to Catholic sainthood in a Christian Syrian setting, see Bandak (2022, 84): "More than stabilizing a particular way of seeing things, the example sets a local world in motion."

15. There is more that could be said on this point, firstly concerning how such symbolism encourages cultures of clericalism within the priesthood (see Plante 2020), and secondly, concerning the way the automatic respect extended to the priest stands in parallel relation to traditions of anti-clericalism. In the latter case, it can be noted that anti-clericalism, at least among Catholics themselves, mainly takes the form of criticism of specific priests rather than of the priesthood per se. On the valence of Catholic priests as living symbols for non-Catholics, see Introduction, n. 9.

16. Questions of exemplarity have reached something of a political tipping point in parts of the world heavily affected by clerical-sexual-abuse scandals. The threshold for that tipping point is arguably already much lower in highly secularized societies like those of Western Europe (Ireland especially), and countries where Catholicism is the minority religion. In such contexts, the positive symbolic power of priests is more diluted, and the priest's individual personality—his actual exemplarity—may carry greater weight.

17. According to the diocesan rule, parish posts are reviewed every six years. Many priests are moved on to a different parish at this point, but in exceptional cases, postings are renewed. In the case of appointing priests as godfathers, a priest godfather cannot also deliver the sacrament of baptism to his godchild. In practice, the child in question becomes vitally connected with *two* priests: the one who presides and the one who becomes her godfather.

3. Faith, Desire, and Machismo

1. Within the anthropology of religion, debates about women's embrace of patriarchal systems has moved from a focus on functionality (i.e., identifying various nonreligious advantages that religious participation affords women)

and resistance (i.e., attention to the way women's piety in fact subverts or resists gendered hierarchies) to a focus on agency. An influential text in this debate has been Saba Mahmood's (2005) critique of Western feminist concepts of agency that revolve around the notion of autonomy and "freedom" and therefore fail to understand the "pious agency" enacted by Muslim women through forms of humility and submission.

2. But see Eriksen (2016) for a critique of Bernice Martin's "Pentecostal gender paradox," which destabilizes the notions of gender and equality that the paradox is built on.

3. Similar arguments can be made for women of Christian Orthodox denominations (Seremetakis 1991).

4. Fluid and nonbinary identities have long been part of the rural gendered landscape, though in the Northeastern interior they tend to be less visible and discursively elaborated than in urban contexts and the south of the country. The predominantly binary concept of gender I work with in this chapter reflects the dominant, heteronormative, and traditionally Catholic concept of gender that shaped (and constrained) the lives of my interlocutors, regardless of their personal inclinations. My focus on "men/women" and "male/female" as gendered categories is offered both as an exploration and questioning of this ethnographically dominant gender ideology.

5. Anthropologists who have written about *machismo* have discussed it as a learned ideological script rooted in patriarchal values and expressed via exaggerated displays of sexual appetite, dominance, and aggression. Above all, *machismo* is a code of conduct based on male ownership of female bodies, which justifies violence toward women (and men) who violate its code (see, for example, Gilmore [2017 (1987); Gutmann 1997). Today *machismo* is quite a polysemic category. While many older people do not use or recognize the term at all, the younger generation increasingly utilizes the term as a pejorative descriptor for men considered to be "backward" in their gender politics and/or overly jealous.

6. Milene had gone from being an acquaintance to a friend who helped me immensely with my research. If I struggle to describe her as my "research assistant," it is because our working relationship always resisted such an explicit definition. Although it was, on one level, asymmetrical in terms of my status as an educated foreigner, Milene had begun helping me years earlier when I was a PhD student out of a mixture of what she described as "interest" in what I was up to and "pity" for the fact that I was, at the time, a young woman with no friends or family in the region and with only a poor grasp of the local tongue. On occasion, she chose to accompany me on research-related visits for no other reason than she had an afternoon free and wished for some distraction. As the years progressed, she allowed me to pay her for longer

stretches of research assistance, but if she ever felt our relationship was tipping too far from friendship into a working contract, she would redress the balance by refusing payment or making me the object of one of her mischievous jokes.

7. Also exemplified by the little clay sculptures of priests with erections found on tourist trails and in folk-art shops throughout the region.

8. Estimates derived from research carried with American priests suggests that 25–60 percent of all priests are homosexual (Cozzens 2000; Plante 2004). Frederic Martel (2019), based on his five-year investigation of the Vatican, estimates that up to 80 percent of Vatican priests are homosexual. Such a figure is remarkable but entirely in keeping with mounting sociological evidence for a connection between homosexuality and the priesthood and with the nature of the Vatican as an exceptionally homosocial milieu built, as Martel (2019, xii) puts it, "both on the homosexual double life and on the most dizzying homophobia." But see also Jordan's critical discussion (2000, 99–112) of attempts to count homosexuality in the priesthood.

9. The *Catechism of the Catholic Church* summarizes the church's teaching on homosexuality as follows:

> Homosexuality refers to relations between men or between women who experience an exclusive or predominant sexual attraction towards persons of the same sex. It has taken a great variety of forms through the centuries and in different cultures. Its psychological genesis remains largely unexplained. Basing itself on Sacred Scripture, which presents homosexual acts as acts of grave depravity, tradition has always declared that "homosexual acts are intrinsically disordered." They are contrary to the natural law. They close the sexual act to the gift of life. They do not proceed from a genuine affective and sexual complementarity. Under no circumstances can they be approved. (*CCC*, §2357–58 *"Catechism of the Catholic Church, 2358–2359,"* Scborromeo.org., October 29, 1951. Last accessed October 29, 2020.)

10. In Brazil, a country that contains some 27,000 ministering priests, not a single one has openly proclaimed himself as homosexual in public. Of the roughly 37,192 priests in the USA, by comparison, just over 10 have spoken publicly about their sexual orientation (Brandalaise 2020).

11. The silence that surrounds homosexuality within the priesthood is a fraught topic, today more than ever, because of the discourse surrounding clerical sexual-abuse cases and the desire of stakeholders to either implicate or disentangle homosexuality from the topic. Within this field of discourse, we might explore the parameters of silence alongside a notion of "doubleness": that broad repertoire of skilled silences, separations, and acts of nondiscernment

that allow conflicting doctrinal norms and alternative values to coexist (Mayblin 2019b).

12. In priests who came of age during the 1970s and '80s, discourses of desire often intersect with psychoanalytical understandings of the person as a result of the popularity of psychoanalysis and psychotherapy among the Brazilian clergy (Serbin 2006).

13. In an analogous discussion of listening as a technique of social action in Italy that crosses Catholic and secular contexts, Andrea Muehlebach (2013a, 460) notes, "It is as though the encounter with poverty must be performed through more than mere material intervention and must instead be enriched by an emotive stance animated by concern and compassion."

14. It is worth noting that this liberation theology understanding of political listening that Padre Marcos puts forward—i.e., listening to a collective in order to address people's material needs—has been superseded in recent times by an identity politics that incorporates a more existential desire to be witnessed and heard simply for who you are. Doubtless, such changing understandings about the role of politics accounts for some of the difficulty liberation theology has encountered among younger generations of Brazilians (Leandro de Paula, personal communication).

15. But the inverse potential of the gendered priestly body in such contexts—to give rise to abuse and therefore feelings not of desire but of revulsion—is equally present.

16. As Hunt (2002, 14) puts it, without misogyny, "There is no Catholicism as we know it." She elaborates on this point in relation to Jordan's thesis on the homoerotic homophobia of clerical power.

> It is not just anyone who is excluded from the gay clerical club, rather it is women, including lesbian women. The reality of women is denied consistently, beginning with the birth of Jesus that is mythologized to erase agency from his mother. The choice of women's names and the stereotypic drag personae of campy priests cannot be explained, as I see it, apart from a however unconscious hatred and/or trivializing of things associated with females. (Hunt (2002, 14)

While I would argue that camp and feminine masculinities have more complicated dynamics than misogyny, I take on board Hunt's point about the worrying erasure of women's agency in much contemporary discourse on the homoerotic homophobic church.

17. I borrow the term "cartography" from Gilles Deleuze, for whom desire is neither restricted to individuals nor an exclusively psychical force; it can be thought of as part of a more collective, materialist cartography (Deleuze 2006). Such a notion helps to convey the vast repetitiveness of this terrain: the

sheer numbers of desiring women who flock around priests, making Catholicism, at the congregational level, a largely female phenomenon.

An interesting comparison could be made on the nature of desire in other Christian traditions. For Bruno Reinhardt, a Deleuzian notion of desire facilitates an understanding of African Pentecostalism as a phenomenon that is simultaneously "desire-repressing and desire-producing." Such a desire, he argues, "envelops Christian docility and ecstasy into a single libidinal economy, wherein lies much of its power . . ." (Reinhardt 2015, 427). Desire in this Deleuzian model isn't just inert longing; it produces more of itself—more sensation, more horizon. Desire as production stands in famous relation to the Nietzschean sense of a force or a "will." As Deleuze's collaborators Guattari and Rolnik once noted, desiring production is:

> . . . the will to live, the will to create, the will to love, the will to invent another society, another perception of the world, and other value systems. . . . (Guattari and Rolnik 2008, 318)

I find Deleuze's notion of desire, both as force and cartography, helpful for understanding certain aspects of the phenomenon I am describing, particularly its institutional scale. However, Deleuze's rejection of the psychoanalytical supposition that desire is rooted in lack is at odds with the ethnographic theory of desire I here elaborate, which combines both absence and presence.

4. Virile Celibacy

1. Comparison could be made with Coleman's (2021, 52) work on pilgrimage, where he expands on the possibilities of movement and journey as a trope that spans the study of religion. Working with the notion of "articulation" as used across the work of Stuart Hall, Coleman advocates for a more flexible and less teleological concept of religious movement, one that entails "the making and remaking of separation and union, dislocation and relocation." The power of pilgrimage, he argues, lies not in any fixed telos or outcome such as unity, contest, or adaptation, but in "its often socially, culturally, and spiritually charged capacities for disassembly and reassembly, autonomy and entrainment" (53).

2. Although municipal politics in the Northeast is considered masculine, women who enter politics are not "butch"—they either play the feminized "caring" card or are cast as "helpers" of a male kin member who performs as though he is really in charge, despite not holding the formal office.

3. Padre Jorge's procession for peace followed a route toward a neighborhood where a large statue of the folk saint Padre Cícero stood in a glass case. For all that the statue had obvious political importance for Padre Jorge,

representing a powerful mayor-priest of the past, it was there because it had been gifted to the neighborhood by Padre Jorge's late father in return for some achieved blessing. So, it also indexed Padre Jorge's material historical and kinship connection to the town.

4. As with other mayor-priests of the past, Padre Aldo's return to ministry was premised on a resacralizing process that could take one of two forms. Either he could spend a year in Rome studying theology or he could leave the area where he was known for an undetermined probationary period to be a curate (a demotion) in another parish.

5. To have one's allied underlings defect to another political faction is cross-symbolized as cuckoldry as well (Aaron Ansell, personal communication).

6. It is worth iterating that Padre Aldo's capacity to straddle worlds went deeper than an appreciation of difference across cultural borders; it enabled him to hold, in tension, a liberal attitude toward homosexuality and a deep understanding of both the problems and possibilities of *machismo* for the male gender. *Machismo* and homophobia were a fairly normative part of the background of many priests growing up in the rural Northeast of the 1970s and '80s; however, in surrendering himself at an impressionable age to the "homoerotic charge" of the priesthood (Jordan 2000), the priest's subjectivity may alter in important ways—firstly, through the discovery that status as a priest exempts a man from some of the rules of *machismo*, and secondly, through the discovery that it is possible in a homophobic society—through the priesthood—to be homosexually inclined, widely respected, *and* institutionally powerful.

7. The priest's mother occupies a complex space. Beset with conflicting desires of her own—for her own prestige and religious respectability on the one hand, and for her son's contentment and grandchildren on the other—she often retains a significant role in the life of her priest son.

8. https://blogcapoeiras.blogspot.com/2011/01/padre-marcos-refeito-de-ibimirim-e.html; last accessed 12/11/2022.

5. Votes of Faith: Force, Power, and Political Form

1. Paulinho, somewhat unusually among his local contemporaries, often explicitly identified himself as "poor and black."

2. The role of belief in religious practice is well debated among anthropologists. Because of its association with scriptural credos and mental states, it has often been critiqued for being a largely Western Christian concept with limited relevance beyond the Judeo-Christian context (Asad 1991 [1982]; Needham 1972; Ruel 1997). Yet it has also received attention as a concept of central importance to understanding cultures of Christianity (Robbins 2007) and as

having varied and nuanced applications beyond Christianity (Lindquist and Coleman 2008).

Moving beyond debates about belief, Joel Robbins has recently pushed anthropologists of religion to think more systematically about the way subjects "know faith." Returning to what might be regarded as the scriptural and intellectual, he has argued that in today's highly educated, globally interconnected, and technically mediated world, "many people now feel it is not enough to proclaim that one belongs to such-and-such a faith. To securely inhabit that religion, one should also know a good deal about it" (Robbins 2019, 17).

3. The synonymous quality of faith and hope, in this context, has to be noted. There is an important philosophical literature on hope, both as an affective and political economy (Bloch 1986 [1956–59], Safatle 2016) and as a method of knowledge (Miyazaki 2004). There is also a strong tradition of thought in Brazilian liberation theology on the active qualities of hope as a theological virtue (Freire 1997). While hope and faith may be somewhat interchangeable, faith is the term more widely in use in everyday life and particularly within this ethnographic context. This may have something to do with its denser relational significance. A person possesses faith (for example, one's own, unalienable source of energy) at the same time that one can *have faith* in a specific relationship or person (a leader or political candidate).

4. Aquinas, *ST* I-II, q. 62.

5. Although the idea of God's presence being in all aspects of creation is fairly well accepted, the notion that it is possible to attribute sentience (and thus "faith" as understood in the Christian tradition) to all creatures and things would be questioned by some of my Catholic interlocutors. Here, it is worth pointing out that Gil's lyrics likely draw influence from the Afro-Brazilian religious universe in which the sacred energy of the gods can be represented by any object or being. *Axé*, the name of this energy in the Yoruba language, means power or strength present in every being or thing. In Afro-Brazilian religions, *axé* can be represented by an object or a being that will be charged with the energy of the spirits honored in a religious ritual.

6. This comment relates to the fact that the Carnival of floats and parades is only really celebrated in the big cities of the coast. In the interior of the state, Carnival isn't marked in the same way, except as a national holiday.

7. As in Acts 2:1–4: "When the day of Pentecost had come, they were all together in one place. And suddenly a sound came from heaven like the rush of a mighty wind, and it filled all the house where they were sitting. And there appeared to them tongues as of fire, distributed and resting on each one of

them. And they were all filled with the Holy Spirit and began to speak in other tongues, as the Spirit gave them utterance" (Revised Standard Version Catholic Edition).

8. For more on electoral campaigns happening at the national level around this time, see Ansell's (2014) discussion of the 2008 "Clean Vote" campaign headed by the Federal Electoral Tribunal and the Organization of Brazilian Attorneys.

9. *Fé* is but one of several Christian idioms to describe sacred forms of power. Across Brazil more broadly, other forces might include *amor* (love) (Mayblin 2012); *força* (strength/power) (Ansell, Forthcoming); *graça* (grace) and *bença* (blessing) (Ansell 2017). While each of these words relates to something quite specific in abstraction, they all refer to largely invisible divine energies that precede human intention. That is, all exist as vital forces before they take form and in this sense work locally very much like the salient key concepts of social theory, performing deep explanatory work of diagnosis but also providing the means through which to act on the world. For a discussion of anthropological investigations of vitality, see Singh (2018).

10. See also Birgit Meyer (2015), whose call for greater attention to "wow" effects focuses on how these might illuminate projects of political and religious world-making. Drawing on the work of R. R. Marett, Meyer argues for an anthropological approach to religion that "neither takes for granted the existence of a god or transcendental force (as in ontological approaches) nor invests in unmasking it as an illusion (as in critiques of religion as irrational), but instead undertakes a close study of the standardized methods that yield the fabrication of some kind of excess that points to a 'beyond' and yet is grounded in the here and now" (7).

11. See "magic," *Online Etymology Dictionary*, https://www.etymonline.com/search?q=MAGIC; last accessed November 1, 2022.

12. In using the term "religiosity," I follow George Simmel (1997), who speculated that religiosity was independent of, and infinitely detachable from, religion as a semantic category and diverse historical-material phenomenon. Simmel argued that while society (and the individual) could do without religion, it could not do without religiosity itself. His thoughts on religion follow a Hegelian style of thinking in which a distinction is posited between that which is shared, affective, and a priori and that which concretizes and condenses into an always particularized form. Religiosity, in this tradition, is an a priori existential or subjective dynamic: "a feeling of being, direction, and energy that cannot be specified more clearly" (24); "a way of the soul to live and experience the world . . . one of the deep forms of movement of the soul" (Simmel, cited in Laermans 2006, 482). Religiosity to religion is as thirst to moisture or hunger to fuel (see also Mayblin 2022b).

6. The Miraculous and the Mundane

1. The last recorded drought lasted from 1997 to 1999 and left large tracts of the surrounding land that were normally full of corn, manioc, and beans overrun by cactus plants. It is reported that even during this comparatively "mild" drought, infant mortality rates jumped by 10 percent, and there was a dramatic decline in school attendance across the region. Schools were shut down as children started being hired to collect water, 60 kilometers away. Young girls turned to prostitution as drought-stricken families resorted to desperate measures, and out of 1,552 municipalities in the drought polygon, 758 suffered serious problems, 336 were declared to be in "official states of emergency," and 442 were labeled in "critical condition" (Arons 2004).

2. See, for example, Jesus's words to the Samaritan woman at the well: "Everyone who drinks of this water will be thirsty again, but those who drink of the water that I will give them will never be thirsty. The water that I will give will become in them a spring of water gushing up to eternal life" (John 4:4–26). Water is a recurring motif in the Gospel of John, where it is said to symbolize the Holy Spirit and to point continually back to God, thus rendering him present (see Jones 1997).

3. According to Albuquerque (1999), a drought industry started to emerge in Northeast Brazil at the end of the nineteenth century with the first-ever government-sponsored drought prevention project. These early drought intervention programs were deeply entwined with the "invention of the Northeast" as a distinctive socio-geographic region because they produced an incentive for regional interests across the North to unify in political pursuit of drought-related federal resources.

4. See Mayblin (2013) for a more detailed discussion of a Catholic-inflected "fluidic economy" in which water, in both its physical and spiritual sense, comes to be constituted as co-extensive with a range of human bodily fluids that must be spent and replenished through never-ending cycles of sacrifice and reciprocity.

5. Webb Keane explains bundling as a kind of "co-presence" between semiotic meanings and material qualities and therefore as a "condition of possibility" embedded in the perhaps obvious but frequently overlooked fact that "qualisigns must be embodied in something in particular" (Keane 2003, 414). Bundling produces the "biography" of things, "as qualisigns bundled together in any object will shift in their relative value, utility and relevance across contexts" (414).

6. For summaries on the prosperity gospel, see Coleman (2011, 2016) and Heuser (2015).

7. As Bialecki (2010; 2017; 2020) and Daswani (2020) have argued, Christianity does not necessarily represent a field in which discrete models of time map onto discrete denominations but one in which multiple models may be concurrently possible. For example, the Ghanaian Pentecostals of Girish Daswani's study place selective emphasis on distinct periods in their lives, sometimes "sacrifice[ing] the present in hopes of attaining some miraculously redeemed future," and other times "work[ing] to bring both the past and the future into a present pervaded by miraculous energy" (Daswani 2020, 68).

8. As with the concepts of perfect kinship, desire, and plenitude encountered in Chapters One to Five, the cosmo-economic principle at work here draws in different ways on a mixture of theologies and ideologies that have been historically prominent across the region, including strong forms of Catholic mystical messianism, rational forms of Marxist liberation theology, and Catholic Social Teaching, as well as the Christian socialism of the peasant leagues (Forman 1975) and the left-wing liberalism of the Brazilian Partido dos Trabalhadores.

9. For Marshall Sahlins (1996), this sense of "doleful abyss" lurks everywhere and has informed all sorts of Western theory, from the model of the relationship between self and nature to social theories that suppose the inevitability of power struggle and miscommunication in human interaction (see also Mayblin 2012).

10. In local parlance *agua encantada* (enchanted water) denotes water that springs from a public source and that cannot, therefore, be owned by individuals or denied to others (Aaron Ansell, personal communication).

11. The speech I refer to is proclamatory in the sense that it announces the miraculous existence of the store cupboard and acclamatory (glory-filled) in its praise for the divine figures mediating that manifestation of plenitude. In such a context, the work of acclamation goes hand in hand with that of proclamation, generating what I would view as an incipient (glimpsed) alternative political order. I am inspired here by Ricoeur's discussion of the "hermeneutic of proclamation," which he describes as the "emergence of the word from the numinous" and as a particular type of poetic language that intensifies the manifestation of the sacred through the employment of paradox and hyperbole (Ricoeur 1995, 65); also by Agamben's discussion of acclamation and glory that, he argues, is still at the center of the political apparatuses of contemporary democracies (Agamben 2011).

12. Different theologies underpin tellings of miraculous economy across the region, and while all involve God, not all entertain the notion of the supernatural. The sense of plenitude created during the "cheap campaign" mirrors a post–Vatican II historical materialist reading of the gospels in which extraordinary abundance is produced by God *via human sharing* and is not, in that sense, miraculous in nature.

At the time of my research, a post-conciliar/liberation theology interpretation of the "miracle of the five loaves and two fish" was popular. In this interpretation of the gospel story, the five small barley loaves and two small fish Jesus uses to feed a multitude of 5,000 is not an act of magic but an accomplished feat of crowd psychology. When a single boy generously offers his meager resources to a crowd of 5,000 people, the crowd, which is made up of individuals hiding food about their bodies, is shamed into sharing what they have. In no time at all, food starts appearing from the folds of biblical rags and, before long, there is plenty for all. In this telling, abundance is created by a sudden and contagious desire to share rather than hoard. Like divine kinship, which is always a priori, such uncalculated sharing is said to be natural and instinctive to the human being, though buried under layers of greed and sin.

13. Padre Jorge later explained to me how Carlos had come to be on his payroll: "When I first started as mayor, I didn't understand why all the local blogs were being so negative about me and my administration. Then someone explained that you had to pay the journalists to be nice—who would imagine? So, Carlos and I came to an agreement."

14. In the comments thread to an article on a regional political news site, Padre Jorge's election defeat is explicitly put down to the reversal of the logic of cheap campaign: by the time the next election came round, it claimed, people were no longer prepared to bankroll his campaign; Roberto Almeida, "Os Padres na Política," http://robertoalmeidacsc.blogspot.com/2017/01/os-padres-na-politica.html.

Conclusion

1. See "All You Need to Know about Most Divisive Vote in Brazil's History," *Aljazeera*, https://www.aljazeera.com/news/2022/10/28/all-you-need-to-know-about-most-divisive-vote-in-brazils-history.

2. See "Voto e religião: Quem são os padres da Igreja Católica que declararam voto em Lula ou Bolsonaro," *O globo*, https://oglobo.globo.com/politica/eleicoes-2022/noticia/2022/10/voto-e-religiao-quem-sao-os-padres-da-igreja-catolica-que-declararam-voto-em-lula-ou-bolsonaro.ghtml?utm_campaign=ebook&GLBID=19ee13edcd5aa96f2cabd8257b3d6eab17142696845446b3470544d46364d4642654355565872 4e72732d4a623654432d71675072777a6b5251586f475547 56334f5838746c65676a66704248314942354359654594e4e315a583657536466 715356555856673d3d3a303a75646d75727377676a65687686e39796d36776b68.

3. See *Folha de S.Paulo*, https://www1.folha.uol.com.br/poder/2022/10/padres-sao-pressionados-a-tomar-posicao-eleitoral-no-interior-do-parana.shtml.

4. See "Padre é ameaçado de morte por apoiar Lula e faz, Boletim de Ocorrência," *pragmatismo*, https://www.pragmatismopolitico.com.br/2022/10/padre-ameacado-morte-apoiar-lula-boletim-ocorrencia.html.

5. Many anthropologists who seek to describe processes of slippage between realms resort to the term "porosity." I have specifically avoided this term because it lacks friction and does not adequately capture the heavy legalistic codes and prohibitions that structure the institution.

Epilogue

1. While it is true that Padre Jorge took a substantial break from his mayoral duties to perform a pilgrimage to the shrine of Padre Cícero—(see http://g1.globo.com/pe/caruaru-regiao/noticia/2015/10/padre-prefeito-anda-mais-de-400-km-para-pagar-promessa-e-espantar-crise.html, last accessed 8/12/22)—Vitor's opinions are not offered here as a definitive summary of why Padre Jorge failed to get re-elected, for there are several other versions of events.

Bibliography

Agamben, Giorgio. 1998. *Homo Sacer: Sovereign Power and Bare Life*. Stanford, Calif.: Stanford University Press.
———.1999. "On Potentiality." In *Potentialities: Collected Essays in Philosophy*, translated by Daniel Heller-Roazen, 177–84. Stanford, Calif.: Stanford University Press.
———. 2011. *The Kingdom and the Glory: For a Theological Genealogy of Economy and Government*. Translated by Lorenzo Chiesa and Matteo Mandarini. Stanford, Calif.: Stanford University Press.
Aidoo, LaMonte. 2018. *Slavery Unseen: Sex, Power, and Violence in Brazilian History*. Durham, N.C.: Duke University Press.
Albuquerque, Durval Muniz de Jr. 1999. *A Invenção do Nordeste e Outras Artes*. Recife: Fundação Joaquim Nabuco, Editora Massangana.
Almeida, Ronaldo de. 2020. "Evangélicos à Direita." *Horiz. antropol.*, Porto Alegre 26 (58): 419–36.
Ansell, Aaron. 2014. *Zero Hunger Political Culture and Antipoverty Policy in Northeast Brazil*. Chapel Hill: University of North Carolina Press.
———. 2015. "Democracy as the Negation of Discourse: Liberalism, Clientelism, and Agency in Brazil." *American Ethnologist* 42 (4): 688–702.
———. 2017. "Democracy Is a Blessing: Phatic Ritual and the Public Sphere in Northeast Brazil." *Linguistic Anthropology* 27 (1): 22–39.
———. Forthcoming. *The Elementary Forms of Corruption: Crisis and Accusation in Brazil, 2003–2022*. Chicago: Hau and University of Chicago Press.
Arons, Nicholas Gabriel. 2004. *Waiting for Rain: The Politics and Poetry of Drought in Northeast Brazil*. Tucson: University of Arizona Press.
Asad, Talal. (1991 [1982]). *Genealogies of Religion: Discipline and Reasons of Power in Christianity and Islam*. Baltimore: Johns Hopkins University Press.
———. 2003. *Formations of the Secular: Christianity, Islam, Modernity*. Stanford, Calif.: Stanford University Press.
Aquinas, Saint Thomas. *Summa Theologica*. Accessed at https://www.ccel.org/a/aquinas/summa/FS/FS062.html#FSQ62OUTP1. Last accessed November 3, 2022.

Babcock, Barbara, ed. 1978. *The Reversible World*. Ithaca, N.Y.: Cornell University Press.

Badone, Ellen. 1990. "Breton Folklore of Anti-Clericalism." In *Religious Orthodoxy and Popular Faith in European Society*, edited by Ellen Badone. Princeton, N.J.: Princeton University Press.

Bakhtin, Mikhail. 1984. *Rabelais and His World*. Translated by Helene Iswolsky. Bloomington: Indiana University Press.

Baldwin, John, and Eros De Souza. 2001. "Modelo de María and Machismo: The Social Construction of Gender in Brazil." *Revista Interamericana de Psicología* 35 (1): 9–29.

Ballano, Vivencio O. 2019. *Sociological Perspectives on Clerical Sexual Abuse in the Catholic Hierarchy: An Exploratory Structural Analysis of Social Disorganisation*. Singapore: Springer.

Bandak, Andreas. 2017. "Opulence and Simplicity: The Question of Tension in Syrian Catholicism." In *The Anthropology of Catholicism: A Reader*, edited by Kristin Norget, Valentina Napolitano, and Maya Mayblin, 155–69. Berkeley: University of California Press.

———. 2022. *Exemplary Life: Modelling Sainthood in Christian Syria*. Toronto: University of Toronto Press.

Banerjee, Mukulika. 2011. "Elections as Communitas." *Social Research* 78 (1): 75–98.

Bialecki, Jon. 2010. "Angels and Grass: Church, Revival, and the Neo-Pauline Turn." *South Atlantic Quarterly* 109 (4): 695–717.

———. 2012. "Virtual Christianity in an Age of Nominalist Anthropology." *Anthropological Theory* 12 (3): 295–319.

———. 2017. *A Diagram for Fire: Miracles and Variation in an American Charismatic Movement*. Oakland: University of California Press.

———. 2020. "Comment" on The Expansive Present: A New Model of Christian Time. *Current Anthropology* 61 (1): 57–76.

Biehl, João, and Peter Locke. 2010. "Deleuze and the Anthropology of Becoming." *Current Anthropology* 51 (3): 317–51.

Björkman, Lisa. 2014. "'You Can't Buy a Vote': Meanings of Money in a Mumbai Election." *American Ethnologist* 41 (4): 617–34.

Blanes, Ruy Llera. 2014. *A Prophetic Trajectory: Ideologies of Place, Time and Belonging in an Angolan Religious Movement*. New York and Oxford: Berghahn.

Bloch, Ernst. 1986. *The Principles of Hope: Studies in Contemporary German Thought*. Translated by Neville Plaice, Stephen Plaice, and Paul Knight. Cambridge, Mass.: MIT Press.

Bloch, Maurice, and Jonathan Parry. 1989. "Introduction." In *Money and the Morality of Exchange*, edited by Maurice Bloch and Jonathan Parry. Cambridge and New York: Cambridge University Press.

Boff, Leonardo. *Fé e Política: Suas implicações.* Accessed at http://www.cefep.org.br/fe-e-politica-suas-implicacoes-leonardo-boff/. Last accessed November 3, 2022.

Boletim do Movimento Padres Casados. 1981.

Braga, Antonio Mendes da Costa. 2008. *Padre Cicero: Sociologia de Um Padre, Antropologia de Um Santo.* Bauru: Edusc.

Brandalaise, Vitor. 2020. "Gelo no pênis, exorcismo e medo: Os padres gays silenciados pela Igreja no Brasil." BBC News. Brazil. March 9. https://www.bbc.com/portuguese/brasil-51554441. Last retrieved June 16, 2022.

Brandão, Carlos R. 1986. *Deuses do povo: Um estudo sobre religião popular.* 2nd ed. São Paulo: Brasiliense.

Brown, Wendy. 2013. "Introduction." In *Is Critique Secular? Blasphemy, Injury, and Free Speech,* by Tala Asad, Wendy Brown, Judith Butler, and Saba Mahmood. New York: Fordham University Press.

Bynum, Caroline Walker. 2011. *Christian Materiality: An Essay on Religion in Late Medieval Europe.* New York: Zone.

Campos, Roberta Bivar C. 2008. "Como Juazeiro do Norte se tornou a terra da Mãe de Deus: Penitência, *ethos* de misericórdia e identidade do lugar. *Religião & Sociedade* 28: 146–75.

———. 2013. *Quando a tristeza é bela: O sofrimento e a constituição do social e da verdade entre os Ave de Jesus (Juazeiro do Norte- CE).* Recife: Ed. Universitária da UFPE.

Cannell, Fennella. 2006. "Introduction." In *The Anthropology of Christianity,* edited by Fennella Cannell. Durham, N.C.: Duke University Press.

Casanova, José. 1994. *Public Religions in the Modern World.* Chicago and London: University of Chicago Press.

Catechism of the Catholic Church (CCC). https://www.vatican.va/archive/ENG0015/_INDEX.HTM.

Chaves, Christine de Alencar. 2000. *A marcha nacional dos sem-terra: Um estudo sobre a fabricação do social.* Rio de Janeiro: Relume Dumará.

———. 2003. *Festas da Política-uma Etnografia da Modernidade no Sertão.* Rio de Janeiro: Relume Dumara.

Ciarallo, Gilson. 2011. "O Tema da Liberdade Religiosa na Política Brasileira do Século XIX: Uma Via Para Compreensão da Secularização da esfera política." *Revista Sociologia e Política* 19 (38): 85–99.

CNBB. [National Conference of Brazilian Bishops]. 2001. *O que é Pastoral Social?* Cartilhas de pastoral social 1. São Paulo: Loyola.

Coakley, Sarah. 2013. *God, Sexuality and the Self: An Essay on "The Trinity."* Cambridge and New York: Cambridge University Press.

Code of Canon Law. https://www.vatican.va/archive/cod-iuris-canonici/cic_index_en.html.

Coleman, Simon. 2011. "Right Now!": Historiopraxy and the Embodiment of Charismatic Temporalities. *Ethnos* 76 (4): 426–47.
———. 2016. "The Prosperity Gospel: Debating Charisma, Controversy and Capitalism." In *Handbook of Global Contemporary Christianity: Movements, Institutions, and Allegiance*, edited by Stephen J. Hunt, 276–96. Leiden: Brill.
———. 2021. *Powers of Pilgrimage: Religion in a World of Movement*. New York: New York University Press.
Collins, John F. 2015. *Revolt of the Saints: Memory and Redemption in the Twilight of Brazilian Racial Democracy*. Durham, N.C.: Duke University Press.
Comaroff, Jean, and John L. Comaroff. 2000. "Millennial Capitalism: First Thoughts on a Second Coming." *Public Culture* 12 (2): 291–343.
Conrad, Robert Edgar. 1986. *World of Sorrow: The African Slave Trade to Brazil*. Baton Rouge: Louisiana State University Press.
Cozzens, D. (2000). *The Changing Face of the Priesthood*. Collegeville, Minn.: Liturgical Press.
Csordas, Thomas J. 1997. *Language, Charisma, and Creativity: The Ritual Life of a Religious Movement*. Berkeley: University of California Press.
Curran, Charles E. 2008. *Catholic Moral Theology in the United States: A History*. Washington, D.C.: Georgetown University Press
Dainese, Graziele. 2017. "Os casos e o gênero: Acontecimentos da moralidade camponesa." *Revista Estudos Feministas* 25 (2): 733–55.
Da Matta, Roberto. 1991a. *Carnivals, Rogues and Heroes: An Interpretation of the Brazilian Dilemma*. Notre Dame and London: University of Notre Dame Press.
———.1991b. *A casa e a rua*. Rio de Janeiro: Guanabara Koogan.
———. 1993. "Antropologica da saudade." In *Conta de mentiroso: Sete ensaios de antropologia brasileira*. Rio de Janeiro: Ed. Rocco.
———. 1994. *Conta de mentiroso: Sete ensaios de Antropologia brasileira*. Rio de Janeiro: Rocco.
———. 1997. *A Casa & a Rua: Espaço, Cidadania, Mulhere e Morte no Brasil*. 5th ed. Rio de Janeiro: Rocco.
Daswani, Girish. 2020. "Comment" on The Expansive Present: A New Model of Christian Time. *Current Anthropology* 61 (1): 57–76.
de Abreu, Maria José de. 2021. *The Charismatic Gymnasium: Breath, Media, and Religious Revivalism in Contemporary Brazil*. Durham, N.C.: Duke University Press.
de Freitas, Dom Geraldo Albano. 1987. *Igreja Brasileira: Abençoada Rebeldia*. São Paulo: CET-ICAB (Centro de Estudos Teológicos).
De Groot, C. F. G. 1996. *Brazilian Catholicism and the Ultramontane Reform, 1850–1930*. Amsterdam: CEDLA.
Deleuze, Gilles. 2006. *Dialogues II*. London: Continuum.

Deleuze, Gilles, and Felix Guattari. 2004 [1987]. *A Thousand Plateaus: Capitalism and Schizophrenia*. London: Continuum.
Denyer-Willis, Laurie. 2023. *Go with God: Political Exhaustion and Evangelical Possibility in Suburban Brazil*. Berkeley: University of California Press.
Dinerstein, Ana Cecilia. 2015. *The Politics of Autonomy in Latin America: The Art of Organising Hope*. Houndmills, Basingstoke: Palgrave Macmillan.
Dodson, Michael. 1997. "Pentecostals, Politics and Public Space in Latin America." In *Power, Politics, and Pentecostals in Latin America*, edited by Edward Cleary and Hannah W. Stewart-Gambino, 25–40. Boulder: Westview Press.
Drogus, Carol Ann. 1995. "The Rise and Decline of Liberation Theology: Churches, Faith, and Political Change in Latin America." *Comparative Politics* 27 (4): 465–77.
Dullo, Eduardo. 2013. "A produção de subjetividades democráticas e a formação do secular no Brasil a partir da Pedagogia de Paulo Freire." Doctoral thesis. Museo Nacional, da Universidade Federal do Rio de Janeiro.
———. 2016. "Testemunho: Cristão e Secular. Religião e Sociedade." *Rio de Janeiro* 36 (2): 85–106.
Dullo, Eduardo, and Rafael Quintanilha. 2015. "Sensibilidade Secular da Política Brasileira." *Debates do NER, Porto Alegre* 16 (27): 173–98.
Durkheim, Emile. 2008 [1912]. *The Elementary Forms of Religious Life*. Edited by Mark S. Cladis. Translated by Carol Cosman. Oxford and New York: Oxford University Press.
Elisha, Omri. 2008. "Faith beyond Belief: Evangelical Protestant Conceptions of Faith and the Resonance of Anti-Humanism." *Social Analysis*, 52 (1): 56–78.
Engelke, Matthew. 2007. *A Problem of Presence: Beyond Scripture in an African Church*. Berkeley: University of California Press.
Eriksen, Annelin. 2016. "Pentecostalism and Egalitarianism in Melanesia: A Reconsideration of the Pentecostal Gender Paradox." *Religion and Society: Advances in Research* 7: 37–50.
Flynn, Alex. 2021. "Once upon a Time in Utopia: Bergson, Temporality and the Re-Making of Social Movement Futures." *Social Anthropology* 29 (1): 156–73.
Frazee, Charles A. 1988. "The Origins of Clerical Celibacy in the Western Church." *Church History*. Supplement: Centennial Issue. 57: 108–26.
Freire, Paulo. 1997. *Pedagogy of Hope: Reliving Pedagogy of the Oppressed*. New York: Continuum.
Freston, Paul. 1994. *Evangélicos na política Brasileira: História, ambígua e desafio*. Curitiba: Encontrão.
Forman, Shephard. 1975. *The Brazilian Peasantry*. New York: Columbia University Press.

Foucault. Michel. 1998 [1976]. *The Will to Knowledge: The History of Sexuality.* Vol. 1. New York: Penguin.

Gamba, Estevao, Eduardo Cucolo, and Fábio Takahashi. 2019. "Prefeitura é maior empregador em 56% das cidades pequenas." Folha de S. Paulo. November 6.

Gay, Robert. 1998. "Rethinking Clientelism: Demands, Discourses and Practices in Contemporary Brazil." *European Review of Latin American and Caribbean Studies* 65: 7–24.

Geertz, Clifford. 1981. *Negra: The Theatre State in Nineteenth-Century Bali.* Princeton, N.J.: Princeton University Press.

Gilmore, David. 2017 [1987]. "My Encounters with Machismo in Spain." In *Gender in Cross-Cultural Perspective*, edited by Caroline Brettell and Carolyn F. Sargent. New York: Routledge.

Giraldi, Alice. 2010. "Textos da Inquisição revelam origens de sexualidade liberal dos brasileiros: Práticas sexuais condenadas pela Igreja Católica grassavam na Colônia. Núcleo da Unesp analisou documentos do Santo Ofício entre 1591 e 1769." *G1 Sciência e Saúde.* https://g1.globo.com/ciencia-e-saude/noticia/2010/05/textos-da-inquisicao-revelam-origens-de-sexualidade-liberal-dos-brasileiros.html. Last accessed September 5, 2022.

Giumbelli, Emerson. 2002. *O fim da religião: Dilemas da liberdade religiosa no Brasil e na França.* São Paulo: Attar.

———. 2013. "The Problem of Secularism and Religious Regulation: Anthropological Perspectives." *Religion and Society* 4: 93–108.

Goldman, Marcio. 2006. *Como funciona a democracia: Uma teoria etnográfica da política.* Rio de Janeiro: 7 Letras.

———. 2013. *How Democracy Works: An Ethnographic Theory of Politics.* Canon Pyon, Herefordshire: Sean Kingston.

Green, James, and Thomas E. Skidmore. 2021. *Brazil: Five Centuries of Change.* 3rd ed. New York and Oxford: Oxford University Press.

Gross, Daniel. 1973 "Factionalism and Local-level Politics in Rural Brazil." *Journal of Anthropological Research* 29 (2): 123–44.

Guattari, Felix, and Suely Rolnik. 2008. *Molecular Revolution in Brazil.* Cambridge, Mass.: MIT Press.

Gutmann, Matthew C. 1997. "Trafficking in Men: The Anthropology of Masculinity." *Annual Review of Anthroplogy* 26: 385–409.

———. 2007 [1996]. *The Meanings of Macho: Being a Man in Mexico City.* Berkeley: University California Press.

Guyer, Jane I. 2007. "Prophecy and the Near Future: Thoughts on Macroeconomic, Evangelical, and Punctuated Time." *American Ethnologist* 34 (3): 409–21.

Halemba, Agnieszka. 2015. *Negotiating Marian Apparitions: The Politics of Religion in Transcarpathian Ukraine.* Budapest: Central European University Press.

Hall, Anthony. 1981. "Irrigation in the Brazilian Northeast: Anti-Drought or Anti-Peasant?" In *The Logic of Poverty: The Case of the Brazilian Northeast*, edited by Simon Mitchell, 157–69. London: Routledge.

Handelman, Don. 1998. *Models and Mirrors: Towards an Anthropology of Public Events.* New York: Berghahn.

Hanley, A. G., and L. S. Lopes. 2017. "Municipal Plenty, Municipal Poverty, and Brazilian Economic Development, 1836–1850." *Latin American Research Review* 52 (3): 361–77.

Harrison, Kelby. 2014. "Learning to Speak." In *More than a Monologue: Sexual Diversity and the Catholic Church*, edited by J. Patrick Hornbeck II and Michael A. Norko. Inquiry, Thought, and Expression. New York: Fordham University Press.

Hatzikidi, Katerina, and Eduardo Dullo. 2021. "Introduction: Brazil's Conservative Turn." In *A Horizon of (Im) Possibilities: A Chronicle of Brazil's Conservative Turn*, edited by Eduardo Dullo and Katerina Hatzikidi. London: University of London Press.

Hauschild, Thomas. 2010. *Power and Magic in Italy.* New York: Berghahn.

Haynes, Naomi. 2013. "Standing in the Gap: Mediation in Ethnographic, Theoretical, and Methodological Perspective. *Swedish Missiological Themes* 101 (3–4): 251–66.

———. 2020. "The Expansive Present: A New Model of Christian Time." *Current Anthropology* 61 (1): 57–76.

Herzog, Hanna. 1987. "The Election Campaign as a Liminal Stage—Negotiations over Meanings." *Sociological Review* 35 (3): 559–74.

Heuser, Andreas, ed. 2015. "Religio-Scapes of Prosperity Gospel: an Introduction." In *Pastures of Plenty: Tracing Religio-Scapes of Prosperity Gospel in Africa and Beyond*, edited by Andreas Heuser. Frankfurt am Main: Peter Lang.

High, Holly. 2014. *Fields of Desire: Poverty and Policy in Laos.* Singapore: National University of Singapore Press.

Hoffman French, Jan. 2007. "A Tale of Two Priests and Two Struggles: Liberation Theology from Dictatorship to Democracy in the Brazilian Northeast." *Americas* 63 (3): 409–43.

———. 2009. *Legalizing Identities: Becoming Black or Indian in Brazil's Northeast.* Chapel Hill: University of North Carolina Press.

Horrocks, Roger. 1997. *An Introduction to the Study of Sexuality.* London: Palgrave Macmillan.

Hoornaert, Eduardo. 1993. "A questão do corpo nos documentos da primeira evangelização." In *Família, mulher, sexualidade e Igreja na história do Brasil*, edited by Maria Luiza Marcilio, 11–28. Loyola: São Paulo.

Hunt, Mary. E. 2002. "Duplicity Writ Large: A Response to the Silence of Sodom." *Theology and Sexuality* 9 (1): 9–17.

Irvine, Richard. 2010. "The Experience of Ethnographic Fieldwork in an English Benedictine Monastery: Or, Not Playing at Being a Monk." *Fieldwork in Religion* 5 (2): 221–35.

———. 2017. "The Everyday Life of Monks: English Benedictine Identity and the Performance of Proximity." In *Monasticism in Modern Times*, edited by Isabelle Jonveaux and Stefania Palmisano, 191–208. London: Routledge.

Jones, Larry Paul. 1997. *The Symbol of Water in the Gospel of John*. Sheffield: Sheffield Academic Press.

Jordan, Mark D. 2000. *The Silence of Sodom: Homosexuality in Modern Catholicism*. Chicago: University of Chicago Press.

———. 2014. "Talking about Homosexuality by the (Church) Rules." In *More than a Monologue: Sexual Diversity and the Catholic Church*, edited by J. Patrick Hornbeck II and Michael A. Norko. Inquiry, Thought and Expression. New York: Fordham University Press.

Kaell, Hillary. 2012. "Of Gifts and Grandchildren: American Holy Land Souvenirs." *Journal of Material Culture* 17 (2): 133–51.

Kaplan, Grant. 2014. "Celibacy as Political Resistance." *First Things*, 49–53.

Kappler, Stephan, Kristin A. Hancock, and Thomas Plante. 2013. "Roman Catholic Gay Priests: Internalized Homophobia, Sexual Identity and Psychological Well-Being." *Pastoral Psychology* 62: 805–26.

Kaczor, Christopher. 2010. *Proportionalism and the Natural Law Tradition*. Washington, D.C.: The Catholic University America, Press.

Keane, Webb. 2003. Semiotics and the Social Analysis of Material Things. *Language and Communication* 23: 409–25.

———. 2007. *Christian Moderns: Freedom and Fetish in the Mission Encounter*. Berkeley: University of California Press.

Keenan, Marie. 2011. *Child Sexual Abuse and the Catholic Church: Gender, Power, and Organizational Culture*. New York: Oxford University Press.

Kenny, M. L. 2002. "Drought, Clientelism, Fatalism and Fear in Northeast Brazil." *Ethics, Place & Environment* 5: 123–34.

Kojève, Alexandre. 1980. *Introduction to the Reading of Hegel: Lectures on the Phenomenology of Spirit*. Assembled by Raymond Queneau. Edited by Allan Bloom. Translated by James H. Nichols, Jr. Ithaca, N.Y.: Cornell University Press.

Lacan, Jacques. 2004. [1977]. *The Four Fundamental Concepts of Psycho-Analysis*. Edited by Jacques Alain Miller. London: Routledge.

Laermans, Rudi. 2006. "The Ambivalence of Religiosity and Religion: A Reading of Georg Simmel." *Social Compass* 53 (4): 479–89.

Latour, Bruno. 1993. *We Have Never Been Modern*. Translated by Catherine Porter. Cambridge, Mass.: Harvard University Press.

Lebner, Ashley B. 2012. "A Christian Politics of Friendship on a Brazilian Frontier." *Ethnos* 77 (4): 496–517.

———. 2021. "The Work of Impossibility in Brazil: Friendship, Kinship, Secularity." *Current Anthropology* 62 (4).

Lederman, Rena. 2001. "Big Man, Anthropology of." In *International Encyclopedia of the Social and Behavioural Sciences*, 2nd ed., 567–73. Amsterdam: Elsevier.

Lee, Christine. 2019. "The Ironic Legacy of an Opus Dei Bishop, Native Priests, and Andean Catholicism in Post-Conflict Apurímac, Peru." *Latin American Perspectives* 46 (5) :59–72.

———. 2021. "You Are a Priest Forever": The Dual Sacramentality and Humanity of Andean Roman Catholic Priests in Talavera, Peru." *Latin American Research Review* 56 (3): 642–54.

Lemenhe, Maria Auxiliadora. 2006. "Uma carreira política e vários modos de legitimaçao." In *Política no Brasil: Visões de antropologis*, edited by Moacir Palmeira and Cesar Barreira. Rio de Janeiro: Ediouro Publicações S. A.

Lester, Rebecca. 2005. *Jesus in our Wombs: Embodying Modernity in a Mexican Convent*. Berkeley: University of California Press.

Levine, Robert M. 1992. *Vale of Tears: Revisiting the Canudos Massacre in Northeastern Brazil, 1893–1897*. Berkeley: University of California Press.

Lévi-Strauss, Claude. 2012 [1955]. *Tristes Tropiques*. Introduction by Patrick Wilcken. Translated by John Weightman and Doreen Weightman. New York: Penguin.

Lindquist, Galina, and Simon Coleman. 2008. "Introduction: Against Belief?" *Social Analysis* 52 (1): 1–18.

Machado, Maria das Dores. 2003. "Existe um estilo evangélico de fazer política?" In *Religião e espaço Público*, edited by Patrícia Birman, 283–308. São Paulo: Attar.

Machado, Maria das D. C., and Cecilia L. Mariz. 1997. "Mulheres e práticas religiosas: Um estudo comparativo das CEBs, comunidades carismáticas e pentecostais." *Revista Brasileira de Ciências Sociais* 34: 71–87.

Mafra, Clara. 2002. *Na posse da palavra: Religião, conversão e liberdade pessoal em dois contextos nacionais*. Lisbon: Imprensa de Ciências.

Mahmood, Saba. 2005. *Politics of Piety: The Islamic Revival and the Feminist Subject*. Princeton, N.J.: Princeton University Press.

Malara, Diego Maria. 2018. "The Alimentary Forms of Religious Life: Technologies of the Other, Lenience, and Ethiopian Orthodox Fasting." *Social Analysis* 62 (3): 21–41.

Malone, Mary. 1993. "Unfinished Agenda: A Critical Look at the History of Celibacy." *Way Supplement* 77: 66–77.

Marder, Michael. 2012. *Groundless Existence: The Political Ontology of Carl Schmitt*. New York: Continuum.

Mariz, Cecília L., and Roberta B. C. Campos, 2011. "Pentecostalism and 'National Culture': A Dialogue between Brazilian Social Sciences and the Anthropology of Christianity." *Religion and Society: Advances in Research* 2: 106–21.

Marmont, Giovanni, and German E. Pereira. 2020. "Propositions for Inoperative Life." *Journal of Italian Philosophy* 3: 9–21.

Martel, Frédéric. 2019. *In the Closet of the Vatican: Power, Homosexuality, Hypocrisy*. Translated by Shaun Whiteside. London and New York: Bloomsbury.

Martin, Bernice. 1995. "New Mutations of the Protestant Ethic among Latin American Pentecostals." *Religion* 25 (2): 101–11.

———. 2003. "The Pentecostal Gender Paradox: A Cautionary Tale for the Sociology of Religion." In *The Blackwell Companion to Sociology of Religion*, edited by Richard K. Fenn. Oxford and Malden, Mass.: Blackwell.

Marques, Ana Claudia. 2002. *Intrigas e questões: Vingança de família e tramas sociais no sertão de Pernambuco*. Rio de Janeiro: Relume Dumará.

———. 2013. "Founders, Ancestors, and Enemies: Memory, Family, Time, and Space in the Pernambucan Sertão." *Journal of the Royal Anthropological Institute* N.S. 19: 716–33.

Massumi, Brian. 1993. "Everywhere You Want to Be: Introduction to Fear." In *The Everyday Politics of Fear*, edited by Brian Massumi. Minneapolis and London: University of Minnesota Press.

———. 1995. "The Autonomy of Affect." *Cultural Critique* 31, *The Politics of Systems and Environments*, Part II: 83–109.

Mauss, Marcel. 2002 [1950]. *The Gift: The Form and Reason for Exchange in Archaic Societies*. With Foreword by Mary Douglas. London and New York: Routledge.

Mayblin, Maya. 2010. *Gender, Catholicism and Morality in Brazil: Virtuous Husbands, Powerful Wives*. New York: Palgrave Macmillan.

———. 2012. "The Madness of Mothers: Agape Love and the Maternal Myth in Northeast Brazil." *American Anthropologist* 14 (2): 240–52.

———. 2013. "The Way Blood Flows: The Sacrificial Value of Intravenous Drip Use in Northeast Brazil." *Journal of the Royal Anthropological Institute* 19 (1): 42–56.

———. 2014. "People Like Us: Intimacy, Distance, and the Gender of Saints." *Current Anthropology* 55: 271–80.

———. 2017a. "The Lapsed and the Laity: Discipline and Lenience in the Study of Religion. *Journal of the Royal Anthropological Institute* 23 (3): 503–22.

———. 2017b. "Containment and Contagion: The Gender of Sin in Contemporary Catholicism. In *The Anthropology of Catholicism: A Reader*, edited by Kristin Norget, Valentina Napolitano, and Maya Mayblin, 139–54. Berkeley: University of California Press.

———. 2019a. "The Ultimate Return: Dissent, Apostolic Succession, and the Renewed Ministry of Roman Catholic Women Priests." *History and Anthropology* 30 (2): 133–48.

———. 2019b. "A Brilliant Jewel: Sex, Celibacy and the Roman Catholic Church." *Religion* 49 (4): 517–38.

———. 2022a. "On the Catholicity of Desire." *Political Theology Network*. https://politicaltheology.com/symposium/on-the-catholicity-of-desire/

———. 2022b. "Afterword" to Engaging Religion. *Religion and Society: Advances in Research* 13: 180–84.

Mayblin, Maya, Kristin Norget, and Valentina Napolitano. 2017. "Introduction." In *The Anthropology of Catholicism: A Reader*, edited by Kristin Norget, Valentina Napolitano, and Maya Mayblin. Berkeley: University of California Press.

Mazzarella, William. 2017. *The Mana of Mass Society*. Chicago: University of Chicago Press.

———. 2020. Further Thoughts on *The Mana of Mass Society*, by way of a response to Jo Richardson. *Global Discourse* 10 (1): 155–15.

McAllister, Carlota, and Valentina Napolitano. 2022. "Introduction: Incarnate Politics beyond the Cross and the Sword." *Social Analysis* 64 (4): 1–20

Medeiros, Melanie A. 2018. *Marriage, Divorce and Distress in Northeast Brazil: Black Women's Perspectives on Love, Respect and Kinship*. New Brunswick, N.J.: Rutgers University Press.

Menezes, Renata de Castro. 2005. "Uma visita ao catolicismo Brasileiro contmporâneo: A Bencão de Santo Antônio num convent Carioca." *Revista USP, São Paulo* 67: 24–35.

Menezes, Renata de Castro, and Lucas Bártolo. 2019. "Quando devoção e carnaval se encontram." *PROA: Revista de Antropologia e Arte* 9 (1): 96–121.

Meyer, Birgit. 2015. "How to Capture the 'Wow': R. R. Marett's Notion of Awe and the Study of Religion. *Journal of the Royal Anthropological Institute (N.S.)* 22: 7–26.

Miyazaki, Hirokazu. 2004. *The Method of Hope: Anthropology, Philosophy and Fijian Knowledge*. Stanford, Calif.: Stanford University Press.

Montero, Paula. 2006. "Religião, pluralismo e esfera pública no Brasil." *Novos Estudos* 74: 47–65.

Moore, Henriette. 2007. *The Subject of Anthropology: Gender, Symbolism and Psychoanalysis*. Cambridge: Polity Press.

Mosse, David. 2012. *The Saint in the Banyan Tree: Christianity and Caste Society in India*. Berkeley: University of California Press.

Mota, Camila Veras. 2020. "Brasil tem milhares de cidades que não arrecadam o suficiente nem para sustentar prefeitura e Câmara." BBC News, Brasil. November 9, 2020. https://www.bbc.com/portuguese/brasil-54669538. Last accessed June 1, 2022.

Motta, Roberto. 2011. "Theology of Liberation and Some Problems of Religious Change in Brazil. *International Review of Sociology* 21 (1): 231–42.

Muehlebach, Andrea. 2009. "*Complexio Oppositorum*: Notes on the Left in Neoliberal Italy." *Public Culture* 21 (3): 495–515.

———. 2013. "The Catholicization of Neoliberalism: On Love and Welfare in Lombardy, Italy." *American Anthropologist* 115 (3): 452–65.

Napolitano, Valentina. 2015. *Migrant Hearts and the Atlantic Return: Transnationalism and the Roman Catholic Church*. New York: Fordham University Press.

Needham, Rodney. 1972. *Belief, Language, and Experience*. Chicago: University of Chicago Press

Negrão, Lísias, Geraldo J. Paiva, Josildeth G. Consorte, and Claude Lepine. 2009. "Considerações iniciais." In *Novas tramas do sagrado*, edited by Lísias Negrão, 9–32. São Paulo: Edusp.

Neto, Lira. 2009. *Padre Cicero: Poder, Fé e Guerra no Sertão*. São Paulo and Rio de Janeiro: Companha das Letras.

Novaes, Regina. 1985. *Os Escolhidos de Deus*. Rio de Janeiro: MarcoZero/ISER.

Nugent, David. 2008. "Democracy Otherwise: Struggles over Popular Rule in the Northern Peruvian Andes." In *Democracy: Anthropological Approaches*, edited by Julia Paley, 21–62. Santa Fe, N.M.: School for Advanced Research Press.

Nunes, Serrano. 2019. "O município na história das constituições do Brasil de 1824 a 1988." *Cadernos Jurídicos, São Paulo* 20 (52): 153–68.

O'Boyle, Edward. 1998. *Personalist Economics: Moral Convictions, Economic Realities, and Social Action*. Dordrecht: Kluwer Academic.

Oliphante, Elayne. 2021. *The Privilege of Being Banal: Art, Secularism, and Catholicism in Paris*. Chicago: University of Chicago Press.

Oliveira, Pedro Ribeiro de. 1992. "Estruturas de Igreja e Conflitos Religiosos." In *Catolicismo: Modernidade e tradição; Grupo de Estudos do Catolicismo do ISER*, org. Pierre Sanchis, 41–66. São Paulo: Edições Loyola.

Orico, Osvaldo. 1948. *A Saudade Brasileira*. Rio de Janeiro: Editora S/A A Noite.

Orsi, Robert. 2017. "What Is Catholic about the Clergy Sex Abuse Crisis?" In *The Anthropology of Catholicism: A Reader*, edited by Kristin Norget,

Valentina Napolitano, and Maya Mayblin, 282–92. Berkeley: University of California Press.

———. 2019. "The Study of Religion on the Other Side of Disgust: Modern Catholic Sexuality Is a Dark and Troubled Landscape." *Harvard Divinity Bulletin*. https://bulletin.hds.harvard.edu/the-study-of-religion-on-the-other-side-of-disgust/. Last accessed September 5, 2022.

Orta, Andrew. 2004. *Catechizing Culture: Missionaries, Aymara, and the "New Evangelization."* New York: Columbia University Press.

Paley, Julia. 2008. *Democracy: Anthropological Approaches*. Santa Fe: School for Advanced Research Press.

Palmeira, Moacir. 1996. "Política, Facções e Voto." In *Antropologia, Voto e Representação Popular*, edited by Moacir Palmeira and Marcio Goldman, 41–56. Rio de Janeiro: Contra Capa.

Palmeira, Moacir, and Beatriz Heredia. 1995. *Os Comícios e a Política de Facções*. Anuário Antropológico 94. Rio de Janeiro: Tempo Brasileiro,

Pang, Eul Soo. 1974. "The Changing Roles of Priests in the Politics of Northeast Brazil, 1889–1964." *Americas* 30 (3): 341–72.

Parker, Richard. 1991. *Bodies, Pleasures, and Passions: Sexual Culture in Contemporary Brazil*. Boston: Beacon Press.

Paul VI. "Sacerdotalis Caelibatus." June 24, 1967. The Holy See. https://www.vatican.va/content/paul-vi/en/encyclicals/documents/hf_p-vi_enc_24061967_sacerdotalis.html.

Paula, Leandro de. 2020. "Um Rio de opinião subterrâneo: Contrapúblicos terrivelmente evangélicos." *Horizonte: Belo Horizonte* 18 (56): 570–99.

Peña, Elaine. 2011. *Performing Piety: Making Space Sacred with the Virgin of Guadalupe*. Berkeley: University of California Press.

Piliavsky, Anastasia. 2014. "Introduction." In *Patronage as Politics in South Asia*, edited by Anastasia Piliavsky, 1–39. Cambridge: Cambridge University Press.

Plante, Thomas G., ed. 2004. *Sin against the Innocents: Sexual Abuse by Priests and the Role of the Catholic Church*. Westport, Conn.: Greenwood.

———. 2020. "Clericalism Contributes to Religious, Spiritual, and Behavioral Struggles among Catholic Priests." *Religions* 11 (5): 217.

Pouillon, Jean. 1982. "Remarks on the Verb "To Believe."" In *Between Belief and Transgression: Structuralist Essays in Religion, History, and Myth*, edited by Michel Izard and Pierre Smith, 1–8. Chicago: University of Chicago Press.

Portella A. P. 2014. "Como morre uma mulher? Configurações da violência letal contra mulheres em Pernambuco." Thesis. Recife: Universidade Federal de Pernambuco.

Prado, Paulo. 1962 [1928]. *Retrato do Brasil—Ensaio sobre a tristeza brasileira*. 6th ed. Rio de Janeiro: José Olympio.

Rancière, Jacques. 2010. *Dissensus: On Politics and Aesthetics*. Edited and translated by Steven Corcoran. London: Continuum.

Rebhun, L. A. 2004. "Sexuality, Color, and Stigma among Northeast Brazilian Women." *Medical Anthropology Quarterly* 18 (2): 183–99.

Reinhardt, Bruno. 2015. "A Christian Plane of Immanence? Contrapuntal Reflections on Deleuze and Pentecostal Spirituality. *Hau: Journal of Ethographic Theory* 5 (1): 405–36.

———. 2017. "The Pedagogies of Preaching." *Journal of Religion in Africa* 47 (1): 72–107.

———. 2018. "Discipline (and Lenience) beyond the Self: Discipleship in a Pentecostal Charismatic Organisation." *Social Analysis* 62 (3): 42–66.

Renzetti, Clare. M., and Sandra Yocum, eds. 2013. *Clergy Sexual Abuse: Social Science Perspectives*. Boston: Northeastern University Press.

Ricci, Magda. 2001. *Assombraçoes de um padre regent: Diogo Antônio Feijó (1784–1843)*. Campinas: Editora da Unicamp.

Ricoeur, Paul. 1995. *Figuring the Sacred: Religion, Narrative, and Imagination*. Minneapolis: Fortress.

Robbins, Joel. 2007. "Continuity Thinking and the Problem of Christian Culture: Belief, Time, and the Anthropology of Christianity." *Current Anthropology* 48 (1): 5–38.

———. 2019. "On Knowing Faith: Theology, Everyday Religion, and Anthropological Theory. *Religion and Society: Advances in Research* 10: 14–29.

Rodrigues, Herbert. 2017. *A Pedofilia e suas Narrativas: Uma Genealogia do Processo de Criminalização da Pedofilia no Brasil*. Rio de Janeiro: Editora Multifoco.

Ruel, Malcolm. 1997. *Belief, Ritual, and the Securing of Life: Reflexive Essays on a Bantu Religion*. Leiden: E. J. Brill.

Sacramento, Octávio, and Fernando Ribeiro. 2013. "Trópicos sensuais: A construção do Brasil como geografia desejada." *Bagoas* 10: 215–32.

Safatle, Vladimir. 2016. *O circuito dos afetos: Corpos políticos, desamparo e o fim do indivíduo*. Belo Horizonte: Autêntica Editora.

Sahlins, Marshall. 1996. "The Sadness of Sweetness: The Native Anthropology of Western Cosmology." *Current Anthropology* 37 (3): 395–415.

———. 2008. "The Stranger King." *Indonesia and the Malay World* 36 (105) (July): 177–99.

Scheper-Hughes, Nancy. 1992. *Death without Weeping: The Violence of Everyday Life in Brazil*. Berkeley: University of California Press.

Scherz, China. 2013. "Let Us Make God Our Banker: Ethics, Temporality, and Agency in a Ugandan Charity Home." *American Ethnologist* 40 (4): 624–636.

———. 2018. "Enduring the Awkward Embrace: Personhood and Ethical Work in a Ugandan Convent." *American Anthropologist* 120 (1): 102–12.

Schmitt, Carl. 1996. *Roman Catholicism and Political Form*. Translated and annotated by G. L. Ulmen. Westport, Conn., and London: Greenwood Press.

———. 2005. *Political Theology: Four Chapters on the Concept of Sovereignty*. Chicago: University of Chicago Press.

Schüssler Fiorenza, E. 1988. *In Memory of Her: A Feminist Theological Reconstruction of Christian Origins*. New York: Crossroad.

Scliar, Moacyr. 2003. *Saturno nos trópicos: A melancolia europeia chega ao Brasil*. São Paulo: Companhia das Letras.

Serbin, Kenneth. 2006. *Needs of the Heart: A Social and Cultural History of Brazil's Clergy and Seminaries*. Notre Dame, Ind.: University of Notre Dame Press.

Seremetakis, Nadia C. 1991. *The Last Word: Women, Death, and Divination in Inner Mani*. Chicago: Chicago University Press.

Santirocchi, Ítalo Domingo. 2011. "Afastemos o Padre da Política! A despolitização do clero brasileiro durante o Segundo Império." *MNEME— Revista de Humanidades* 12 (29): 187–207.

Shapiro, Matan. 2016. "Paradoxes of Intimacy: Play and the Ethics of Invisibility in North-east Brazil." *Journal of Latin American Studies* 48 (4): 797–821.

———. 2021. "Brajisalem: Biblical Cosmology, Power Dynamics and the Brazilian Political Imagination." *Ethnos* 86 (5): 832–52.

Singh, Bhrigupati. 2015. *Poverty and the Quest for Life: Spiritual and Material Striving in Rural India*. Chicago: University of Chicago Press.

———. 2018. "Anthropological Investigations of Vitality." *HAU: Journal of Ethnographic Theory* 8 (3): 550–56.

Silva, Ana Rosa Cloclet da. 2012. "Padres políticos e suas redes de solidariedade: Uma análise da atuação sacerdotal no sertão de Minas Gerais (1822 e 1831)." *Revista Brasileira de História* 32 (63): 119–42.

Silva, Claudia Neves da. 2006. "Igreja católica, assistência social e caridade: Aproximações e divergências." *Sociologia, Porto Alegre* 8 (15): 326–51.

Silva, Edlene Olivera. 2008. "Entre a Batina e a aliança: Das mulheres de Padres ao Movimento de Padres Casados." Tese apresentada como requisite final para a obtençao do título do doutor junto ao Programa de Pós-Graduação do departamento de História da Universidade de Brasília.

Silva, Isabel Correa da. 2014. "A Rosa brasileira que incendiou a questão religiosa em Portugal: O Caso Calmon (1899–1901)." *Revista Tempo* 20.

Silva, Maria da Conceicao, and Wellington Moreira Coelho. 2013. "O sacerdócio goiano celibato e historiografia." *Varia Historia*, Belo Horizonte 29 (50): 553–S69.

Simmel, Georg. 1997. *Essays on Religion*. Edited and translated by Horst Jurgen Helle, in collaboration with Ludwig Nieder. Foreword by Phillip. E. Hammond. New Haven, Conn.: Yale University Press.

Sipe, A. W. Richard. 1990. *A Secret World: Sexuality and the Search for Celibacy.* New York: Routledge.

Skidmore, Thomas. 1992. *Black into White: Race and Nationality in Brazilian Thought.* Durham, N.C.: Duke University Press.

Sloterdijk, Peter. 1987. *Critique of Critical Reason.* Minneapolis: University of Minnesota Press.

Spencer, Jonathan. 2007. *Anthropology, Politics, and the State. Democracy and Violence in South Asia.* Cambridge: University of Cambridge Press.

Stoler, Ann Laura. 1995. *Race and the Education of Desire: Foucault's History of Sexuality and the Colonial Order of Things.* Durham, N.C.: Duke University Press.

Strathern, Marilyn. 1992. "Parts and Wholes: Refiguring Relationships in a Post-Plural World." In *Conceptualising Society*, edited by Adam Kuper. London: Routledge.

Steil, Carlos Alberto, and Rodrigo Toniol. 2013. "O Catolicismo e a igreja Católica no Brasil à luz dos dados sobre religião no censo de 2010." *Debates do NER, Porto Alegre* 14 (24): 223–43.

Sullivan, LaShandra. 2017. "Black Invisibility on a Brazilian 'Frontier': Land and Identity in Mato Grosso do Sul, Brazil." *African and Black Diaspora* 10 (2): 131–42.

Taussig, Michael. 1999. *Defacement: Public Secrecy and the Labor of the Negative.* Stanford, Calif.: Stanford University Press.

Taylor, Charles. 2007. *A Secular Age.* Cambridge, Mass.: Harvard University Press.

Taylor, Lawrence. 1990. "Stories of Power, Powerful Stories: The Drunken Priest in Donegal." In *Religious Orthodoxy and Popular Faith in European Society*, edited by Ellen Badone. Princeton, N.J.: Princeton University Press.

Thurian, Max. 1993. "The Theological Basis for Priestly Celibacy." The Holy See. https://www.vatican.va/roman_curia/congregations/cclergy/documents/rc_con_cclergy_doc_01011993_theol_en.html.

Tomlinson, Matt. 2020. *God Is Samoan: Dialogues between Culture and Theology in the Pacific.* Honolulu: University of Hawaii Press.

Torjesen, K. J. 1995. *When Women Were Priests: Women's Leadership in the Early Church and the Scandal of Their Subordination in the Rise of Christianity.* San Francisco: HarperSanFrancisco.

Turner, Neil. 2018. "Brazil's Dichotomous Treatment of Corruption." Parts 1–3. *Perspectives in Anthropology.* Online Magazine, available at https://perspectivesinanthropology.com/2018/01/02/brazils-dichotomous-treatment-of-corruption-pt-1/.

Velho. Otávio. 1991. "The Peasant and the Beast." *European Review of Latin American and Caribbean Studies* 51: 7–25.

———. 1995. *Besta-Fera: Recriacão do mundo; Ensaios críticos de antropologia*. Rio de Janeiro: Relume Dumar.

Villela, Jorge Mattar. 2004. *O povo em armas: Violência e política no sertão de Pernambuco*. Rio de Janeiro: Relume Dumará.

———. 2005. "O dinheiro e suas diversas faces nas eleições municipais em Pernambuco. *Mana* 11 (1). Online version.

———. 2012. "Confiança, Autonomia e Dependência na Política Eleitoral no Sertão de Pernambuco." In *Cultura, Percepção e Ambiente—Diálogos com Tim Ingold*, edited by Carlos Alberto Steil and Isabel Cristina de Moura Carvalho, 211–27. São Paulo: Terceiro Nome.

Villela, Jorge Mattar, and Ana Claudia Marques. 2006. "Municipal Elections: Favour, Vote and Credit in the Pernambucan Sertao of Brazil." *Latin Americanist* (Spring): 25–63.

Weber, Max. (2013 [1922]). *Economy and Society*. Edited by Guenther Roth and Claus Wittich. Berkeley: University of California Press.

Werbner, Richard. 2011. *Holy Hustlers, Schism, and Prophecy: Apostolic Reformation in Botswana*. Berkeley: University of California Press.

Walker, Gillian M. S. W. 2004. "Fragments from a Journal: Reflections on Celibacy and the Role of Women in the Church." *Studies in Gender and Sexuality* 5 (1): 81–101.

Warner, Michael. 2002. *Publics and Counterpublics*. Durham, N.C.: Duke University Press.

White, Thomas Joseph, OP. 2020. "On the Sanctification of the Catholic Priesthood." *Nova et Vetera*. English ed. 18 (1): 1–13.

Woodhead, Linda. "Religion and Gender." In *Religions in the Modern World: Traditions and Transformations*, edited by Linda Woodhead, Christopher Partridge, and Hiroko Kawanami. London and New York: Taylor and Francis.

Žižek, Slavoj. 2005. "From Revolutionary to Catastrophic Utopia." In *Thinking Utopia: Steps into Other Worlds*, edited by Jörn Rüsen, Michael Fehr, and Thomas W. Rieger, 247–62. New York: Berghahn.

Index

abundance, as religio-political discourse, 154–156, 159–162, 164, 213–214n12
Agamben, Giorgio, 57, 179–180, 202n4, 213n11
agape, 54, 202
agreste, 12, 28
alter Christus, 16, 69, 195n7, 198n21
Ansell, Aaron, 14, 39–40, 45, 48, 104, 105, 140–144, 197n16, 201n4, 209n5, 211n8n9
anti-clericalism, 77, 197n16, 204n15
assistencialismo, 14, 47–51; 201n3.
 See also patron clientelism
Augustine, Saint, 23, 57
axé, 210n5

Base Ecclesial Community, 155, 194n6
Batista, Padre Cicero Romão, 11, 156, 162, 176, 187; and Doctor Feitosa, 155, 196n9
belief, 78, 127–128, 198n21; in anthropological theory, 209–210n2
bishop, 1–3, 5, 9–10, 54, 56, 59, 60–63, 88, 99–101, 115–117, 121, 156, 189, 193–194n3, 198n19; in story of Padre Jorge, 99, 101. See also Câmara, Dom Hèlder; Duarte Costa, Dom Carlos; Feijó, Padre
boundaries as "set in passage," 19–20, 29, 101–102, 107, 123, 180–183.
 See also Massumi, Brian

Canudos, 5
câmara, 13. See also Chamber of Councillors
Câmara, Dom Hélder, 156, 162
carnival, 133–134, 210n6
Catholic Church: and charitable works, 194–195n6; as elastic institution, 19–20; and ideas about kinship, 53–55; as "imponderable" construct, 185–186; as "passionate machine," 79; as "political form," 79 (see also *complexio oppositorum*); reform of, 59; relation to independence, 8; and relation to Portuguese Crown, 8; structural position of women within, 57, 77–78
Catholicism: as bureaucratic system, 97–98; demographic in Brazil, 195n7; as "gymnastic," 199n24; as "libidinous" cartography, 91
Catholic Social Teaching, 213n8. See also pastoral commissions
Chamber of Councillors, 13, 42,47, 158
charisma, religious, 17, 175; and the Catholic charismatic movement, 195n7; and charismatic leaders, 52, 69, 126, 156
chastity, clerical vow of, 2, 17. See also celibacy
celibacy: clerical, 17–18; in history of Brazilian priesthood, 58–64; and ideal of social unity, 73–74; and Romanization, 203n7; as "sign" of end times, 56; theology of, 55–57, 202n3; as "virile celibacy," 99–124, 184; and women's position in Church, 57
clericalism, 204n15. See also anti-clericalism
clerical sexual abuse, 23, 62, 98, 204n12, 204n16, 206n11, 207n15
Coleman, Simon, 180, 208n1
colonial era, 8, 12; Catholicism during, 58–59
complexio oppositorum, 18–19, 199n24.
 See also Schmitt, Carl

confession, sacrament of, 91, 92, 95
Constituent Assembly (of 1823), 194n4
corruption, 4, 14, 28, 30, 35, 41; and anti-corruption, 41, 50, 55, 141, 151, 201n2. See also *politicagem*
Council of Trent, 59
cynical reason, 145. See also Sloterdijk, Peter

Da Matta, Roberto, 14, 104, 134
Deleuze, Gilles, 22, 24, 97, 184, 200n27, 207–208n17; in anthropology of Christianity, 200n27; and Guattari, 22, 29
democracy, 6, 18, 39–41, 48, 196–197n14; as "anarchic element," 137–138, 178; structural relation of Church towards, 181–182; as theological problem, 55, 66–67, 122, 127. See also race
desire, 20–24; in anthropology of Christianity, 22–24; in Christian theology, 80; in continental philosophy, 21–23, 208n17; psychoanalytical theories of, 20–22; as utopia, 97
dictatorship, 5, 7,8, 63, 196–197n14. See also Vargas era
"double life," 113, 123, 206n8. See also doubleness; secrecy
doubleness, 18, 88, 113, 184, 206n11
drought, 5, 11, 12, 61 150–152, 155, 163, 212n1, 212n3
Duarte Costa, Dom Carlos, 60

economy, 30, 184, 201n5; in Catholic theology of celibacy, 41, 56–57; and Christian eschatology, 154–155; as divine abundance, 175; as "miraculous" versus "mundane" in nature, 151–164, 202n1, 212n4, 213n12; and municipal budgets, 169; in relation to "being versus praxis," 179–180; as "sexual economy," 96
election campaigns: and Brazilian legal code, 142; cost of, 157–159, 214n14; at national level, 194n4, 211n8; and relation to gift-economy, 161–162
elections, 1–6, 9, 13, 23, 24, 29, 33, 49, 55, 65, 176, 177, 178; as aesthetic and ritual forms, 125–150; in anthropological discussion, 138, 201n1; mayor-priests' elections, 99–122, 174, 187, 190, 194n4, 214n14; relation to hope, 138 (*see also* hope). See also election campaigns
época da política, 125–127, 130, 133, 138–140, 146, 164, 175
eros, 23, 182
ethics, of research, 26–27
ethnography, and data collection, 24–26. See also methods
Eucharist, 10–11, 16, 58
evangelicals, 10, 95, 128, 130, 131; in contemporary Brazilian politics, 177–178, 196n8. See also Protestantism
exemplarity, 16, 69

faith, 20, 24, 125–149; in anthropological literature, 130–131; as Catholic theological virtue, 130; and divine agency, 130; as embodied force, 146; ontology of, 127–129; as passion, 139–140; and politics, 131; and relation to "thirst," 152; as "species of power," 145. See also *fé*
father, 6, 53,54, 59, 68, 90, 94, 129, 208n3; as form of address for priests, 72
fatherhood: as political role, 14, 84, 104, 106, 113, 120, 122, 161, 168, 181,182, 195n7; as spiritual, 10, 64, 70–73, 131, 198n20
fé, 20, 24, 80–81, 125–149. See also faith
fieldwork. See ethnography
friendship, 14, 41, 47, 50, 93, 112, 197n16, 201n3; between ethnographer and interlocutors, 82, 136, 189, 191, 205–206n6; between women and priests, 91
Frei Damião, 150–151
folk religion, 15, 127, 141
food, 53, 92; in gift-exchange, 32, 49, 156, 159–162, 171, 213–214n12
Foucault, Michel, 22, 57, 58, 88; 203n5
Freud, Sigmund, 21

gender, 10, 20, 23, 26, 29, 54, 57, 69, 73, 104, 105, 112, 123, 124, 178, 181, 182, 204–205n1, 207n15, 209n6; "binary model" of, 205n4; gender-based-violence, 81–83; and religious

"paradox," 77–79, 86, 89, 93, 96.
  See also women
gift: celibacy as, 17–18; in Christian ritual and practice, 153, 208–209n3; of God to humanity, 54, 128; as sacerdotal act, 173
gift-exchange, 30, 38–39; Marcel Mauss's theory of, 38–39; moral dimension of, 45; and patronage, 39; in politics and electoral cycles, 46, 50–52, 105, 158, 160–162, 175, 188; with priests, 79, 103
godparenthood, 72, 204n17
Goldman, Marcio, 40

hierarchy, 40, 54, 125, 185, 202n2
homosexuality: in catechism of the Catholic Church, 209n6; in Catholic Church, 206n8nn9–11; of priesthood, 86–90, 96–97, 103, 105, 113–114, 183
homosociality, of Church institution, 20, 88, 206n8
hope, 76, 127, 129, 138, 145, 147, 180; anthropological literature on, 201n3

Igreja Católica Apostólica Brasileira, 60. *See also* Duarte Costa, Dom Carlos
independence, Brazilian, 8, 59
Indigenous, 12, 194n5, 196n13
inequality, 39, 126, 151; in Northeastern society, 12, 13; and "perfect kinship" as solution to, 54; and in social history, 151. *See also* hierarchy
inoperativity, 57, 73, 104, 123, 182, 202n4. *See also* Agamben, Giorgio

kinship, 5, 10, 16, 28, 37, 93, 112, 202n2, 208–209n3; in Catholic theology, 53–55; as "perfect," 53–55, 68, 69, 71, 73, 156, 181–182, 213n8, 213–14n12

Lacan, Jacques, 20–21, 22, 80
lack: in discourse of priests, 92, 97, 98; in local discourse, 80–81, 152; in philosophy of desire, 20–24, 179, 207–208n17; as *saudades*, 200n28
laicisation, 100
leadership, in anthropology of Christianity, 197n17

Lebner, Ashley, 50, 193n2, 202n2
liberation theology, 5, 9, 26, 32, 33, 43, 60, 61, 62, 63, 155, 156; demise of, 62–64, 207n14, 210n3, 213n8, 213–14n12
lived religion, 15, 199n25
Lula, Inácio da Silva, 48, 177, 178

machismo, 81–83, 95, 104–105, 119, 183; and homophobia, 209n6; literature on, 205n5
mana, 147
marriage, 53–54, 57, 58, 61, 62, 64, 71, 95, 114, 116
Massumi, Brian, 19–20, 101, 102
mayor-priest: as cohort for study, 25; electoral campaigns, 107–121; spatio-temporal strategies in office, 165. *See also* secular passage
mayors, 11–15; attending to citizens, 168–17; and masculinity, 13–14; and moral virtue, 14; and use of publicity, 167
messianic movements, 213n8. *See also* millenarian movements
methods, for data collection, 24–26
military dictatorship. *See* dictatorship
millenarian movements, 5
miracles, 11, 24, 69, 155, 157, 163, 176, 180, 187, 196n9
misogyny, in Catholic Church, 207n16
mothers, 70, 76, 78, 90, 171; in Catholic commentary and theology, 54, 131, 194n6, 207n16; of priests, 100–107, 120, 209n7
Movimento dos Padres Casados do Brasil, 60–61, 203n9
municipal counsellors, 46–49; history of in Brazil, 196n14; legal definition of in Brazil, 196n11. See also *vereador*

Napolitano, Valentina, 30, 97, 182
Northeast: history of, 12; "Biblical culture," 49; cultural identity, 209n6; social stereotype, 119

ontological mistrust, 49–52. *See also* Lebner, Ashley; Northeast; suffering
ordination, and notion of charismatic "seal," 16, 69

Padre Feijó, 59–60
passage. *See* pilgrimage; secular passage
passion, 182; definition in catechism of the Catholic Church, 140; The Passion, 151
"passionate machine," 79, 97, 182
pastoral commissions, 8, 194n6. *See also* Catholic Church: and charitable work
paternalism, Catholic forms of, 202n1
patriarchy, 20, 78, 79; in institutions of local church and government, 124, 202n7; and positionality of researcher, 27; in priesthood, 96
patronage, 14; anthropological discussions of, 41; emic critique of, 41; and "poetics of manhood," 104
patron clientelism, 14, 104, 170–171. See also *assistencialismo*; patronage; *politicagem*
proportionalism, 203n10
Pentecost, 140, 210n7
Pentecostalism, 108, 153–154, 200n27, 207–208n17, 213n7; as "gender paradox," 77–78, 205n2
Pernambuco, 31, 150, 167; history of, 12–13
pilgrimage, 11, 187, 208 n1; as metaphor to think with, 180. *See also* Coleman, Simon
politicagem, 35, 41, 44–45, 55
politicians, and general mistrust of, 49. *See also* mayor-priests; mayors; municipal counsellors
politics: and factionalism, 35, 135–136, 143; as festivity, 133; as an "impossibility," 41; as masculine pursuit, 104; and political parties, 13; as "political time," 125–126; as publicity, 169; and religion in Brazilian media, 178; as seduction, 105. *See also* *época da política*
Pope Benedict XVI, 63
Pope John Paul II, 8, 63
Pope Paul VI, 17, 56
positionality, of fieldworker, 26–27
poverty, 12–14, 32, 36, 51, 56, 61, 89, 145, 152, 159, 177, 194–195n6, 207n13
priesthood, 15–20; and charisma, 17; gender and sexuality, 17; homophobic/homoerotic duality of, 88–89; homosexuality in, 86–89, 113, 183, 206n8, 206n10; as patriarchal institution, 86; as queer institution, 81, 96; and transgression, 19. *For sexual abuse see* clerical sexual abuse
priests, 15–20; in anthropological literature, 15, 197n17; and canon law on political involvement, 9; and Catholic social action, 8; as exemplars, 69; as "listeners," 92–93; and literacy, 8; as living symbols, 68–70; married priests, 199n; parish duties, 76, 85; as public figures, 67; and relation to authoritative center, 180; religious versus secular, 193n1; role in *abertura*, 8; role in Independence, 82; as "sensitive," 89; and sexual scandal, 110–116. *For pedophile priests see* clerical sexual abuse
prosperity gospel, 153–154, 212n6
Protestantism, and nature of conversion to in Brazil, 195n7. *See also* evangelicals; Pentecostalism
psychoanalysis, clergy embrace of, 207n12

quilombo, in settlement of interior, 12

race: in culture of Northeast, 196n13; ideology of, 12; intersection with sexuality, 203n6; and mayor-priest identities, 201n29
Rancière, Jacques, 137–138
republic, 7, 11, 59, 197; and role of priests in establishing, 193–194n3
religiosity, Simmel's concept of, 211n12
religious authority: clerical, 16, 18; ecclesial, 9; Weberian "types" of, 17, 30
Ricoeur, and "hermeneutic of proclamation," 213n11
ritual: in anthropological theory, 146; and role in building social intimacy, 71. *See also* sacraments
Romanization, 203n7

Sacerdotalis Caelibatus, 18, 56
sacraments, 16, 17, 19, 69, 70, 71, 74, 76, 81, 91–92, 103, 116, 180, 182, 198n19, 204n17

sacrifice, 18, 56, 61, 153, 159, 173, 190, 212n4, 213n7
saints, 69, 76, 160, 164, 186, 195n7, 204n14
saudades, 81, 200n28
Schmitt, Carl, 18–19, 123, 199n25
secrecy, "culture of," 27; and sex-lives of priests, 61, 88–89
secularism, 7, 193n2; in Brazilian public discourse, 177–178; Catholic versus evangelical, 196n8; local concept of, 9; and relation with Catholicism, 7; secular as religious concept, 198n22
secular passage, 99–124, 180–181; gendered construction of, 102, 183–184; as journey of sexual outing, 106
sex: and sexual revolution, 62; and "libidinous cartography" of Church, 96–97. For sexual abuse see clerical sexual abuse
Sipe, Richard, 56
slavery, 12, 13, 37–38, 58, 59, 196–197n14, 200n28
Sloterdijk, Peter, 145
sonic dominance, 137
suffering: in notion of "lack," 81; and ontological mistrust, 50–52; as political trope, 46–47

Taylor, Charles, 181, 193 n2
temporality: in anthropology of Christianity, 138–139, 213n7; in election ritual, 125–150

ultramontanism, 11, 60, 193–194n3
unity, Catholic Church as, 68, 104

Vargas era, 197n14. *See also* dictatorship
Vatican II, 60, 63, 64, 213n11
vitalism, 22; ethnographic concepts of, 201n9. *See also* Deleuze, Gilles; *fé*
vereadors, 46–49. *See also* municipal counsellors
vote-buying, 14, 39, 46, 108, 117, 157–159, 201n1. *See also* corruption

water: and "fluidic economy" in Northeast, 151–152, 171–172, 212n4; in Gospels, 212n2; and miracles, 155–157, 213n10
Weber, Max, 17
women: in history of Church, 57; in local politics, 104; as mayor-priest supporters, 112; as "shadow partners," in mayor-priest campaigns, 120–124; relationship to priests, 183; and "agency" in patriarchal religions, 205n1. *See also* gender

MAYA MAYBLIN is Senior Lecturer in Social Anthropology at the University of Edinburgh. Her work explores religion, theology, politics, and gender in Brazil and beyond. She is the author of *Gender, Morality and Catholicism in Brazil* and co-editor of *The Anthropology of Catholicism: A Reader.*

CATHOLIC PRACTICE IN THE AMERICAS

James T. Fisher and Margaret M. McGuinness (eds.), *The Catholic Studies Reader*

Jeremy Bonner, Christopher D. Denny, and Mary Beth Fraser Connolly (eds.), *Empowering the People of God: Catholic Action before and after Vatican II*

Christine Firer Hinze and J. Patrick Hornbeck II (eds.), *More than a Monologue: Sexual Diversity and the Catholic Church. Volume I: Voices of Our Times*

J. Patrick Hornbeck II and Michael A. Norko (eds.), *More than a Monologue: Sexual Diversity and the Catholic Church. Volume II: Inquiry, Thought, and Expression*

Jack Lee Downey, *The Bread of the Strong:* Lacouturisme *and the Folly of the Cross, 1910–1985*

Michael McGregor, *Pure Act: The Uncommon Life of Robert Lax*

Mary Dunn, *The Cruelest of All Mothers: Marie de l'Incarnation, Motherhood, and Christian Tradition*

Dorothy Day and the Catholic Worker: The Miracle of Our Continuance. Photographs by Vivian Cherry, Text by Dorothy Day, Edited, with an Introduction and Additional Text by Kate Hennessy

Nicholas K. Rademacher, *Paul Hanly Furfey: Priest, Scientist, Social Reformer*

Margaret M. McGuinness and James T. Fisher (eds.), *Roman Catholicism in the United States: A Thematic History*

Gary J. Adler Jr., Tricia C. Bruce, and Brian Starks (eds.), *American Parishes: Remaking Local Catholicism*

Stephanie N. Brehm, *America's Most Famous Catholic (According to Himself): Stephen Colbert and American Religion in the Twenty-First Century*

Matthew T. Eggemeier and Peter Joseph Fritz, *Send Lazarus: Catholicism and the Crises of Liberalism*

John C. Seitz and Christine Firer Hinze (eds.), *Working Alternatives: American and Catholic Experiments in Work and Economy*

Gerald J. Beyer, *Just Universities: Catholic Social Teaching Confronts Corporatized Higher Education*

Brandon Bayne, *Missions Begin with Blood: Suffering and Salvation in the Borderlands of New Spain*

Susan Bigelow Reynolds, *People Get Ready: Ritual, Solidarity, and Lived Ecclesiology in Catholic Roxbury*

Katherine Dugan and Karen E. Park (eds.), *American Patroness: Marian Shrines and the Making of U.S. Catholicism*

Sandra Yocum and Nicholas Rademacher (eds.), *Recovering Their Stories: US Catholic Women in the Twentieth Century*

Maya Mayblin, *Vote of Faith: Democracy, Desire, and the Turbulent Lives of Priest Politicians*

www.ingramcontent.com/pod-product-compliance
Lightning Source LLC
Chambersburg PA
CBHW031146020426
42333CB00013B/532